S0-DMQ-846

MALPRACTICE
A Guide to Avoidance & Treatment

MALPRACTICE
A Guide to Avoidance & Treatment

Kenneth E. Brooten, Jr., M.A., J.D.
Attorney and Counsellor at Law
Washington, D.C.

Stu Chapman
Executive Editor, Data Centrum
New York, New York

Grune & Stratton, Inc.
Harcourt Brace Jovanovich, Publishers
Orlando   New York   San Diego   London
San Francisco   Tokyo   Sydney   Toronto

Library of Congress Cataloging-in-Publication Data

Brooten, Kenneth E.
    Malpractice: a guide to avoidance & treatment.

    Includes index.
    1. Physicians—Malpractice.   I. Chapman, Stu.
II. Title. [DNLM: 1. Malpractice. W 44 B873m]
RA1056.5B76   1987   346.7303'32   86-26953
ISBN 0-8089-1849-4   347.306332

Grune & Stratton, Inc.
Orlando, Florida 32887

Distributed in the United Kingdom by
Grune & Stratton, Ltd.
24/28 Oval Road, London NW1

Library of Congress Catalog Number 86-26953
International Standard Book Number 0-8089-1849-4
Printed in the United States of America
86 87 88 89   10 9 8 7 6 5 5 4 3 2 1

DEDICATIONS

Kenneth E. Brooten, Jr.

To Patricia who stood beside me for 21 years and without whose help and uncommon dedication this work would not have been written.

Stu Chapman

To my parents, for their love, good humor and respect for the printed word.

CONTENTS

ACKNOWLEDGMENTS

This book reflects the experience and thoughtful contributions of many of our friends, relatives and colleagues. We are grateful to them for their generosity, guidance and encouragement. They are attorneys, physicians, nurses and health care professionals whose experience with the legal system— often as clients or witnesses— provided much of the framework for the material contained in this work.

We also thank Bob Feigenbaum, Editor of *Physicians Management*, for his keen interest in solving the malpractice problems that face each of us.

Special thanks are due to two distinguished medical malpractice defense attorneys, William H. Ginsburg, Esquire, of Los Angeles, California, and Barry A. Gold, Esquire, of Albany, New York, for sharing with us their ideas and allowing us to use some of their material. We also wish to thank Dr. Robert H. McCollough and the Gainesville, Florida Medical Group for the use of their medical history form.

A special acknowledgment is due to Whitmore Jensen and *Data Centrum*, a medical journal that served as a resource for information.

INTRODUCTION

The purpose of this book is to help you avoid being sued for medical malpractice. It is intended to be a day-to-day practical guide for "avoidance." Many books have been written on the subject of malpractice— some aimed at lawyers, still others at physicians and other health care providers. This nation's billion dollar malpractice crisis is and continues to be a major enigma of our time.

Something is terribly wrong with a system in which some physicians who practice in high-risk specialties can expect to appear in court to defend themselves more often than common criminals. Malpractice premiums for a single year for some physicians now approach the figure of their annual net income. Today, no health care professional is immune from a lawsuit. Today's malpractice crisis permeates virtually every phase of the professional and personal lives of health care providers.

Those who look for a solution to the malpractice crisis often rest their hopes on the avalanche of state legislation designed to limit or curb the litigious atmosphere that pervades our daily lives. Even a simple analysis indicates that tort reform legislation has achieved mixed and often unexpected results. Organized medical groups have kept a high profile on risk management while playing key roles in the passage of hundreds of state laws.

Ultimately, the final decisions rest with the individual physicians and health care providers. In the final analysis it is the individual physician and health care provider who shares the final responsibility to practice in such a manner as to curtail the filing of unwarranted malpractice actions. The adage, "Physician, heal thyself," has assumed a newer and perhaps truer dimension as physicians reassess the effectiveness of risk management procedures in their offices and hospitals. Now more than ever before, incompetent or impaired colleagues pose a "clear and present danger" by involving other health care professionals in their lawsuits.

How many physicians who have needlessly lost malpractice cases have questioned why they did not institute the safeguards that could have prevented the "malpractice meltdown"? Still others are left— like the proverbial Monday-morning quarterbacks— reclusively pondering how their cases were handled— or mishandled.

"Was the case settled for the convenience of the malpractice carrier as is increasingly the case? To whom did the carrier's attorney owe an allegiance? Was I adequately prepared for a deposition? Was I told what to expect before a jury? How much time was spent preparing me? Did I really have confidence that the attorney was exercising his judgment for my benefit?" These are the haunting, provocative questions that many of you may ask. If they are asked after the fact it is too late.

This book is dedicated to helping you answer those questions. It is a desk reference— a practical daily guide for every health care professional to assist in the prevention of unfounded malpractice claims. This reference also alerts you about what to do and what to look out for if you are sued.

This is not a legal case book that cites chapter and verse cases from various jurisdictions that have no bearing on how to solve your daily medical-legal problems. It does provide an analysis of "black letter" legal principles and how they directly affect you. This book reflects the experience of the two of us from the battlefield of the courtroom in more than 100 trials involving allegations of professional negligence, thousands of hours of pretrial preparation of clients and expert witnesses, analysis of testimony, negotiations, tactics and the "art of the practice of law." This work also involves years of experience from the actual day-to-day operation of a hospital to interviews with medical-legal experts throughout the nation. This work is predicated upon actual practical problems encountered by both authors, who have dealt with these problems and sought real solutions.

Beginning with a basic understanding of malpractice and related legal theories, we move to the most common situations and relationships that trigger the filing of a malpractice claim, from the recording of medical records to appropriate methods of discharge of patients. Continuing with an orientation to the legal process, we cover a range of issues related to the defense of a suit. We suggest a checklist of practical procedures to follow when served with a summons. We review what to expect at every stage of the legal process and provide practical advice on strategies to follow and guidelines about how you can evaluate the progress of your case and the performance of your attorney.

This book is a primer for all health care providers, with practical information for the prevention and treatment of malpractice in a simple, direct manner. Our sole allegiance is to provide practical, easily accessible information to the profession we serve.

Like any manual, the success of this book depends on how often and how well you apply the lessons contained within its covers. It will not pry the malpractice monkey off your back; however, it is a first strike toward lightening that load with principles of good risk management. Good risk management is as much an art and science as the practice of medicine or law.

Finally, everyone must recognize the fact that we have at least 51 different legal systems in the United States - one for each state and a Federal system. Wherever you practice your profession— you should consult with experienced medical counsel for specific answers to specific medical-legal questions which may arise. This work is not intended to be relied upon as the giving of specific legal advice and accordingly should not be relied upon by you to answer what may be a complex legal question.

1

MALPRACTICE
WHAT IS IT?

"But where shall I begin?"
"Begin at the beginning go to the end and then stop," said the King sternly.

Like Alice's adventures in Wonderland the "law" in its "majesty" does not always make the sense that we expect it to. Malpractice is negligence. Negligence is a tort. A tort is a civil wrong. Therefore malpractice is wrong. Sound like Alice in Wonderland?

Malpractice, in its simplest terms has four essential elements:

1. **Duty.** Every health care provider assumes a "duty" when he commences consultation, diagnosis or treatment of a patient. The duty arises from an express or implied contract. For example, if you go to a lawyer to prepare a deed to real property, the lawyer assumes a duty to prepare a "correct" deed. If you see a patient with abdominal pain, you undertake to diagnose and you assume a duty to diagnose correctly. It matters not whether you are paid or whether the patient was referred to you for a consultation, what you are undertaking is a "duty."

2. **Breach:** If you fail to make a correct diagnosis once you have assumed a duty to do so, you have created a "breach of the duty" due and owing to the patient. Even if you were only a consultant, you have assumed a duty.

3. **Causal Connection:** We now know that you have assumed a duty to diagnose the etiology of the abdominal pain. Let us suppose you diagnose the condition as simple gastritis when in fact it is not; that the patient has an acute appendicitis, which subsequently ruptures causing peritonitis, a prolonged hospital stay, loss of bowel and every other complication you can possibly think of. In legal terms, as a direct and

1

proximate result of your failure to correctly diagnose "duty" you "breached" the duty due and owing to the patient and as a direct and proximate result of your breach caused *damages*.

4. **Damages:**   As a result of your failure to correctly diagnose, the patient sustained damages in the form of an additional hospital stay, complications that may or may not be of a permanent and continuing nature. The critical element is that the patient sustained damages as a result of your breach of duty.

We often hear the term "medical negligence." Negligence is the doing of something that a similar health care provider would not do or the failure to do something that a similar health provider would do. It's simple: you did not do something that you should have done or you did do something that you should not have done. In our example, you should have correctly diagnosed acute appendicitis, therefore you failed to do something that a similar health care provider would have done.

STANDARD OF CARE

By what standard are you measured? Although there is no universal standard adopted by every state, the majority of states require that you provide the standard of care of a "similar health care provider." What is a "similar health care provider"? If you are a Board Certified General Surgeon, you are held to the standard of care of every other Board Certified General Surgeon without regard to locality. Some states still have the "locality rule." The locality rule is a limitation; for example, a Board Certified General Surgeon in the City of Waldo would be judged against the standards of his peers in Waldo or a similar sized city in the surrounding locality.

Standard of care is critical because it determines whether you committed a *breach*. It is also critical in the selection of expert witnesses who may be called upon to testify that you did not commit a *breach*. We will address the subject of expert witnesses later, but for our purposes it is important to understand now where each piece of the "malpractice puzzle" fits.

A simple illustration of "negligence" with which we are all familiar is the automobile accident. In law the standard imposed upon the driver of a car is that of the "reasonably prudent man," whoever that may be. In some jurisdictions violation of a statute constitutes "negligence." If you run a stop light, are speeding or commit a number of other violations, that may constitute negligence. Let's examine a typical example. Driver "A" is driving his car down the road at 75 MPH, crosses the center line and hits car "B" head on. Driver "A" had a duty to drive his car at the posted speed of 55 MPH and he had a duty not to cross the center line; he breached that duty when he crossed the center line, collided with the oncoming car "B" and killed the driver. Duty → Breach → Causal Connection → Damages. Standard of care ↔ reasonably prudent man. No reasonably prudent man would drive down the road at 75 MPH, cross the center line and create a head on collision with car "B".

Of course, in medicine, we are not examining speed limits or crossing center lines, what we are dealing with is much more complex— often we are dealing with differences of medical opinion, medical judgment; with complications that seldom occur, or with an unexpected result (i. e., the operation was technically perfect but the patient could not get off the heart–lung machine and died on the table). That is not "medical negligence," although to the family and their attorney it may appear to be.

Medical malpractice is nothing more or nothing less than the basic tort of "negligence." The application of the complexities of medicine and the lack of understanding by attorneys, judges, jurors and most importantly, litigants, are perhaps the primary factors that have caused the malpractice crisis.

HOW YOU CAN BE LIABLE WITHOUT EVEN TRYING

"Sentence first— verdict afterwards," said the Queen.

Like Alice in Wonderland you may be liable for other than your own acts. Let us examine the ways.

Respondeat Superior

Basically, this doctrine of law places the liability on you for the actions of those in your employ. It differs from the "Captain of the Ship" doctrine— unless of course you own the ship and employ the crew.

With the application of this doctrine, *you* can be liable without even trying. Let us examine a prime example. Your trusted office nurse takes the patient's vital signs. She inadvertently transcribes them on the wrong patient's file. She also fails to note, as is clearly indicated on the patient's chart that he is allergic to penicillin. You see your patient for a simple URI and prescribe an agent to which the patient is allergic, resulting in an anaphalactic reaction causing death. Liable— yes. The legal principle of *Respondeat Superior*: you are responsible for the actions of your employees. If they are negligent, that negligence is imputed to *you!!!*

Application of the legal doctrine of *Respondeat Superior* can dramatically increase your exposure to malpractice liability. How many little mistakes have you discovered, and how many times have others on the health care team discovered simple errors on your part? The delivery of health care is a team effort, but the ultimate liability may rest with you even though you have done nothing negligent.

Joint and Several Rule

The majority rule of law in the United States is that you may be held jointly and severally liable. The doctrine of Joint and Several is neither new nor novel; however, its application to health care delivery is rapidly expanding. Joint and Several means that if there is more than one person who is negligent they are all liable for the total damages.

How does it work? Let us suppose that you order an agent for an in-patient in the hospital. The hospital formulary does not contain the specific agent that you ordered for your patient. The hospital pharamacist substitutes another agent, which though therapeutically equivalent has ototoxic effects. Without checking you ratify the use of the agent. The patient has a permanent hearing loss. You, the hospital and the hospital pharmacist are sued. Clearly, the hospital pharmacist was negligent but he is an employee of the hospital (remember *Respondeat Superior*). The jury returns an interrogatory verdict finding you one percent negligent for failing to check the PDR for adverse reactions to the substituted drug. They find the pharmacist ninety percent negligent for the substitution, and they find the hospital nine percent negligent for having the agent on the formulary. Can they collect the full amount of the verdict against you? Yes!!

Another scenerio is being played out daily across the nation. Most states do not have mandatory medical malpractice coverage. Let us suppose that you are assisting in a procedure as a first assistant to a surgeon who either has no insurance or is underinsured. Let us further assume that you commit some minor error that is compounded by the primary surgeon. Again, if the jury finds you even one percent negligent you may be liable for the full amount of damages.

Of course, there are other remedies for contribution as between tort feasors, i. e., one who commits a tort. But as you may expect, if John Q. Surgeon has all his assets neatly tucked away because of previous lawsuits and recoveries against him, you are not going to collect from him. Your rates will increase as dramatically as his. The application of the joint and several rule is similar to being a "little bit pregnant."

2

RELATIONSHIPS WITH PHYSICIANS AND OTHER HEALTH CARE PROFESSIONALS GIVING RISE TO LEGAL LIABILITY

MALPRACTICE CHECKLIST

- You are required to give patients reasonable notice that another physician will substitute for you.
- Noncoercive confrontation by a colleague is the best hope for modifying behavior in an impaired physician.
- If there is a general taint or rumor of professional incompetence because of age or alcoholism, do not refer a patient to that doctor.
- Diagnosis is the crucial area where physicians need to limit the role of the Physician Assistant.
- Regard PAs as an extension of a physician's practice but not as a substitute for making decisions that you should make.
- For the first three months after an employee is hired, he or she should be closely supervised.
- If an employee is called upon to do anything invasive with which he or she is not yet familiar enough, the physician should supervise.
- If it is a "nurse's diagnosis" it should be called that in the patient's medical chart.
- One of the most serious errors is a report of an abnormality that is filed in the patient's record before the physician has seen it.

VICARIOUS LIABILITY AND RESPONDEAT SUPERIOR

Few malpractice claims are apt to shock you as much as the one that arises from vicarious liability when you are held responsible for another health care professional's negligence. As one physician who was sued describes the theory of vicarious liability: "It suggests the medical-legal equivalent of a sexually transmitted disease." For physicians who have caught it, the lessons learned are painfully obvious and the experience of defending oneself is anything but "vicarious."

The safety net provided by the extended family of colleagues, nurses, physician assistants and staff can become an entangling web. It can snare you when these additional personnel become "agents," that is, are authorized to act for or represent you. The legal doctrine is called *Respondeat Superior*, or "let the master answer," but simply stated it generally means that you can be held liable for the negligence committed by a partner or someone under your control. This area of law is expanding, too. In some jurisdictions, for example, physicians have been held responsible for "negligent referrals," and this seems to be an emerging trend. Another trend concerns the duty to report incompetent and impaired colleagues on the hospital staff if you knew or should have known about the professional's disability prior to the filing of a liability claim in which you may also be named. If you are not named in a civil suit, you may be held to answer before licensing authorities for not blowing the whistle.

Assessing liability in these situations may be complex because of the different ways in which relationships arise in the heatlh care setting. Part of the complexity is in establishing who is in control in a situation. For example, a scrub nurse is frequently under the control of a surgeon, but an anesthesiologist may not be under a surgeon's control. These finer points of law are often decided on a case-by-case basis or are reviewed in legal texts that dwell on matters beyond the scope of this manual.   The practical relevance of vicarious liability is suggested by the following questions: What are the typical situations that can expose you to vicarious liability? How can your staff get you into malpractice trouble? What are your obligations to report incompetent or impaired colleagues?

COLLEAGUES AND REFERRALS

As long as you have used due care in selecting a physician to cover for you, ordinarily you will not be held liable. The reason is that the employer–

employee relationship so vital to vicarious liability is not established. Problems arise, however, when the substitute physician is on a salary from the treating physician. You must ensure that the substitute is qualified and if you have not done so, in selecting him, you could be held liable. What's more, you are required to give patients reasonable notice that another physician will substitute for you. Without such notice, physicians can be held liable in situations where they might not otherwise have been implicated in a case that arises from a substitute's negligence. One ruling that illustrates the problem involves an obstetrician who provided a substitute while he was on vacation. The substitute delivered the plaintiff's child, a healthy baby, but the mother sued because the substitute had failed to give her a general anesthetic as the original physician had promised. Since she had no notice of any substitution prior to her going to the hospital, the OB was liable.

Although you may share offices with a colleague, but do not share responsibility for each other's patients, you will usually not be held liable for the other's negligence. In situtations where you refer a patient to a specialist, and then withdraw from the case, you will not usually be held liable unless the patient can show that the specialist was unqualified or incompetent— and that you should have known it.

The problem that often arises is when two physicians treat a patient jointly, each seeing the patient on a continuing basis. Both will be liable for any negligence within the area in which both are involved. On the other hand, if you assist a specialist in a procedure after a referral, you should not expect to be found liable for negligence arising from the surgery. However, do not forget the joint and several rule.

The governing factor in determining whether liability has occurred is usually the degree to which one physician's care overlaps another's. For example, imagine you sent a patient to an allergist who sent the patient back to you with an indication that he needs allergy shots. The malpractice net might widen if the allergist is negligent and the problem is not allergy-related. If you administer the allergy shots and the patient suffers an injury, an attorney might be able to argue well for "agency" or "joint enterprise" liability.

Confusion over responsibility for different aspects of care may be a central factor in vicarious liability. Negligence arises when physicians fail to specify what services they are requesting of each other. If it's a consultation, then say so: "I'd like you to take a look at this patient and evaluate him for such and such and make a recommendation back to me." On the other hand, an actual referral should be no less clear: "I don't know anything about this problem. It's really in your area. I'd like you to take this patient as your own."

Clear delineation of duties also prevents awkward (and potentially disastrous) situations, such as the patient being billed by two doctors or a patient returning to you unexpectedly. Avoidable fumbling like this only confuses a patient; and confusion— when someone feels their health is at stake— is only one step away from hostility.

Along with spelling out responsibility, a referring physician should provide a complete medical history to the consultant before the visit. This is more than a courtesy. Don't assume a patient is able to fill the doctor in on what drugs and what therapy have been prescribed. Also, a specialist might spot something relevant in the chart that you overlooked. Your patient will be impressed if the consultant is well briefed on the problem.

SURGEONS AND THE "CAPTAIN OF THE SHIP DOCTRINE"

The "captain of the ship doctrine" was once the gold standard for evaluating whether a surgeon could be held liable. The theory held that the operating surgeon, as "captain of the ship," could be sued if anyone in the OR made a mistake that left the patient injured. But recent decisions have chipped away at the doctrine and have undermined its influence in medical malpractice cases. Nevertheless, most states still hold a surgeon responsible for all negligence that occurs in the OR at the time he is performing surgery. While the staff working with him technically may be employees of the hospital, most courts hold that they are, for the purpose of performing surgical procedures, "borrowed servants." With that type of responsibility, they are under the control of the operating surgeon.

Some courts, however, have recently been taking a somewhat different direction. In Texas, for example, the state's supreme court has held that when the surgeon leaves the OR after having instructed the hospital employees in what to do, the hospital will be liable for any negligent acts performed in the surgeon's absence. The court has stated that a surgeon's mere presence does not make him or her automatically liable for the negligence of others. For example, it found that a scrub nurse who had miscounted sponges was a hospital employee and not the surgeon's "servant." The hospital was held liable for the nurse's negligence when an injury was attributed to her role in the operation.

Anesthesiology suggests its own set of rules, depending on whether a nurse anesthetist is present. In most cases when anesthesia is given by a nurse, the surgeon is liable for his or her negligence, because the surgeon usually directs the type of anesthesia and route of administration. Some state courts have ruled differently, however, finding that the hospital, as the nurse's employer, is liable for any negligence. But these rulings are rare and generally physicians are liable for the negligence of nurse anesthetists. Since anesthesiologists, however, are in charge of their own sphere of activity, the surgeon is not liable for their negligence. The anesthesiologist is considered an independent agent rather than an assistant to the surgeon, since the anesthesiologist decides the type and route of administration.

INCOMPETENCE AND IMPAIRED COLLEAGUES

The AMA estimates that 10–15 percent of physicians are impaired by either alcohol or drug dependence or from mental illness. When *Physician's Management* recently conducted a telephone survey of 28 physicians, 22 of them reported some experience with impaired colleagues.

The situation involving an impaired colleague represents a double-edged sword. On the one hand, many states have enacted new laws requiring physicians to report impaired doctors. But the reason why only a few cracks have developed in the "conspiracy of silence" is that circumspect physicians fear litigation from those whom they accuse of being impaired. Many doctors feel that they can be sued for slander if they blow a whistle on a colleague. Partly because of such fears, only 2 of the 22 physicians in the *Physician's Management* survey who knew of cases of impaired colleagues, actually had an active role in reporting cases.

But case law and new regulations are making it harder for physicians to duck the issue of reporting. Some cases involving incompetent physicians have raised frightening and bizarre implications in the way entire medical staffs have been snared in a malpractice suit because of one impaired colleague whom the plaintiff claimed the staff should have weeded out. In imposing tougher obligations on physicians to police their own ranks, courts and regulatory agencies have left doctors with little choice but to report cases of impairment.

The scope of the problem of the impaired physician has been put in sharper perspective by estimates from Blue Cross and Blue Shield. It estimates that impaired physicians are involved in providing compromised quality care in 100 million patient visits per year.

CAN MANDATORY REPORTING WORK?

States have enacted "Impaired Physician" statutes that provide either mandatory or voluntary reporting of the physician. Some states that have mandatory reporting requirements exempt therefrom the physician who is treating an impaired physician on grounds of the physician–patient relationship.

The American Medical Association's Council on Mental Health concludes: "It is a physician's ethical responsibility to take cognizance of a colleague's inability to practice medicine adequately by reason of physical or mental illness, including alcoholism or drug dependence." The consensus of licensing boards, medical societies, and state committees is that noncoercive confrontation by a colleague is the best hope for initiating modification of behavior in the impaired physician.

Advocates of mandatory reporting argue that the only effective means of prompting physicians to identify their impaired colleagues is to impose a statutory duty to report. The failure of a physician to report an impaired colleague is unprofessional conduct and grounds for discipline against the non-reporting physician by the regulatory board. If a known impaired physician injured a patient because of his impairment, a physician who failed to make a mandatory report would be personally liable for the injury. To avoid potential personal liability or discipline, physicians must report their impaired colleagues.

Proponents of voluntary reporting criticize mandatory reporting requirements as conflicting with the rehabilitative purposes of impaired physician programs. They argue that if impaired physicians think a program administrator is required to report them to a regulatory board having punitive powers, few will voluntarily submit themselves for treatment. Moreover, physicians will be fearful that they may cost a colleague his license and will be dissuaded from urging an impaired colleague whose quality of practice has not significantly suffered to seek rehabilitation. Proponents of voluntary reporting view the matter as an ethical responsibility rather than a legal duty. Initial reports from two states that enacted mandatory reporting requirements, after previously functioning with a voluntary reporting program, did not reveal an increased rate of reporting. Additionally, in New York, the physician-administrators of the Voluntary Physician's Committee charged that the mandatory reporting requirement undermined their efforts. With the implementation of mandatory reporting, the voluntary committee stopped receiving reports of impaired physicians. The New York Legislature recognized this problem and amended their mandatory reporting requirement to exempt from general reporting requirements those physicians who are members of a state medical society's voluntary committee for the rehabilitation of impaired physicians. Since then, better cooperation has existed between the New York Legislature, the state medical society, and the state department of health. Whether the threat of disciplinary action against a non-reporting physician is an effective method of promoting the identification of impaired physicians is questionable. A survey of states having mandatory reporting requirements reveals no instance where a physician received discipline for failure to report an impaired colleague.

The AMA's standard for ethical conduct states that physicians are ethically responsible to take cognizance of their impaired colleagues. This standard for ethical conduct is violated by the medical staff member who knows of a colleague's drug dependence and does not take action. Hospitals are legally required to restrict medical staff membership to those physicians competent in their respective fields and who meet standards of professional ethics. Silence and inaction of a medical staff member could be construed as a violation of this ethical standard and serve as grounds for dismissal from the medical staff.

As the AMA has moved to strengthen its stand on ethical conduct concerning the impaired physician, courts have moved to impose stringent obligations on physicians who fail to heed the warning signified by an impaired colleague. Consider a remarkable 1975 New Jersey case, *Corletto v Shore Memorial Hospital*, which set broad standards for the inclusion of physicians in a suit and suggests a new dimension behind the concept of vicarious liability. This case shows that the web of potential malpractice liability may extend to ensnare an entire medical staff that might be considered to be on notice that the doctor is incompetent or impaired. In addition to suing a doctor for alleged negligence in performing abdominal surgery, the plaintiff here also sued the hospital where the patient had died and the entire medical staff— a group of 141 independent contractor physicians. The plaintiff argued that they knew or should have known that the doctor was not competent to perform the surgical procedure and allowed him to remain on the case when it was obviously beyond his control.

In addition to allowing this suit against the hospital, the court allowed the complaint against the 141 physicians, rejecting their procedural argument that they could not be sued because they were an unincorporated association.

SUING THE WHOLE HOSPITAL

The frightening implication is that a physician could be named in a suit like that. The court in the Corletto case never decided whether the 141 physicians could be held liable. It only ruled that they could be named in the suit. The case was settled by the defendant physician before the case went to trial. The merits were never argued and the case against the 141 physicians may have been dismissed.

Nevertheless, the case is important because it points to the reponsibility of physicians who have the power to do something about an incompetent physician. If the physicians know about a physician who practices poor medicine and don't do anything about it, they can be held liable. If a physician on the staff is impaired or alcoholic or has some other problem, then it seems fair to attribute the negligence of the doctor who is the alcoholic to the physician who knew about him and did nothing about it.

While courts have spun an expanding web of case law that includes decisions like *Corletto's*, what are the practical implications? In recent years, your obligation has grown increasingly clear. If you know a physician is an alcoholic, you have a duty by statute to report him. If you have a patient requiring his care and you know that Dr. White has a tremor, you've seen him and strongly suspect he's an alcoholic, then you have a greater duty not to refer a patient to him. A good rule to follow is if there's a general taint or rumor of professional ineptitude because of age or alcoholism and you are aware of it, you should not refer a patient to that doctor.

You need stronger criteria to refer a doctor to an ethics committee. Usually your information doesn't come from colleagues. Patients may tell you about him directly, but it's more likely to come from operating room personnel, nursing supervisors, and nurses on the floor.

In the case of one physician covering for another, there's a clear link of liability if something goes wrong. If one physician misses something and the patient did not have the opportunity to select that doctor, he comes along as part of the package. There's more of a connection between the two. A doctor who leaves on vacation without adequately briefing the physician who covers for him has breached the standard of care. What safeguards can a physician build into his practice to prevent such liability from cropping up?

One method suggested for referrals is to refer to Dr. M, Dr. N, and Dr. O and let the patient make the choice. If the patient chooses Dr. N, then there's no negligence for referring because the patient made the choice.

Secondly, as long as Dr. N has a good record in the community and you as the referring physician have no reason to know that Dr. N is an alcoholic or is not board-certified or really botches that kind of surgery, then there's no negligence on your part.

Above all choose carefully whom you're working with. If you're on a hospital staff and you know there's a bad apple, then you have an obligation to report him, to try to get him off the staff or prevent him from doing surgery.

WALKING THE FINE LINE ON PHYSICIAN PERFORMANCE

Except for the obvious circumstance, where there is culpability on the part of a physician being reviewed, it's very difficult to carry out quality assurance with any degree of certainty. There is a lot of difference of opinion about whether an individual is a risk and is practicing less than the standard of care. Just because he doesn't do it your way doesn't mean he's not doing it within acceptable limits. And that bothers many physicians the most.

The time to catch the problem is at the initial credentialing process, but even then one doesn't know what kind of physician a person is going to be. The significant majority of malpractice cases are gray— they could go either way. And if that's true of malpractice suits, then it's true of the whole area of physician performance. You can criticize a person, but for every criticism there is a counterargument for explaining why he acted the way he did.

If a physician feels that a reasonable doctor confronting the same or similiar circumstance would be apprehensive about the quality of care to be rendered, he must understand that by referring a patient to that physician he is assuming a certain risk of liability. If you have apprehension or doubt, don't send a patient to that physician.

PHYSICIAN'S ASSISTANTS

In the race against the clock, a physician often wishes for a clone to attend to those routine tests for which there never seems enough time. For many doctors who employ them, physician assistants are the next best thing. They save time in obtaining histories, performing simple diagnostic tests and treating emergencies, but the convenience provided by PAs can carry an expensive price tag for the physician who begins to rely too heavily on them to achieve practice shortcuts.

In the 20 years, since the first physician assistant program was organized, the use of these paramedical assistants has spiraled. More than 15,000 of them now work in the U.S., and 1500 more graduate each year from the nation's 55 programs. As the fear of malpractice grew in the wake of the crisis of 1975, use of physician assistants continued to be popular. Physicians tended to practice more defensively, administering more diagnostic tests and routine procedures that can be carried out by assistants. "Qualified to perform a minimum of 70% of the clinical procedures carried out by general practice physicians," according to the American Academy of Physician Assistants, these medical personnel have filled a vacuum in health care.

The road to certification is rigorous. A PA must pass a stringent exam developed and administered by the National Board of Medical Examiners, must be supervised by a physician, and is subject to varying state regulations. For example, 14 states have granted PAs prescriptive authority, allowing them to prescribe all but controlled substances.

While state laws are clear on what they are allowed to do, case law is also clear on how they can expose a physician to malpractice. The same rules that govern the standard of care of a physician in the performance of his duties also applies to physician assistants. A physician assistant is held to the same standard of care had the physician performed the same service. Under the legal doctrine of respondeat superior, the physician is responsible for the acts of an employee.

Some Guidelines for Physician Assistants

As an example of the kinds of guidelines that states have enacted, a number of provisions in Ohio law governs the use of PAs. The Ohio law prohibits the PA from the following:

• Making a diagnosis of a disease or ailment or the absence thereof, independent of the employing physician.

• Prescribing any treatment or regimen not previously set forth by the employing physician.

• Prescribing medications, signing or stamping a prescription blank on behalf of the employing physician.

• Having prescription blanks available that have been presigned or prestamped by the employing physician.

- Signing a physician's name to authenticate any prescription or orders, or in any situation that gives the indication of the physician's approval.
- Supplanting the employing physician in making visits outside the physician's office.
- Initiating or changing any orders on the patient's chart in the hospital, nursing home, or clinic, or places other than the physician's office.
- Maintaining an office, independent of the employing physician.
- Admitting a patient to or releasing a patient from a hospital, independent of an employing physician.

Diagnosis is the crucial area where physicians need to limit the role of the PA. Physicians need to be wary of allowing a PA to diagnose ailments outside the scope of common problems. If they are not limited in this area, PAs could leave a physician more vulnerable to a malpractice suit than a nurse. It's a different type of practice, it's more direct. The PA is actually diagnosing and sometimes testing. A nurse treats under a doctor's supervision, but rarely makes a diagnosis of his or her own. The PA is semitrained as a physician, and a doctor has to trust and know this person's capabilities more than those of the nurse. In outlying areas, some PAs work almost exactly like the doctor— they go in and make rounds and write the necessary orders.

The rule to follow: Regard PAs as extensions of a physician's practice but not as a substitute for making decisions that only the physician should make. If they do their job, they can be a comforting presence. They can hold down the fort so the doctor can have more thinking time.

NURSES AND STAFF: MALPRACTICE PROPHYLAXIS

In addition to physician assistants, your office or hospital staff should be the first line of defense in a malpractice suit. Skilled, professional personnel who are attuned to situations that set the stage for a malpractice action can form a protective barrier to buffer you from liability claims long before they start.

The staff may also be a pressure point for malpractice, however. It can leave you vulnerable to suits if you have problems determining where their jobs end and where the scope of your practice begins. Working smoothly with your staff during a busy schedule, you generally can neither afford the time nor indulge the inclination to consider exposure from your staff to a malpractice suit.

What's more, studies have shown that efficient physician assistants (PAs) and nurse practitioners are readily accepted by patients. A recent *New York Times* survey found that 58 percent of respondents would rather have their illnesses treated by a nurse or a PA than a doctor, and 33 percent were willing to give up their right to sue if these factors could lower their costs of medical care.

Vaguely aware that your staff members are conducting WBC counts, x-rays, and the myriad of other laboratory tests and support services that you need, you may tend to overlook distinctions between your role and their's. Pressed for time, and burdened with a staggering patient load, you may delegate areas of practice to PAs, nurses or others in whom you have begun to vest too much responsibility.

Physicians may fail to realize that certain aspects of a practice have crossed into an area where they could be sued for the liability created by a staff not as skilled as a doctor in many situations. Physicians can also be taken to court for aiding and abetting the illegal practice of medicine.

In what areas of your practice are staff members most apt to expose you to liability? Where should you look for guidelines to define the nature and scope of their jobs? What areas of their work should you personally supervise to minimize your risk for vicarious liability? Should you set up a quality assurance program to regularly monitor the work of your staff?

Assuming that you are satisfied with certification and references, it is crucial to match your new employee with responsibilities you are comfortable with and conform to guidelines in your state law. In the last ten years, more than half the states have revamped their nurse practitioner acts, increasing the scope of practice for nurses. Two states have given them limited power to prescribe drugs, while others allow for "nursing diagnoses."

A wide gap exists between what some states permit and what others disallow, and before you begin to rely on nurses or PAs to achieve practice short cuts, you should consult your state's licensing laws that define appropriateness of practice and required supervision. Supervision may take three forms— over the shoulder, on the premises, or at a distance, with regular monitoring and review.

SUPERVISION IS CRITICAL

For the first three months after an employee has been hired, he or she should be closely supervised— either by a physician or someone who is competent in the procedures that the new employee will be doing. This is critical where immunizations are being performed on children, when x-rays are taken, or in the conducting of pregnancy tests and biopsies. Physicians have often been sued for negligence arising from an employee's actions in these areas.

Generally, if an employee is called upon to do anything invasive or with which he or she is not yet familiar enough, the physician should supervise. A frequent source of litigation, for example, is the failure to take skull x-rays and x-rays to locate foreign bodies in the eye. A physician should have a standing protocol that x-rays be taken when patients present with signs and symptoms of such problems at the office or a hospital emergency room. The protocol that sets forth these and other responsibilities is crucial to managing risk. These responsibilities— what your staff can and should not do— should not exceed what state guidelines suggest.

CLARIFYING DIAGNOSIS

The nurse's obligation to know what clinical signs are important and to call these to the attention of a physician can quickly shift into a grey area bordering on diagnosis. For example, a nurse must recognize emergency situations, postoperative and pregnancy complications, sick children who may be labile and threatened by coma, untoward drug reactions, or synergistic drug reactions. Any change in a patient's vital signs would require a nurse to inform a physician.

But where is the line drawn? It's a thin one because courts have differed on how they view diagnosis. Some jurisdictions hold that the nurse is properly allowed to judge the gravity of symptoms without engaging in diagnosis. Others have ruled that when a nurse evaluates a symptom and decides no serious disease is indicated, she is diagnosing. Interpretations of the word must be seen in the context of the particular law. The definition is complicated because diagnosis and the obligation to observe symptoms and reactions seem to be intertwined.

Most states have wrestled with the problem and seem to be making headway. Many have amended the scope of a nurse's practice and tried to define diagnoses and treatment from a nursing perspective. Some of these nursing practice acts are abandoning the position that strictly prohibits a nurse from diagnosing. They have coined a new term: "nurse's diagnosis." If such diagnoses are made in your practice, it would be wise to call it by that name in the patient's medical chart to avoid confusion with a diagnosis made by you or another physician.

ROUTINE MONITORING

Aware of the pitfalls of vicarious liability that have trapped their colleagues, physicians should routinely examine their own practices, monitor the work of their staff through a conscientious effort of quality assurance, and candidly discuss their concerns about risk with members of their staff, soliciting their ideas for managing the problem.

As part of that review, consider how well instructions are communicated to nurses, PAs and technicians. Orders should be written instead of oral; for example, are drugs spelled legibly and written out as they are referred to in the office or hospital formulary? Are dosage requirements indicated clearly— 0.2 mg, for example, instead of .2 mg, which may leave room for misinterpretation if the decimal point is not clearly marked?

It is a good idea to consult and maintain in your files the books, monographs, and other material that can help you recognize the risk that may have taken root in your office. By monitoring these problems and nipping them in the bud, managing the risk from your staff will not be a capricious concern, but an everyday fact of life in your practice.

Regardless of the emphasis you place on risk management in your office and the concern instilled among hospital personnel, your staff and those who work with you may not be attuned to specific situations that tend to set the stage for the filing of a suit. They may have a theoretical understanding of the problems but lack an awareness of the practical considerations that lead to trouble. The following discussion suggests how clear delineation of roles and responsibilities, meticulous record keeping and careful attention to protocol can keep vicarious liability out of your practice.

INACCURATE READINGS OR REPORTS

Physicians rely heavily on office staff to obtain and record objective data. Errors can set the stage for a malpractice suit. Consider the following: The nurse records the blood pressure accurately, but takes the pulse in a cursory manner and fails to detect obvious irregularities. The physician glances at the readings— "BP 128/78, pulse 84 and regular"— and relies on them. Or the laboratory technician, or whoever performs simple tests such as hematocrits and urinalysis, mixes up the samples or records results on the wrong lab slip. The physician relies on a normal result, when in fact the patient's test was highly abnormal. Moreover, the patient whose test actually is normal may be treated based on the abnormal result. Similarly, the test may be performed in a manner that results in an invalid result. For example, the staff person might be using an outdated reagent, fail to follow the protocol accurately, or generate incorrect results because of a quality control breakdown.

INAPPROPRIATE PRESCRIPTION REFILLS

Occasionally, office staff will exceed their authority and approve a prescription refill over the telephone without having consulted the physician— particularly when the patient is well-known, the physician has always refilled it without question (but is unavailable), and the patient needs the prescription that day.

Consider a generally stable cardiac patient for whom the physician has prescribed nitroglycerin over the past several years. The nurse, knowing the physician has always authorized a refill in the past and believing the patient should never be without a "fresh" supply, authorizes the refill in the physician's name. Unfortunately, the patient had called because she wasn't getting relief from her chest pain with tablets from her current supply. She had erroneously assumed it was because the tablets were no longer active. In fact, she was having an MI, but did not tell the nurse about the chest pain because the nurse quickly authorized the refill. This example, although hypothetical, is not farfetched.

Most office personnel will not exceed authority in this context, but can still create a malpractice risk for the physician who does authorize the refill. First, the staff person requesting the refill for the patient might fall into the same trap described earlier with regard to the nitroglycerin scenario. The physician, assuming the patient was fine but simply wanted the refill before exhausting her current supply, authorizes it. Second, the staff person might write the prescription for the physician to sign. This is not an uncommon practice, yet a simple error in medication or dosage can be catastrophic for the patient if the physician does not detect it. Consider, for example, a patient needing a prescription for propranolol who receives furosemide by mistake— or who needs 0.125 mg/d of digoxin, but receives 0.25 mg/d. Third, the staff person might be unaware that the previous prescription is no longer appropriate because of a recent change in the patient's condition. For example, take the digitalized patient who has lost renal function and requires a downward adjustment of the dosage. Although the physician thinks the dosage appropriate, the staff member is unaware of the patient's recent out-of-state hospitalization and newly diagnosed renal dysfunction. A more careful history by the office staff might have detected this "red flag." Most patients, of course, would volunteer the information, but some, for reasons that may be legitimate, might not. Whatever the reason for the failure to communicate, the physician is accountable for prescribing errors.

FAILURE TO INSTRUCT APPROPRIATELY

Physicians frequently delegate patient education responsibilities, including instruction for follow-up care and "what to do" if particular symptoms change. Again, most of the time office staff do a thorough and competent job— sometimes better than a physician would do. But time pressures, personal problems, miscommunication with the physician, or a variety of other factors can lead to erroneous or incomplete instructions.

RECORDING THE CHIEF COMPLAINT

A thorough understanding of the patient's complaint is essential to providing quality care— and therefore integral to "risk management." Although obtaining the history is usually considered the role of the physician, many physicians rely on office staff to interview the patient, determine the chief complaint, and enter this information into the record along with basic objective data such as vital signs and necessary lab tests.

Most office personnel are sensitive to the desirability of communicating directly to the physician any unusual aspects of the patient's history or situation. The more effective this "screen," the more likely the true nature of the patient's complaint will come to light. A patient might be complaining of "dry skin" or a "mild headache," but really be in the grip of a serious depression. A sensitive office assistant might pick this up and convey his or her concern to the physician.

ROUTINE TESTS IN THE
PHYSICIAN'S ABSENCE

Physicians sometimes book a patient for routine office testing while they are making rounds or doing surgery— or for that matter, during their day off. This may be convenient for all concerned and a cost-effective practice, but it is not without risks.

Consider this hypothetical situation: A middle-aged patient is seen in the doctor's office, complaining of chest discomfort of several months' duration. He denies any recent changes or disabling symptoms. The physician, after performing a complete history and physical examination, recommends certain diagnostic tests, including an ECG, blood tests, and x-rays. The patient's ECG is scheduled for later that week, on a day the physician will not be present. The office nurse performs the ECG and leaves the tracings on the physician's desk for interpretation. While running the test, the nurse does not detect an injury pattern or a serious arrhythmia, and the patient goes home with a follow-up appointment.

THE TRIAGE FUNCTION

Office assistants frequently have telephone discussions with patients who ask to see the physician before the next "available" appointment. With or without physician input, the assistant might determine the urgency of the patient's condition and when that patient should see the physician. This is a very important function; yet the nature of a busy practice often minimizes the time an assistant has to handle triage calls. Particularly difficult are well-known patients with multiple medical and psychological problems— and a tendency towards hypochondriasis. It is not unusual for certain patients to call their doctor's office several times a week about one problem or another. Generally, their condition is the same stable problem, not needing urgent attention; occasionally, however, such patients do develop a life-threatening condition.

Consider the highly neurotic middle-aged patient who calls in complaining that he is "tired and weak," and who has had similar complaints over the years— followed by negative work-ups. It requires a competent office assistant to obtain more history that may suggest other symptoms compatible with severe hyperglycemia, a GI bleed, or an MI.

OUT OF SEQUENCE FILING

Probably, the most serious error is the abnormal report filed in the patient's record before the physician has seen it. An abnormal Pap smear report is a typical example. Many offices tell the patient that "no news is good news"— in other words, the office will notify the patient of the result only if it is abnormal. Although this policy cuts back on phone calls, it effectively removes an important "tickler": the patient.

Consider the following: The physician performs the routine Pap smear. The abnormal report is filed without the physician's seeing it. The patient, assuming the report is normal, returns for her next routine examination a year later. Adenocarcinoma of the cervix is diagnosed.

Another pitfall exists, even if the physician has reviewed the report before it was filed. The physician may have determined that it is appropriate to wait until the next scheduled visit (for example, in six weeks) to inform the patient and act on the report. The report is correctly filed. If the patient returns for the scheduled visit, the physician will note again the abnormal report and follow through as necessary. However, the patient or physician might cancel the visit. Unless there is some indication in the appointment book that a cancellation should trigger notification of the physician, who then can determine the urgency of notifying the patient and arranging follow-up, the necessary visit might be significantly delayed— or missed altogether.

Another problem can arise when the staff submits only abnormal reports to the physician for review, filing the normal reports on receipt. Consider a patient whose most recent hematocrit is well within normal range. The previous hematocrit, however, was significantly higher, and the office assistant files the report without noting the decrease. The patient might be having a slow GI bleed or other condition requiring physician assistance. Put simply, a report that is in the "normal range" may not be normal for that patient, but may constitute an important positive sign of a new condition.

Related to this is the normal report, duly filed, which the physician thought would be abnormal. For example, a physician might order gallbladder tests after the history and examination have made the diagnosis of gallbladder disease likely. He never sees the normal report and forgets to follow up with other recommendations. The patient might assume that since the "tests" were normal (i.e., he didn't hear again from the physician), his abdominal pains aren't serious. As most physicians are aware, failure to diagnose, or delay in diagnosis, is a common cause of malpractice suits.

THE MISFILED REPORT

With the enormous number of reports flowing through a physician's office every day, the occasional misfiled report is inevitable. Harm can result in several ways. The staff might misfile the report after the physician has reviewed it, but before follow-up has been scheduled, as in the example just described. Not only might there be a risk of delay from cancellation, but with the report in the wrong file, it won't be available to jog the physician's memory if the patient does return as scheduled.

Similarly, the report might be entered into the wrong section of the medical record—or in the correct section, but out of sequence by date. In either case, the physician, on the patient's next visit, might be less likely to review the report, particularly if the subsequent treating physician is not the physician who ordered the test.

Misfiling of the reports, particularly when the reports contain sensitive information, can result in an unintentional but harmful breach of confidentiality. Consider a positive G/C culture report erroneously filed in a patient's record, and subsequently released to a third party for medical-legal or insurance purposes.

IMPROPER RELEASE OF RECORDS

Physicians receive requests daily from insurance companies, attorneys, government agencies, and others for release of medical records. Most experienced office staff obtain appropriate authorization before releasing records. Nonetheless, mistakes happen, some of which carry criminal penalties.

For example, the staff might release records on the authorization of someone they wrongly believe to have such legal capacity in the patient's behalf. Also, a staff assistant might release the entire record— even though the patient authorized release of material only from a specific date or with regard to a specific condition.

Physicians should use release forms that provide them with maximum protection. This is particularly important when records document a history of substance abuse or mental illness and the treatment was funded either directly or indirectly by the Federal Government. There are strict laws on even identifying a patient by name and a physician should consult an attorney prior to the release of such records.

INAPPROPRIATE DELAY OR FAILURE TO RELEASE RECORDS

Failure to release records despite a request and an appropriate authorization is another pitfall. Consider the following: A patient with a lengthy record authorizes release to another party. Usually the office assistant, after consulting with the physician, would compile the required pages from the record and convey them to the party requesting them. However, this time several busy days pass, and the records remain on the assistant's desk. The patient returns to see the physician because of a new or urgent condition, and the records are subsequently refiled.

The office assistant might assume someone else took care of the request— or, for various reasons, the patient may not think to question the fact. The requesting party has already written three times for the records and assumes they will not be forthcoming.

THE LOST MEDICAL RECORD

In an office with several thousand active records, it is not unusual to occasionally lose one "to the system." A record can be misfiled, for example, or mislaid. Often, the impact of the loss of a record is either minimal or can be minimized. However, in some clinical and medical-legal situations, the loss of a record can have serious ramifications. For example, there is always the potentially disastrous situation involving an already hostile patient who has suffered an untoward result of treatment. Unfortunately, there is a very good chance that that patient might become even more hostile.

Similarly, an attorney who has been consulted by the physician's patient as to "whether the patient has a case" usually requests medical records. Reporting that they have been lost will do little to persuade the attorney against bringing suit.

Finally, once a suit is filed, good documentation can be integral to a good defense.

ERRORS IN ADDRESSING LETTERS OR BILLS

Office assistants frequently send notices of one sort or another to patients. For example, a patient might be advised that the physician would like him to return for another examination, or to receive treatment for a specific condition. Also, the individual responsible for billing routinely sends bills to large numbers of patients. In either case, sensitive and confidential information could end up in the wrong hands. The same type of problem can arise when an office assistant leaves a telephone message for the patient.

ULTIMATE RESPONSIBILITY LIES WITH THE PHYSICIAN

Physicians rely on office staff to a great degree and should be aware of the major administrative and direct patient care responsibilities office staff carry. It's up to the physician to communicate closely with the office assistants, to ensure that they have the opportunity for ongoing training, and to review the more important protocols and procedures staff are asked to follow on a regular basis. Failure on the part of office staff to avoid common pitfalls can translate into a malpractice suit. Successful avoidance can result in better medical care for the patient, and one hopes, better legal "odds" for the physician.

3

THE MALPRACTICE
PRODROME
AND THE
THERAPEUTIC ALLIANCE

MALPRACTICE CHECKLIST

- Avoid showing support for patients who seem compelled to disparage a physician they have just seen.
- Refrain from passing judgment on previous care and suggest that the patient needs an independent evaluation.
- If an overdue bill is large enough for aggressive collection, review results of treatment with a personal malpractice defense attorney to assess liability potential.
- A lawsuit for fees owed does not have to be brought until the statute of limitations for malpractice has expired.
- Compliance is so crucial that you should set aside time at the end of a patient visit to explain why.
- Don't ignore the patient's spouse— soliciting his or her comments can help in assessment of progress.
- Office-based practitioners cannot leave informed consent responsibility to a non-physician.
- You are obliged to advise patients that alternatives exist to a treatment that entails certain risks.
- If risk is statistically low, but consequences of untoward result extremely severe, you should still inform the patient.
- If statistical risk is low and severity of untoward result not great, you can modify warning so as not to interfere with consent.

- You are only expected to explain risks "reasonably foreseen."
- The more elective the procedure, the more detailed the informed consent.
- Do not think of informed consent as a formality— recital of options, signing of forms.
- Empathize with the patient's attitudes and fears.
- Build a relationship based on honesty in facing the "uncertainty inherent in clinical practice."

No one can predict with certainty which patients are most likely to sue for medical malpractice, but in selected patients, you can identify early signs and symptoms. There is a "malpractice prodrome," a series of telltale warning signs that should alert you that a claim may be brewing as reliably as clinical signs can foreshadow the deterioration of a condition. If you can spot them soon enough when they occur— an unexplained lack of payment, a chronic lack of compliance or poor communication— you can nip a claim before it reaches the stage where you need to notify your carrier or personal attorney.

The "malpractice prodrome" may prompt you to reassess your management strategies. In some cases, you may conclude that you are likely to be sued no matter how good the care is that you are providing, in which case you may want to carefully discharge the patient to avoid being accused of abandonment. With other patients, however, certain adjustments, such as improved communications, can reestablish a good relationship, easing tensions so that a disgruntled patient or family is more willing to accept an untoward result that will never measure up to unreasonable expectations. Similarly, they may reconsider the idea of suing you for malpractice because their anger has been replaced by the recognition that you have conformed to the standard of care.

Unreasonable expectations can assume an important role in raising false hopes concerning the outcome of treatment. Thus, a lack of informed consent or poorly obtained informed consent represents one of those breakdowns in communication that set the stage for the filing of a claim. If malpractice hinges on matters of choice, what tests were ordered and treatments followed, it also hinges on the kinds of communication that suggest to the patient risk/benefit ratios associated with such tests and treatment.

Maintaining a sense of the quality of communications between you and a patient can help you predict which patients are most likely to sue for malpractice. A lack of communication or poor communication between patient and physician is part of the "malpractice prodrome," an element that can help you spot which patients may have liability on their minds.

Predicting which patients are most likely to sue is an art and science in some ways as much so as the practice of medicine. Spotting these patients in advance can also save you countless hours in defending liability claims that you might have defused before the plaintiff's attorney gets around to calling you.

Identifying the litigious patient is an inexact science at best. Some lawsuits appear to have no rhyme or reason and may simply represent a "fishing expedition" by an attorney who has taken the case on a contingency basis. Even among those patients who have been injured by a physician and have a cause to sue, less than one in ten will actually file a claim, according to a California study conducted be Dr. Don Harper Mills, a Los Angeles physician and attorney.

Your first step in spotting liability prone patients is to discard the stereotypes that physicians tend to harbor about litigious patients. They may not be loud and aggressive or manipulated by an attorney. In the proper context, such as failure to warn patients about certain complications following surgery or drug interactions, any patient is capable of suing if the result falls short of expectations. But what about the borderline cases where it might be more of a judgment call? The circumstances do not always dictate whether a patient will file suit.

Despite the undeniable importance of circumstance and the result of care in triggering a lawsuit, not all patients are prospective plaintiffs. Given the same result, some patients sue while others forgive and forget. Those patients most apt to file malpractice cases can be categorized into distinct categories. Certain traits and idiosyncrasies can provide you with valuable clues about the likelihood of their taking you to court.

THE SHOPPER

Consider the shopper, the malcontent patient who never seems pleased with the care rendered by the physician who previously treated him or her. The patient may be attributing the persistent complaints of blurred vision to a growing list of physicians who failed to measure up to the patient's impossible standards. The patient may not be willing to acknowledge that such problems stem from his or her advanced stage of diabetes and that until the blood pressure is under control there is little that a physician will be able to do to curb the retinopathy.

If you are unfortunate enough to become this patient's physician, you may fail, as others before you, to resolve the patient's complaints. Whatever the ocular problem, however, the tip off should be the litany of complaints often heard from these patients who seem compelled to disparage the physician they have just seen. The crucial medical legal point to remember in treating them is to avoid showing support for the criticism leveled at another physician.

These patients are not only shopping for another physician, they're in the market for the confirmation they need to file a malpractice claim. Even if your support is tenuously provided, and that may be so subtle as a raised eyebrow or some other expression of surprise at or disapproval of the previous treatment by another physician, the patient may have found the convincing proof to file an action or seek legal advice.

As in all situations, meticulous record keeping is especially important because these patients may misconstrue your comments or reactions. Refrain from passing judgment on previous care rendered, suggesting to the patient that his or her condition deserves an independent evaluation and that previous care was rendered at a different time and is not a matter for you to evaluate. When the patient seems particularly difficult to relate to urge him or her to bring a family member or friend to the next appointment to verify what you have said. At all times, documentation in the medical chart is essential.

THE RELUCTANT PAYER

A long overdue bill is one of the best barometers that a liability claim may be brewing. If it is overdue, aggressive efforts at collection may even encourage the patient to retain an attorney and sue you. It is usually easy to discover the reason underlying a patient's reluctance to pay.

Gentle reminders and customary dunning techniques from office staff will generally fail to produce payment in these cases. Since filing a suit for collection can precipitate a countersuit from the patient for malpractice, collection efforts must be handled gingerly. It can be a minefield. Sometimes an expression of genuine personal concern is the gesture that may help an individual excuse treatment that did not meet expectations, even though a court may indicate that you conformed to the best standards of care.

Practice management consultants and malpractice defense attorneys frequently advise that it may not be worth the effort to press hard for collection. At such a point, if the bill is large enough for more aggressive collection efforts, wisdom dictates that you review the results of treatment with a personal malpractice defense attorney to decide whether the potential exists for liability. If it does, legal experts advise that you write off the bill rather than risk further angering the patient to the point of filing a claim.

Many of these billing disputes can be peacefully resolved because they are often a sign that the patient poorly understood the nature and scope of treatment. If that is true, a straightforward explanation of the need for the course of care should suffice.

But a fear of a counterclaim for malpractice should not be the only reason to back down from pursuing your claim for fees. In most jurisdictions, the physician who wants to sue for payment owed can use the statute of limitations to his advantage. In virtually all states, the statute of limitations for recovery of money owed by a breach of contract is substantially longer than the statute of limitations for initiating a malpractice action. The important point to remember is this: A lawsuit for fees owed does not have to be brought until the statute of limitations for medical malpractice has expired. What's more, in some states the law clearly forbids a counterclaim of malpractice or negligence to a claim based on a contract (the refusal to pay the agreed fee). You should consult your personal attorney to clarify how state laws apply to your situation.

THE EXPERT

Inspired, no doubt, by Ralph Nader, these archtypical consumers will try to convey the impression that none of your explanations are beyond their depth of medical knowledge. In fact, they will insist, you may be surprised by how much they know.

The pitfalls in dealing with the "consumerists," may be that they will even try to set traps for you, either seeking to confirm for themselves the sophisticated level of their knowledge or to corner you into suggesting that a certain sequence of symptoms and signs makes you suspect a certain diagnosis. It's best to concede that their medical knowledge is indeed better than what you have seen from other patients. By praising them, you have taken off some of the edge. But if they persist in questioning your judgment, beware of reacting defensively. That means you have gone for the bait, and you may run the risk of hasty judgments. You may want to suggest that they should confirm your diagnosis or choice of treatment by obtaining a second opinion.

THE PATIENT WHO FAILS TO COMPLY

Unlike the other groups of patients whose propensity to sue may only come to light after you learn more about their backgrounds and attitudes toward your care, uncooperative patients often provide you with early warning signs long before you suspect that they are liability minded. For example, the patient who is a constant "no show" for appointments, refuses to follow instructions or fails to contact you within a specified time suggests a troublesome individual who expects you to produce a cure without his or her cooperation.

These patients are frustrating because successful therapy hinges on a patient's compliance. Consider your duty to refer a patient to a neurologist. What if the nearest neurologist is not easily accessible because the patient lives in a rural area? Once the referral is made, however, it becomes the patient's obligation to make an appointment with the specialist based on your advice.

Whenever you refer, make sure that you have documented your recommendation in the record. Thus, the patient who may later seem confused about the sequence and timing of events surrounding your referral, or who even contradicts your recollection of what happened, cannot torpedo you in a deposition or in court.

By adequately documenting the patient's need for referral, you will lay the groundwork for your defense. Compliance is so crucial that it is advisable to set aside time at the end of a visit to explain in considerable detail why cooperation is essential.

EMOTIONALLY DISTURBED PATIENTS

Taxing personal problems, emotionally or financially based can also play a role as a precipitating factor in the filing of a malpractice claim. Such anxiety can lead to unrealistic demands on health care professionals and unreasonable expectations of treatment. Perhaps unaccustomed to coping with such problem patients, physicians may not be as attuned as they should be to recognizing affective disorders or other psychiatric problems. Since these emotional problems may be overlooked or not reported during the taking of a medical history, they may only be revealed later.

As always, carefully documenting your course of care and the responses of the patient, if need be in the presence of someone on your staff who initials the chart as a witness, can help establish that you followed appropriate standards. Do not treat such patients in a vacuum because you need the confirmation of others concerning their emotional upset.

It may be that personal problems in a patient's life are overwhelming. If that is true, certain aspects of care may need to be postponed until he or she is better able to understand the nature and scope of treatment. However, you may not have that luxury. If that is the case, consulting with other family members and expressing your concerns about the patient's mental health is preferable to ignoring emotional upset that may manifest as unreasonable expectations by the patient.

While the emotionally disturbed patient, the reluctant payer, the shopper and other selected patients may perk your index of suspicion that they are prone to filing malpractice claims, such signs are less obvious with other patients. For the vast majority of patients who file claims, anger is the key ingredient, and a breakdown in rapport is often the underlying factor that precipitates the filing of a claim. A patient spurned ("He said he would call me and let me know the test results, and he never called") or a patient insulted ("He told me I didn't need his help, I needed a psychiatrist!") are those who might otherwise overlook a poor result if they had only been handled with more consideration and understanding. There are a number of techniques you can use to optimize rapport and improve the sense of mutual trust and respect.

OFFICE PERSONNEL

Your office staff and the attitude that you engender toward patients is the logical place to begin building rapport. The reception given your patient can help set the tone for your relationship. By ensuring that your staff recognizes the importance of showing concern for the patient's problem and respect for the patient, you will not be burdened during the office visit itself with making excuses for their rudeness.

HIRE A QUALIFIED STAFF

Qualified people are happier employees, and they convey that feeling to the patients. When a patient first arrives at the doctor's office, he or she is probably greeted by a receptionist.

If this person is competent, friendly and courteous, he or she can have a positive influence on the patient's entire attitude. A competent outer office persuades the patient that the doctor is also competent; an inefficient, un-friendly outer office creates precisely the opposite impression. The physician who allows such conditions to exist is asking to be sued.

KEEP PATIENT WAITING TIMES SHORT

A critical element in the patient's mental framework is how long he or she has to wait before seeing the doctor. Timeliness is a component of respect and courtesy; the more thoroughly an office practices it, the happier the patient will be. The happier the patient, the less likely he or she is to file suit against the doctor.

DON'T IGNORE THE PATIENT'S SPOUSE

The sued doctor may have had excellent rapport with the patient, but never took time to listen to the patient's spouse. The office personnel and the physician need to realize that many married couples are governed or controlled by one spouse, who must not be ignored. If the doctor fails to solicit the spouse's comments, he may never know how the patient is really doing, and may blindly assume there are no problems.

KEEP THE PATIENT INFORMED

A physician and his staff should keep the patient informed regarding medical problems. Patients experience tremendous anxiety about their ailments, and the physician must put the ailments in perspective for the patient. A patient told of a potential treatment complication will be less likely to sue if he or she understands the complication. Without being previously informed and warned, he or she may believe the doctor made an error and caused the complication.

LEARN TO LISTEN

Probably the most simple, yet least practiced aspect of communication, is listening. The only way to correctly diagnose is to listen to the patient's descriptions of the condition; the only way to know whether treatment is correct is to listen to the patient. Not listening, or listening but not hearing, contributes to more malpractice cases than any other single failure on the part of the physician or his staff. Normally, the doctor will say he was never told something when, in fact, the patient claims he told the doctor several times.

INFORMED CONSENT

If rapport forges good communication, it pays off in tangible ways such as obtaining informed consent. The duty to inform a patient raises questions about the kinds of information that you must disclose to a patient to allow him or her to make an intelligent decision. Recent court decisions have also raised questions about your obligations in situations where patients refuse certain diagnostic tests. How much information do you need to disclose? In addition, what must be consented to? Must you explain all the risks and benefits of a throat culture? an injection?

POTENTIAL RISKS

The rule of the road is that anything that carries a potential risk must be explained and consented to. Some procedures do not need consent if the risk is so minor, the likelihood of its occurring so small, or the benefits so overwhelming. What is a small likelihood? Estimates vary, but in a Washington case, *Mason v. Ellsworth* (1970), the court held that if an unanticipated result occurred in only 0.25–0.75 percent of cases, it could be considered remote as a matter of law.

Unlike the hospital setting in which other personnel might obtain consent, an office-based practitioner cannot leave the responsibility to a nonphysician. It is often helpful for a nurse to be present during treatment or the explanation of a diagnostic procedure. You might follow the common practice of maintaining a running conversation and explanation with your nurse while the patient is being examined and treated. Since the nurse has heard the explanation many times, the informed consent discussion is for the patient's benefit. The nurse, however, is also serving as a witness.

EXPLANATIONS OF ALTERNATIVES

You are obliged to advise patients that alternatives exist to a treatment method that entails certain risks. Even if you do not consider the alternative to be the best approach, as long as reasonable medical opinion considers it acceptable, you are obligated to tell the patient the treatment is available elsewhere. For example, a woman with breast cancer may choose a lumpectomy over a modified radical mastectomy if the choice is proposed. But if you do not think that an alternative will work in the patient's case, you need not suggest it. The rule? Alternatives must be suggested if they are accepted by at least a respectable minority of medical opinion. For example, you could not be held liable if you failed to suggest laetrile to the same women with breast cancer. On the other hand, if some form of adjunct therapy is available, you might be obligated to review such alternatives.

WHEN CAN YOU WITHHOLD INFORMATION?

If your patient is unreasonably fearful of a procedure and if you believe that explaining all the risks will lead him to refuse the necessary treatment, you need not offer explanations beyond those you consider safe for him to know. This is especially true when the risks are highly improbable. The general rule: If the risk of an untoward result is statistically high, inform the patient regardless of its effect on informed consent. If the risk is statistically low, but the consequences of the untoward result are extremely severe, you should still inform the patient. But if the statistical risk is low and its severity is not great, you can modify your warning so that it does not interfere with obtaining consent. Some situations require full disclosure of risks (e.g., angiograms). Warnings of serious side effects of drugs must always be given before prescriptions are written.

RIGHT OF "INFORMED REFUSAL"

A recent California case should alert physicians to still another situation in which a communication breakdown can leave them vulnerable to suit. In the 1980 case of *Truman v. Thomas*, a family practitioner was held liable for neglecting to tell a woman of risks in failing to have a Pap smear performed. The woman subsequently developed cervical cancer and died.

The trend in the courts has been to expand the doctrine of informed consent so that you need to warn the patient not only about factors that influence his or her consent to treatment but to consequences of refusing treatment, too.

DISCLOSE ONLY WHAT IS "REASONABLY FORESEEN"

You are only expected to explain risks that are "reasonably foreseen." Unexpected after effects of procedures or unexplained events during surgery go beyond what is required. For example, you need not explain that infections have been known to occur postoperatively. Confine your discussion to risks that are considered inherent in the procedure.

A GOOD BAROMETER: HOW ELECTIVE IS IT?

A yardstick used by many doctors is to what extent the procedure is considered elective. The more elective the procedure, the more detailed is the informed consent. Consider the severe arthritic for whom you may suggest cortisone treatment or immunosuppressive therapy. In cases like this involving long-term therapy in which the patient must balance suffering with the symptoms as opposed to getting some relief with risk of side effects, the patient is entitled to a detailed explanation before you can assume consent is "informed."

DOCUMENTATION

As in other phases of malpractice prevention, documentation is a pivotal factor in your defense. A patient may not recall that he or she consented to treatment, but if it is charted, the jury will not be left trying to decide between your credibility and the plaintiff's.

THE THERAPEUTIC ALLIANCE

The impact of informed consent is double-edged. Although it clarifies options and can encourage mutual understanding, the procedure also has its dangers in that you are calling attention to risks. These risks, when covered in an informed consent form, can trigger feelings of helplessness "by crystallizing the patient's awareness that the situation really is uncertain," say three authors whose recent article in the *New England Journal of Medicine* (311:49-51, 1984) suggests how a physician's communications skills can be used to obtain informed consent and build a "therapeutic alliance" with a patient. That alliance, helping the patient confront and become reconciled to the uncertainty of medical choices and chances, works in a physician's favor by deepening the patient's trust. A trusting patient is less likely to sue for malpractice.

However, Drs. Thomas G. Gutheil and Harold Bursztajn and researcher Archie Brodsky suggest that before you can build that alliance you and the patient face several hurdles. In addition to calling attention to risks, the consent form also discloses a seemingly authoritative list of complications with numerical probabilities. In reviewing that list with you, the patient may cling to the magical hope that "all bases have been covered." Disappointment that everything has not been covered may lead to a malpractice suit if the result is unfortunate. Thus, these authors say, the twin dangers lie in exaggerating how little or how much you know.

MAKING INFORMED CONSENT WORK

The key to the effectiveness of informed consent is to stop thinking of it as a formality (the recital of options and the signing of forms). Instead, you should enter into it with your patients as a process of mutual discovery. The communication between you and the patient should be directed not only at satisfying the legal requirements but toward addressing that all-important question of uncertainty. The uncertainty of medical treatment should not pose a threat but can be the basis for your alliance with the patient, according to the book, *Medical Choices, Medical Chances*. The importance of this lies in the fact that the patient feels a sense of working together with the doctor. That feeling of cooperation, becoming part of a partnership, is one of the major elements in avoiding negative reactions to treatment and consequently, a malpractice suit.

PATIENT FANTASIES OF UNCERTAINTY:
HOW DO YOU RESOLVE THEM?

Fears, doubts and the disabling nature of illness trigger memories of childhood helplessness. When illness threatens, the patient longs for a feeling of power that is vested in the physician. It is almost magical power that, in effect, says, "You will make me good as new," much as a child might resort to magical thoughts.

In this context, the patient is unwilling to accept your suggestion that the prognosis is not as certain or predictable as he would like it to be. That is because magical notions of science play a key part in such fantasies of what to expect. You represent science, perceived as certain knowledge. But the patient is easily prey to feelings of paranoid distrust. Already a helpless victim of illness, the patient may feel helpless in the face of science. If the outcome is less than expected, the patient may not only refuse to assume responsibility for his or her own care but may consider litigation as the only resort.

You cannot take away the patient's wishful thinking without replacing it with a different comfort, a different alliance that tests your ability to effectively communicate. During your explanation of possible risks, you can empathize with the patient's attitude with remarks such as, "I wish I could give you a medication that was sure to have only positive effects," and "There is just no guarantee you'll live through this, I wish there were."

Drs. Gutheil and Burztajn and researcher Brodsky suggest that statements like these make it possible for the patient to "approach the physician not as a childhood fantasy ideal but as another vulnerable human being, and hence, sharing the same uncertainty. Instead of squaring off defensively against each other, doctor and patient are brought together by the shared acknowledgement of clinical uncertainty and of the fantasies used to deny it."

WEANING THE PATIENT FROM THE FANTASY OF CERTAINTY

Once the patient and physician are looking at the fantasy together, the physician can guide the patient in seeing it for what it is. The choice of words is once again crucial. Expressions like, "I wish it were possible . . .", even as they validate the wish, imply tactfully that it is contrary to fact. Clarifying statements ("Many people do believe that one can specify in advance every possible complication of an operation") offer the patient tactful suppport in taking a critical look at beliefs that he or she may share with "many people."

With that groundwork, the physician can move on to explain how uncertain some aspects of treatment may be, giving the patient a more realistic sense of what to expect. Now the patient is a participant-observer rather than feeling like a participant in "an experiment." But the physician cannot stop there. The alliance with the patient and the new awareness it generates means that the physician must still be there to share the uncertainty. Use of statements like, "I'll be with you every step of the way" are helpful. It conveys the promise of a continuing relationship if there is a poor or even tragic outcome. When this promise is fulfilled, the patient is less likely to make the physician pay for an untoward result through a lawsuit.

The value in this approach is that it stresses what you say rather than following the conventional path of taking more time or telling patients more. Practically, it actually requires less time, yet more is understood because your communication is efficient.

HOW THIS APPROACH YIELDS LEGAL BENEFITS

The usual approach to informed consent is generally considered a form of defensive medicine. It is primarily used to protect the physician from a malpractice suit, but it often fails to do even that. However, by developing the "therapeutic alliance," the physician discourages that simplistic blaming and alienation that leads the patient to file a liability claim. As the physicians who promote the idea have written: "This is true malpractice prevention, which offers the physician stronger legal protection by allowing both doctor and patient to deepen their understanding while building a supportive and trusting relationship, a relationship based not on unrealistic certainty but on honesty in facing the uncertainty inherent in clinical practice."

4

ESTABLISHING EFFECTIVE PATIENT RELATIONSHIPS

MALPRACTICE CHECKLIST

- Patients should bring all medications to initial visit and phone other physicians for release of records.
- Time spent in obtaining a history safeguards you from a lawsuit.
- Patients who do not complete the history probably have something to hide and you should not accept them as patients.
- Beware of patients who praise you as the only physician who "understands them."
- Your staff should be "attitudinally cloned" after you. If you are neat and cordial, your staff should be, too.
- Grade yourself on the four A's— Accessibility, Affability, Availability and Affordability.
- Being a good listener can put you on good footing.
- Instructions are more likely to be followed if given in short segments so the patient has time to absorb each one.
- To avoid noncompliance: Be positive about your therapy, prescribe a regimen you know they can follow, suspect noncompliance.
- Let the patient blow off steam.
- Document that every effort was made to explain why the course of treatment is important.

- If a patient refuses treatment, have the patient sign a statement releasing you and your staff from liability.
- ER staff should work as a team to discover why the patient is refusing treatment.
- If a patient is mentally incompetent, substitute consent should be obtained from a family member.
- Treating without consent applies to true, life-threatening emergencies.
- Child neglect presenting in ER: notify social services department or inform hospital administrator immediately.
- Questions about DNR orders should be raised with the patient as early as possible.
- DNR: patient should be terminally ill, response of family should be documented, and order must be written in record.
- One or more consultant's opinion should be obtained on DNR.
- There must be evidence that competent patient consented or next of kin or guardian agreed if patient is incompetent.

ESTABLISHING EFFECTIVE PATIENT RELATIONSHIPS

No health care provider should initiate immediate non-life-threatening treatment without first obtaining a complete and comprehensive patient history. In many areas "shoppers" are becoming an increasing problem. We often think of the shopper as an individual with a chronic pain condition that requires higher and higher doses of controlled substances. They may be seeing two or three physicians simultaneously and simply add another physician so they leave the appearance of being maintained on a constant dose of the particular substance.

The most insidious of the shoppers are those who, unknown to one physician, are seeing several others for various conditions which often may be real. The danger arises from the lack of knowledge of what all the other physicians are doing and, most importantly, prescribing. Without a complete comprehensive patient history the physicians are subjecting themselves unnecessarily to litigation or sanctions for providing class II narcotics for chronic pain patients. At the onset, no single documentation is more important than a comprehensive patient history. How can you take the time to do a ten-page patient history? You don't— the patient does. As is indicated by the forms that follow this chapter, the burden is on the patients to complete the form and to sign a statement that they have not withheld answers on the questionnaire and that they are fully aware that you will rely on the information *they* provide to care for them.

The form may be initially mailed to the patient when they make an appointment so they will have adequate time to complete the questionnaire. If they are making an initial appointment they should bring all their medications, phone other physicians for release of their records and be scheduled so that they may complete the form prior to being seen. An office nurse may review the form with the patient, initialing and dating the time of the review and interview with the patient, and the physician should also review the questionnaire with the patient. In terms of time and accuracy, the physician or other health care provider should have the best possible patient history available. The time spent to obtain the history is an investment in safeguarding yourself from a lawsuit and providing the best care and treatment to your patient. By following this procedure, you will find that those who do not want to complete the history probably have something to hide and should not be accepted as a patient.

Following completion of your questionnaire, you should communicate with any other physician, dentist, psychologist or other health care provider who has rendered treatment to the patient within the past five years. You should not simply contact them but clearly document that fact in your records. To do so is to ensure that you have a complete patient profile. A complete patient profile is absolutely essential to protect you from your patient. Remember, it is not another physician's patients who will sue you, it will be your patients. You will find from other physicians how compliant the prospective patient is; you will find out if they are constantly changing physicians. Beware of the patient who praises you as the only physician who "understands them." They are the very ones who will point an accusing finger from the witness stand. In short simple terms, we have arrived at the stage of health care delivery that mandates that we literally do a background check on potential patients. The forms that are contained at the end of this chapter may be modified for your individual office use. There is no "single form" to meet the needs of every health care provider. Let's examine some examples of how the procedure works and more importantly what to look for.

A 35-year-old white male presents at your office with a history of kidney stones and renal cholic. He tells you he has had problems for years and wants to establish a physician–patient relationship because he has severe pain at times. He is young, intelligent and articulate and has just arrived in your area. He completes the form in its entirety. When you check with his previous physicians in another geographical location you find that he has had only minor problems with kidney stones and major problems with the abuse of narcotics, which led to the loss of his job. You do not need this individual as a patient— he is fraught with danger.

An 82-year-old woman moves from another area to live with her son. She has multiple physical problems. She completes the form. However, because of her lack of memory, she leaves out certain critical information. Her previous physician, who treated her for the past 30 years, can provide an excellent insight as to the type of patient and human being you are dealing with. Even though she omitted certain information, you will know that she has not knowingly done so and you will also be aware of the necessity to give instructions about the taking of medications to her son or daughter-in-law to ensure compliance.

The authors have compiled various patient questionnaires in an effort to provide you with various formats that you may adapt for your office use. Once you have formulated a final form, you may have it printed on NCR paper to give the patient one copy, have one for your office records and to have one in a hospital record if you see the patient for the first time in the hospital. In a lawsuit, it may be the most important document for your defense.

COMMUNICATIONS: WHAT YOU DON'T SAY CAN HURT YOU

The patient history forms are the first step toward building effective communications and rapport. As long as the lines of communication between you and the patient remain clear and strong, a malpractice suit will not have fertile ground in which to take root. Most patient problems that set the stage for a lawsuit arise from a combination of two factors: The first is a poor result, which may or may not be attributable to negligence. The second is a breakdown in communication. In numerous claims filed by patients, the physician did not spend enough time discussing the problems of medical management and what patients should expect. When a patient feels offended because the doctor has ignored legitimate complaints or behaved in a way that implied to the patient that the physician "couldn't care less," that dissatisfaction and anger will likely make the patient feel uninhibited about consulting a lawyer and filing a suit if anything less than a perfect result occurs. Communication is the common denominator in a practice. It cuts across virtually every facet of patient care— from the efforts to obtain informed consent to how you achieve compliance during follow-up therapy. Good rapport begins with your office staff and the moment the patient walks into the waiting room. Your staff should be somewhat attitudinally cloned after you. If you pride yourself on a neat appearance and a cordial attitude, your staff should too.

For starters, office staff should offer patients explanations for a late or cancelled appointment instead of letting them stew until it's time for them to see you. Scheduling should be done with care to ensure the patient will have enough time with you— especially if the patient is new. Allow more time than usual for that first visit, because you never know what may happen and what the patient may reveal about the source of a problem. Patients tend to be more forgiving later in the course of care when you rush them if you gave them a leisurely first visit. It's their first impression and, like meeting anyone for the first time, the first impression is lasting. The staff should be trained to know that patients are not numbers and are never to be treated as a diagnosis. Patients do not like to be sitting in the waiting room and hear themselves referred to as a disease. Staff should be discreet about payments. These fees should be made clear to patients at the time appointments are made. If you require payment after an office visit, a sign in the office should be clearly visible and your staff should gently remind patients of that fact. Fees can be included in an office brochure that also spells out other features of office policy.

BASIC QUESTIONS

There are five basic questions that the most successful physicians answer for the patient: What's wrong with me? What caused it? What are you and I going to do to treat my condition? How long will it take? How much will it cost?

If you can put yourself in the role of the patient, you might ask yourself how you fare in these areas:

- Accessibility: How easily can I approach the doctor?
- Affability: How pleasant and friendly is the physician?
- Availability: Can I see the physician when I want? How much time will he give me?
- Affordability: Can I afford to see the doctor? Are the insurance matters handled efficiently?

It may sound simplistic, but just being a good listener can quickly put you on good footing with a patient. What's more, in the long run you will save a lot of time. If a patient is allowed to explain the onset of illness and symptoms, he is likely to provide information that is often missed by rapid-fire questioning. As you listen, you may look for body language that is often more revealing than what the patient is saying. If the patient is sitting on the edge of a chair, for example, or with arms clutching his or her sides, you may detect anxieties that need to be approached.

INSTRUCTIONS

Instructions are more likely to be followed if they are given in short segments, so the patient has enough time to absorb each one. Listening is also important at this stage, since most patients feel embarrassed about their lack of knowledge. They are afraid to confess that they do not understand instructions or the diagnosis. For that reason, don't be afraid to ask them how much of what you have said they understand. Patients should be allowed to interrupt explanations instead of being told to "wait until I'm finished." Further, when you ask a patient whether there are any other questions, it should not be a curt "Any questions?" but a genuine request to make sure the patient understands. When time allows, it's a good idea to have the patient explain the treatment back to you so that you are sure.

CONFRONTING PROBLEMS OF NONCOMPLIANCE

Many medical-legal complaints originate when a physician fails to investigate the reasons for noncompliance or does not adequately confront the problem.

Be Positive about Your Therapy

Carefully wording your explanation for why you have adopted a treatment approach will encourage compliance. For example, phraseology such as, "Maybe we should try a dose of this to see if it will make you feel better" will leave the patient with the idea that you are too tentative. Instead say something like, "I'm prescribing this medication because it's been effective in controlling problems such as yours— but it can't help if you're not careful to take it on schedule."

Prescribe a Regimen You Know They Can Follow

If you prescribe eye drops containing pilocarpine for a truck driver who works at night, you have wasted everyone's time. Tailor your treatment as much as possible to your patient's lifestyle and habits.

Go with the Simplest Regimen, If Possible

Most patients are faithful to a once-a-day regimen and are usually good about twice-a-day programs. But the curve of compliance takes a nose dive with a t.i.d. regimen. And if you do prescribe a regimen of three or four times a day, make sure you allow extra time to explain the importance of the patient's compliance with your instructions.

Suspect Noncompliance

If you inquire carefully about compliance after the patient has been on a regimen for a while, you may discover how lackadaisical a patient has been. When you discover a patient's shortcomings, avoid displays of anger or temper and try to work out a program or a method of ensuring better compliance.

Watch the Cost of Medications

Many patients have a good excuse for not complying with regimens if the cost becomes more than they can bear. Generic medications are not always advisable but are one solution in some cases. Another cost-cutter is to order double-strength doses when you have prescribed scored tablets. If a 50 mg tablet costs 20 cents, then a 100 mg tablet may cost 30 cents. Over time this will add up to a considerable cost savings.

Let the Patient Blow Off Steam

Patients who refuse to comply with your instructions or who set strict limits on what they will and will not let you do need to be handled gingerly. If mishandled or antagonized, they could easily turn into a medical-legal problem. Many of these patients have decided what their problems are, what "impossible" remedies you are suggesting and what they will tell you. Since they have anticipated a confrontation with you, let them blow off steam before you reply. In many cases the root of their problem is unrelated to the fight that they have picked with you and if you probe beneath the surface with comments such as "Why don't we find out first what the problem is? Who knows, maybe I'll agree with you," you will reflect a concern that can help to defuse their anger. Fear is such a basic motivator of patients that physicians often overlook how it can affect their relationships. In such cases, you may not be able to turn things around in one office visit. It may take several for you to gradually build up a trust. During the second visit and subsequent ones the patient will begin to realize that the setting of limits does not work and that what you are suggesting as a workup or treatment is not so drastic or unreasonable, after all.

REFUSED CONSENT: A TEST OF COMMUNICATIONS SKILLS

If a noncompliant patient signals the need for renewed efforts at communication, the patient who refuses consent is the supreme test of those communication skills. But when the patient outright refuses to consent to treatment, a new set of malpractice risks arises. Generally, a competent, conscious adult has the right to refuse to consent to medical treatment— as does an emancipated minor. In one of the earliest cases dealing with consent to medical treatment, Justice Cardozo of the Court of Appeals of New York ruled: "Every human being of adult years and sound mind has a right to determine what shall be done with his own body; and a surgeon who performs an operation without his patient's consent commits an assault, for which he is liable in damages."

Fear of results or side effects, embarrassment over techniques used, and the influence of alcohol or drugs are among the leading reasons for a patient's refusal of treatment. Women over 50, for example, often refuse Pap smears because they do not want a pelvic examination. Yet a recent California case broadened the concept of informed consent when a woman who had refused a Pap smear and subsequently developed cervical cancer sued a physician for failing to warn her of the risks of refusing that test. But the Pap smear, like other tests such as sigmoidoscopies and barium enemas, are part of a constellation of techniques about which the patient must be informed concerning the risks of refusal. The intoxicated patient or drug overdosed patient brought into the emergency room who becomes combative and agitated presents additional problems concerning refusal as they waver between competence and possible coma.

Every effort should be made to explain to the patient why the course of treatment is important, and this effort should be documented in the record. If that fails, the physician should inform the patient that by refusing, the patient now accepts the responsibility for not having the procedure done. Consequences or the refusal (such as possible malignancy, etc) should be outlined as well. Another effective way is to involve members of the family, particularly a spouse. But it is important not to overuse the family with the patient who refuses. Involve them in significant areas of care. For example, if a patient presents with angina and you think it is advisable for him to be admitted in the hospital because of the possibility of an impending MI, the family can help. A patient is less apt to give the physician a hard time after arguing with his family. Acknowledging a patient's apprehension will provide the patient with evidence that you are listening rather than showing a perfunctory attitude. It is also advisable to have the patient sign a statement that releases the medical staff from all liability since the patient did not permit them to proceed with treatment.

REFUSAL OF CONSENT IN AN EMERGENCY

The belligerent, hostile or intoxicated patient who refuses to consent to treatment is a frequent visitor to the emergency room. Such a patient poses a special challenge to the staff. They should determine if the patient is clinically competent to make an informed decision to forego treatment— not always an easy judgment call in cases of overdose, for example, when a patient may be drifting in and out of altered states of consciousness. The entire ER staff should work as a team to discover why the patient is refusing treatment. Did one of the staff make the patient hostile or uncooperative? If so, the staff member should apologize or avoid contact with the patient. The patient and any family or friends present should be made aware of the consequences of his not being treated. If the patient is mentally unable to refuse treatment because of his condition, substituted consent should be obtained from a family member. The ER staff should bear in mind that the emergency doctrine that allows them to treat without a patient's consent applies to true, life-threatening emergencies. However, when the patient is conscious, competent and expressly refuses treatment, an express refusal overrides any implied consent.

No matter how many times a physician confronts such refusals, each one presents a slightly different set of problems. Consider, for example, the 24-year-old man brought into the ER who has swallowed 200 tablets of a tranquilizer and tells you he wants to die. His friends may have brought him in forcibly and he informs you that he will sue you for assault and battery if you put down an NG tube. You have two choices: (1)wait until the patient becomes so comatose that he won't resist treatment and try to save him from that time on; or if you (2)do nothing and you lose him, his relatives may sue you for not saving the man, who they could claim was incompetent for trying to commit suicide. Although you may be able to obtain a court order for cases involving religious objections to life-saving treatments, such as in cases of a parent who is a Jehovah's Witness and who refuses treatment for his or her child, in the ER you may not have the time to contact a judge. Physicians who have weathered similar episodes in the ER report that they generally try to convince intoxicated patients to remain in the ER until the effects of alcohol or a drug overdose have worn off. On the other hand, you may decide that it is probably worth it to take a chance against a suit for assault and battery, convinced that by saving a life you will not be found guilty of such a charge.

Jehovah's Witnesses who require elective surgery but who waive life-saving administration of blood often present with special medical-legal problems. There is no prohibition against a patient's donating his own blood in advance of surgery, and that is how physicians usually try to resolve it if they have the time. If there is no time for donation of blood, use blood substitutes. When confronted with this problem, physicians and hospitals may find themselves with no alternative but to seek a court order that will authorize the transfusion or treatment.

TREATING THE MINOR WHOSE PARENT REFUSES TREATMENT

The Baby Doe cases have turned this area into one of the most volatile medical-legal issues. Your choices in other situations also loom complicated if your state has passed an emancipated minor statute. In most cases in which parents refuse treatment recommended by physicians, the hospital or social service agency either seeks temporary guardianship of the child to authorize treatment or charges the parents with neglect. Usually, when parents object to life-threatening surgery because of religious tenets, courts approve the request for surgery when the primary care physician recommends it, if the risks of the surgery are small. For example, if a child has acute appendicitis, courts routinely authorize treatment, since fatalities from such procedures are so rare and the risk of death without the operation great. However, if the treatment is experimental or risky, courts have upheld the parents' rights to prevent treatment. That happened in the 1980 California case involving Philip Becker, a 12-year-old boy with Down's syndrome and a congenital ventricular septal defect.

The trial judge said the major cardiac surgery had a mortality rate of 10 percent and said four factors must be considered before the state intervenes. They are the likelihood the child will suffer serious harm, the evaluation of medical professionals involved in the child's treatment, the risks involved in that treatment and the preference of the child. He upheld the parents' right to leave the heart untreated.

A court's decision often hinges on whether the physician knows that with a certain kind of standard treatment, the child will have a full recovery. Parents cannot confine their child to death, but the physician should not treat a child himself or herself without consent before a court order. It is considered assault and battery to touch the child without consent.

Physicians must be aware of mandatory reporting statutes. Whereas the laws dealing with child neglect for refusing medical treatment vary from state to state, advice about what to do is uniform— notify the social services department or immediately inform the hospital's administrator, and follow hospital procedure.

Although infants obviously cannot make medical preferences known, in some states young teens can consent to surgery without their parent's permission. All states say that when a child is old enough to understand the risks, benefits and alternatives, the child can sign a consent form. In fact research shows there has not been a successful suit in 30 years against a doctor who provided care for a teenager over 14 without parental consent.

A physician would be well-advised to talk with his or her own attorney about the state laws dealing with this well in advance of the situation in which that advice is needed because of the impact of emancipated minor statutes. These statutes generally allow you to treat minors for venereal disease and alcohol or drug problems without parental consent. Court injunctions allowing treatment without consent for parents whose religious beliefs won't allow treatment are nearly always granted in life-threatening situations. In fact, there are times when the parents actually want the court order for treatment that is not accepted by the church. To protect you from possible criminal action, if a parent refuses treatment deemed necessary, get a second opinion. Try to get a second opinion in any case, especially if you are starting child neglect proceedings.

IS IT LIFE-THREATENING?

Courts will usually not overturn a parent's medical choice if treatment is optional and not life-threatening. Courts are more apt to make a quick decision if the nontreatment is life-threatening. Courts would rather err on the side of life.

In cases of refusal in which the treatment is not life-threatening, the physician should still contact the social welfare agency, but allow the parents to take the child home with them. However, if a child is brought to your office with acute appendicitis and the child may die, go into the next room and call juvenile court. If the child will be disabled or dead before a hearing can be held, the court can order treatment on the phone.

WRITING NO CODE ORDERS:
WHAT ARE THE GUIDELINES?

> *"There is nothing anyone can do," the old man whispered. "Even without your gadgets, medic, you know what's wrong with me. You can't mend a whole body, not with all your skills and all your fancy instruments. The body wears out... And even if you gave me a new body, you still couldn't help me, because down deep where your knives can't reach and your instruments can't measure, is the me that is old beyond repair."*
> *—Journal of Medical Ethics, 1982.*

The order not to resuscitate can be the ultimate challenge to your ability to effectively communicate with your patient. The guidelines for writing DNR orders have undergone rapid change in the last five years as the AMA and other groups have revamped recommendations for terminally ill patients. One set of guidelines for example, recently published in *The New England Journal of Medicine* proposes that "severely and irreversibly demented patients need only care given them to make them comfortable. If such a patient rejects food and water by mouth, it is ethically permissible to withhold nutrition and hydration artificially administered by vein or gastric tube." The guidelines add that it is ethical for physicians to withhold antibiotics for pneumonia and appropriate "not to treat intercurrent illness except with measures required for comfort."

Writing a no-code order is least troublesome when a competent, informed patient and a sensitive physician can view the issues in clear perspective. Thus a "living will," written when a patient is competent, can help clarify a physician's options when the patient is in extremis. But if the patient is ambivalent about such orders and choices, if the family disagrees with what is recommended by the physician, no-code decisions can become a potential minefield of medical-legal problems, raising questions of criminal liability as well.

Approaching the Decision Early in Care

Questions about DNR orders should be raised as early as possible. Primary care physicians have an opportunity to discuss them early in the illness even before admission to the hospital when a disease is chronic and progressive. If a physician has good rapport with a patient, it is easier at that time to begin the discussion than to wait until the patient is incompetent to comprehend the choices. Physicians need to recognize that among patients with chronic degenerative diseases, it is fairly certain that at some point down the line, these decisions will have to be made.

Patients already seriously ill upon entry to a treatment center are the candidates for whom a discussion is most appropriate. The staff should stay alert for patients with a strong feeling on the subject because sooner or later the patient will initiate the discussion. These patients may eventually be asked a question similar to this: "While you are here, there may come a time when you become too ill to communicate with us about your medical care. Are there any specific instructions you might want us to follow at such a time?" The response provides the basis for further discussion and exploration of the concept of DNR and what it will mean.

In his study published in *The Journal of the American Geriatric Society*, Dr. Steven A. Levenson, medical director at the Levindale Hebrew Geriatric Center and Hospital in Baltimore, reviews a classification scheme that is working well, The scheme proposes classifications for terminal and critical illness (see **Table 4-1** for classification). Patients are initially placed in Class A or B until the staff can establish the extent of a patient's problems. After assessing and evaluating the patient's capacity for rational thought and decision making, that classificaton may change. These classifications are indicators of the kind of therapeutic measures that are required. Within one to two weeks after admission, a multidisciplinary conference discusses the care plan in more detail and the staff exchanges observations on the patient's mental competency. One key question asked: "Could this patient, now or at some future time, participate in discussion in his best interest about his care?" Based on interviews with the patient, the medical condition or prognosis, classifications of treatment are then made (see **Table 4-1**). The patient is further classified according to what resuscitative steps should be taken. Subsequent conferences— at least every two

TABLE 1
Classifications for Terminal and Critical Illness

CLASS A: MAXIMUM THERAPEUTIC EFFORT

Transfer to acute care hospital without hesitation, if necessary. Patient is candidate for intensive care unit (ICU), respirator, if necessary.

CLASS B: MAXIMUM THERAPEUTIC EFFORT WITHIN LIMITS OF THIS INSTITUTION

Transfer to acute care hospital, if necessary (where reevaluation may occur). Not an ICU candidate. Some invasive procedures, special tests, may be appropriate. Try to avoid transfer to general hospital.

CLASS C: LIMITED THERAPEUTIC MEASURES

X-ray examination, blood tests may be in order. Intravenous therapy (IV) may be appropriate. Antibiotics should be used sparingly. Invasive procedures and transfer to general hospital for special tests should be avoided. Change to Class B or D depends on patient's response to initial treatment.

CLASS D: NO THERAPEUTIC EFFORT

Only that which enhances comfort and minimizes pain. No x-ray examinations, blood tests, antibiotics. IVs ought not to be started unless they will enhance comfort or minimize pain.

On admission, patients should be treated as Class A or B until further designation is made.

This patient should be considered Class__ if critically ill. "Critical illness" means an illness that could lead to imminent death, but might respond to treatment, i.e., pneumonia, pulmonary embolus, or myocardial infarction.

This patient should be considered Class__ if terminally ill. "Terminal illness" means an illness that will result in imminent death regardless of treatment, i.e., metastatic cancer, or certain neurologic disease.

In all cases, the floor nurse will notify the attending physician or on-call physician before any action is taken or any treatment withheld.

Scheme indicates a method for classifying patients based on medical condition and prognosis upon entry to care facility.
Classes denote level of therapy considered appropriate.

months— review this decision and the impact of changes in the patient's condition.

Resolving Questions of Ambivalence

Even when questions of the risk/benefit ratio of treatment have been decided, the decision to write a DNR order is complicated by other considerations. A patient's ambivalence can make the decision extremely difficult. These expressions of ambivalence— such as a patient's wavering on whether to be removed from a respirator— make the concept of patient "autonomy" difficult to define. In still other cases, a patient's request for DNR status may be influenced by depression. The astute clinician must remain alert for a history of endogenous depression, vegetative signs of depression and any acute condition that could precipitate a reactive depression.

One case history in the literature cites how these problems are resolved. A 76-year-old man had been transferred to an intensive care unit after surgery for diverticulitis. The patient's hospital course was complicated by a urinary tract infection and aspiration pneumonia, which required orotracheal intubation. Before intubation, however, he had emphasized his strong desire to return to his previous state of health. However, when the patient became delirious as a result of sepsis, his wife and daughter urged that no "heroic" measures be taken. The conflict between the patient's statements and the family's wishes led to sharp staff disagreements on the level of supportive care. On the basis of the patient's previous statements, the hospital's terminal care committee recommended that "vigorous supportive intervention" be continued but reviewed on a daily basis. Five days later the patient contracted a nonresponsive superinfection, became transiently hypotensive and developed progressive renal failure. A DNR order was written and was implemented when the patient expired in the ICU.

Writing the Order

The irreversibility of disease is among the most important criteria for writing the order. Three guidelines are generally in order:

1. The patient should be irreversibly and terminally ill so that resuscitation would merely delay the inevitable outcome.
2. The patient, his family or both should be counseled concerning the order, and the response should be documented by a note in the progress record.

3. The order must be written. Nurses should not be the ones to write the order.

These additional precautions should also be taken:

- There should be complete documentation of the terminal state and prognoses.
- One or more consultants' opinions affirming their agreement should be obtained.
- Opinions of the "ethics" committee, if available, should be secured.
- Agreement by the institution should be required.
- The order should be written on the order sheet, dated and signed. Verbal no-treatment or CPR orders are not appropriate and do not meet with accepted medical standards.
- There must be evidence that a competent patient consented, or that the next of kin or guardian agreed if the patient is incompetent.

Nevertheless, legal questions of patient, family and physician rights in withholding resuscitation and life support have not been clearly answered by the courts. Although a competent patient generally has the right to reject resuscitative treatment, the courts may restrict that right in protecting third parties such as spouses or children. A patient not irreversibly, terminally ill and with a dependent spouse or child might not be allowed to refuse life-saving treatment if the courts are called upon to decide such issues. But in general, if a competent, irreversibly and terminally ill patient consents to or requests a do-not-resuscitate status, the decision cannot be overridden by family members without a court order even if the patient subsequently becomes incompetent. On the other hand, if a competent patient requests resuscitation in the event of an arrest, a no-resuscitation status cannot be ordered without a court order even if the patient subsequently becomes incompetent and the family requests such a status.

Current Trends

Recent decisions seem to be sending this message from the courts to physicians: "Come to us only when there is disagreement in the family concerning the decision." The trend is to allow physicians and the family to make the decision in cases where the patient has not clearly indicated a preference. Nevertheless, physicians cannot unilaterally make the decision without having discussed it as openly as possible, informing the nurses and obtaining the agreement of the family. The courts say that if there is a conflict, physicians should not touch the decision without obtaining a judicial ruling.

MEDICAL HISTORY FORM

DATE: _____

NAME _____ Birth Date _____ Age _____

ADDRESS _____ CITY _____ STATE _____ ZIP _____

PHONE NUMBER HOME: _____ WORK: _____

REFERRING PHYSICIAN _____

INSURANCE &/OR MEDICARE # _____ SOCIAL SECURITY # _____

MEDICAID # _____

WHO IS FINANCIALLY RESPONSIBLE FOR YOUR MEDICAL CARE? _____

PROBLEMS: (State reasons you want to see a doctor. List in order of importance to you.) You may use last page to describe in detail if you wish.

1. _____
2. _____
3. _____
4. _____

LIST OTHER PHYSICIANS SEEN IN LAST TWO YEARS AND WHY. _____
_____
_____

PAST MEDICAL HISTORY:

1. Illnesses (requiring hospitalization, list problem and year, do not list operations here)
(a) _____ (d) _____
(b) _____ (e) _____
(c) _____ (f) _____

2. Accidents (list broken bones, injuries, etc.)
(a) _____ (d) _____
(b) _____ (e) _____
(c) _____ (f) _____

3. Operations (list all and give year)
(a) _____ (d) _____
(b) _____ (e) _____
(c) _____ (f) _____

4. Allergies (have you had reactions to any of the following medications (yes or no) and describe the reaction; for example, "Rash, asthma, hives, blackout")
(a) Penicillin _____ (e) Demerol _____
(b) Sulfa _____ (f) Barbiturates _____
(c) Aspirin _____ (g) Anesthetics _____
(d) Codeine _____ (h) Other _____

5. Pregnancies _____ Miscarriages _____ Weight of largest child at birh _____

6. Medications (list all you are now taking or have taken [in the past month] and indicate how often you have taken them): BRING ALL MEDICATIONS WITH YOU
(a) _____ (e) _____ (i) How much aspirin _____
(b) _____ (f) _____ (j) Laxatives _____
(c) _____ (g) _____ (k) Oral contraceptive _____
(d) _____ (h) _____ (l) Sleeping pills _____

REVIEW OF SYSTEMS: Review the list below and CIRCLE any number that describes a problem you are currently having and UNDERLINE those problems you have frequently had in the past.

1. Headaches
2. Seizures or fits
3. Numbness or tingling in hands, feet, arms or legs
4. Weakness in hands, feet, arms or legs
5. Difficulty maintaining balance
6. Dizziness
7. Fainting or balckout spells
8. Strokes
9. Ringing in ears
10. Difficulty with hearing
11. Difficulty with vision
12. Double vision
13. Difficulty smelling things
14. Excessive sneezing
15. Trouble breathing through nose
16. Nose bleeds
17. Change in voice
18. Shortness of breath at night
19. Shortness of breath while walking
20. Swelling of ankles or feet
21. Palpitaions
22. Chest pain or tightness in chest
23. Heart attacks
24. High cholesterol
25. Swelling of legs
26. Cough
27. Cough up blood
28. Wheezing during breathing
29. Sugar diabetes
30. High blood pressure
31. Night sweats
32. Continuous fever for greater than 5 days
33. Nausea, chronic
34. Trouble with swallowing
35. Vomiting
36. Diarrhea, chronic
37. Constipation, chronic

38. Vomit blood
39. Have blood with bowel movements
40. Black, loose bowel movements
41. Stomach pain
42. Jaundice (yellow skin)
43. Stomach ulcers
44. Hemorrhoids
45. Weight loss
46. Weight gain in past year
47. Loss of appetite
48. Frequent urination or passing water
49. Urination at night
50. Pain on urination
51. Pus or milky color of urine (water)
52. Blood in urine
53. Pass a stone in urine
54. Reduction in force or size of urine
55. Difficulty starting urine stream
56. Leakage of urine
57. Difficulty with erection
58. Difficulty with ejaculation
59. Discharge from penis
60. Onset of menstruation (age)_____
61. Duration of menstruation in days _____
62. Length of interval between periods_____
63. Bleeding between periods
64. Painful periods
65. Irregular periods
66. Last menstrual period_____
67. Last pelvic_____
68. Vaginal discharge
69. Back pain— high

70. Back pain— low
71. Change in glove size, shoe size or hat size
72. Muscle cramps in arms, legs, hands or feet
73. Pain in legs while walking
74. Joint swelling
75. Joint pain
76. Pain in hands or feet on cold weather exposure
77. Skin rash
78. Dry skin
79. Increase in hair growth
80. Loss of hair
81. Increase in oiliness of skin
82. Hives
83. Excessive sweating
84. Prefer hot water
85. Prefer cold water
86. Itching of skin
87. Skin pallor (paleness)
88. Breast discharge
89. Lumps in breast
90. Painful breast
91. Excessive blistering after sun exposure
92. Change in facial cutting skin
93. Easy bruising
94. Excessive bleeding after appearance
95. Crying spells
96. Insomnia
97. Mood swings
98. Nervousness
99. Difficulty with memory
100. Problem with thinking clearly
101. Chronic fatigue or weakness
102. Depression and anxiety

Weight Age 20_____   Weight 1 year ago____   Weight now _____

59

FAMILY HISTORY:

	Age	State of Health	Cause of Death
Father	_____	_____	_____
Mother	_____	_____	_____
Brothers	_____	_____	_____
	_____	_____	_____
	_____	_____	_____
Sisters	_____	_____	_____
	_____	_____	_____
	_____	_____	_____
Spouse	_____	_____	_____
Children (circle one) M F	_____	_____	_____
M F	_____	_____	_____
M F	_____	_____	_____
M F	_____	_____	_____

WHO IN YOUR FAMILY HAD:	Father	Mother	Sister(s)	Brother(s)	Other
1. Goiter					
2. Cancer					
3. Tuberculosis					
4. Allergies or asthma					
5. Strokes					
6. Nervous breakdown					
7. Suicide					
8. Convulsions/epilepsy					
9. Headaches					
10. Diabetes					
11. Arthritis					
12. Heart attack					
13. High blood pressure					
14. Gout					
15. Kidney stone					
16. Bleeding problem					
17. Ulcers					
18. Stroke or heart attack prior to age 60					

PERSONAL HISTORY:

1. Occupation: Yours_____ Spouse's_____
2. Place of employment:_____
3. Education: (circle level completed) High School   College   Masters   Ph.D.   Others
   9 10 11 12   1 2 3 4
4. Marital status: (circle)   Single   Married   Widowed   Separated   Divorced
5. Religious preference:_____
6. Hobbies: (list) _____
7. Smoking history: Packs each day?_____ For how many years? _____
8. Drinking history: Ounces each day? _____ For how long in years? _____
9. List the individuals that live in your home: _____

10. Whom should we contact in the event you develop a medical emergency (give name, address, phone number and relation to you) _____

11. How much exercise do you get (walking, jogging, bicycling, swimming, golf, tennis, other: circle please). Min each day? _____ Hours per week? _____ Moderate occupational and recreational exercise? _____ Sedentary work and light exercise only? _____

12. What additional information should the doctor have about you? _____

_____

_____

13. Comments

_____

Patient's signature

SUPPLEMENTAL PATIENT HISTORY FORM

This form is intended to supplement your medical history since your last complete examination. If we have hospitalized you in the interval, a complete summary of the hospitalization will already be in your record.

Date _____

Name _____   Age _____

(Please indicate any change in address or phone number)

Address _____   **Phone (home)** _____
City/State/Zip _____   **(business)** _____

PAST MEDICAL HISTORY: Please indicate any serious illness, serious injuries, operations (give type and date) or pregnancies that you have had <u>since your last physical exam</u>. Please indicate any other physicians you have seen in the interim and why.

_____

PLEASE BRING ALL OF YOUR MEDICATIONS!!!!!!

DRUGS YOU ARE TAKING:

1. _____   4. _____   7. Laxatives? _____
2. _____   5. _____   8. Oral contraceptives? ___
3. _____   6. How much aspirin? ____   9. Sleeping pills? _____

List all medications to which you are allergic, or which have produced adverse side effects.

_____

REVIEW OF SYSTEMS: Review the list below and circle any number that describes a problem <u>you are currently having</u> or <u>have had in the past six months</u>.

1. Headaches
2. Seizures or fits
3. Numbness or tingling in hands, feet, arms, legs
4. Weakness in hands, feet, arms, legs
5. Difficulty maintaining balance
6. Dizziness
7. Fainting or blackout spells
8. Strokes
9. Ringing in ears
10. Difficulty with hearing
11. Difficulty with vision
12. Double vision
13. Difficulty smelling things
14. Excessive sneezing
15. Trouble breathing through nose
16. Nose bleeds
17. Change in voice
18. Shortness of breath at night
19. Shortness of breath while walking
20. Swelling of ankles or feet
21. Palpitations
22. Chest pain or tightness in chest
23. Heart attacks
24. High cholesterol
25. Swelling of legs
26. Cough
27. Cough up blood
28. Wheezing during breathing
29. Sugar diabetes
30. High blood pressure
31. Night sweats
32. Continuous fever for greater than five days
33. Nausea, chronic
34. Trouble with swallowing
35. Vomiting
36. Diarrhea, chronic
37. Constipation, chronic
38. Vomit blood
39. Have blood with bowel movements
40. Black, loose bowel movements
41. Stomach pain
42. Jaundice (yellow skin)
43. Stomach ulcers
44. Hemorrhoids
45. Weight loss
46. Weight gain in past year
47. Loss of appetite
48. Frequent urination or passing water
49. Urination at night
50. Pain on urination
51. Pus or milky color of urine (water)
52. Blood in urine
53. Pass a stone in urine
54. Reduction in force or size of urine
55. Difficulty starting urine stream

56. Leakage of urine
57. Difficulty with erection
58. Difficulty with ejaculation
59. Discharge from penis
60. Onset of menstruation (age) _____
61. Duration of menstruation in days _____
62. Length of interval between periods _____
63. Bleeding between periods
64. Painful periods
65. Irregular periods
66. Last menstrual period ___
67. Last pelvic ___
68. Vaginal discharge
69. Back pain— high
70. Back paon— low
71. Change in glove, shoe or hat size
72. Muscle cramps in arms, legs, hands, feet

73. Pain in legs while walking
74. Joint swelling
75. Joint pain
76. Pain in hands or feet in cold weather
77. Skin rash
78. Dry skin
79. Increase in oiliness of skin
80. Loss of hair
81. Increase in hair growth
82. Hives
83. Excessive sweating
84. Prefer hot weather
85. Prefer cold weather
86. Itching of skin
87. Skin pallor (paleness)
88. Breast discharge
89. Lumps in breast
90. Painful breasts
91. Excessive blistering after sun exposure

92. Change in facial appearance
93. Easy bruising
94. Excessive bleeding after cutting skin
95. Crying spells
96. Insomnia
97. Mood swings
98. Nervousness
99. Difficulty with memory
100. Problem with thinking clearly
101. Chronic fatigue or weakness
102. Depression and anxiety
103. Weight change
104. How many ounces of alcohol consumed a week _____
105. How many packs of cigarettes do you smoke each day? _____

WHO IN YOUR FAMILY HAS DEVELOPED
SINCE YOUR LAST PHYSICAL EXAM:

1. Cancer	
2. Tuberculosis	
3. Allergies	
4. Heart disease at an early age	
5. High blood pressure	
6. Gout	
7. Strokes	
8. Mental disorder	
9. Convulsions or epilepsy	
10. Diabetes	
11. Rheumatoid arthritis	
12. Other	

WHAT ADDITIONAL INFORMATION SHOULD
THE DOCTOR HAVE ABOUT YOU?

_____

_____

_____

_____

_____

5

THE ROLE OF
THE CONSULTANT

MALPRACTICE CHECKLIST

- You must communicate not simply with the referring physician, but also with the patient— after you have communicated with the referring physician.
- You must involve the patient in decisions about whom to see.
- Where the diagnosis remains elusive or therapy has not met expectations, wisely refer to a colleague.
- Confusion over responsibility for different aspects of care may be a central factor in triggering a claim.
- When referring, don't rely solely on doctor's academic and professional qualifications, ask physicians who know him.
- Take charge: arrangements for referral can be made from your office so patient can be seen within reasonable amount of time.
- Beware of delays that can worsen a patient's condition.
- Referring physician continues to have duty to treat patient even though he has referred.
- Define scope of referral and follow-up arrangements.
- Document your differences of opinion with consultant.
- Coordinate follow-up visits.
- Keep track of phone conversations with consultant— at home as well.

- Establish a "tickler" system alerting you to fact that you need report from referral doctor in reasonable amount of time.
- Do not assume care and become primary physician if patient is referred to you.

THE ROLE OF THE CONSULTANT

Physicians often find themselves inextricably intertwined in a lawsuit where their only contact with the patient was as a consultant. Beware of doing a consult and leaving your further role ill-defined or undefined. Recall the Joint and Several Rule? The function of a consult is fraught with Joint and Several Liability.

You must follow the rule of clearly defining what duty you are assuming. Let us examine some examples that many of you face in your daily practices. A patient has as his primary physician a family practitioner who has cared for the patient for a number of years. The patient develops transient ischemic episodes and his physician refers the patient to you— a board certified internist and cardiologist. Your office staff makes an appointment for the patient in your office. You see the patient and determine that he will need to see a neurologist and possibly a vascular surgeon if he has a blockage in the carotid arteries that will require an endarterectomy. The same patient may have ischemic heart disease that requires a non-invasive modality of treatment and he can be monitored by his primary physician.

How do you handle it? First, ask yourself, "What am I supposed to do as a consultant?" Certainly, you have found that the ischemic heart disease requires only a regimen of medication, but additionally, you have found other problems that require further exploration and work up by other medical specialties. The threshold question of whether you should refer to those specialties or whether you should refer the patient back to his primary physician for other direct referrals should be immediately determined. You must communicate not simply with the referring physician but also with the patient— after you have communicated with the referring physician. You may make a recommendation for further workup— but it is the decision of the primary treating physician unless that physician specifically requests you to proceed with your recommendations and make necessary referrals. In that case you must next communicate with the patient, advising him that he has other problems that require further workup by other specialists and that his physician has requested you to make those referrals.

What have you accomplished? First, you have not assumed a duty beyond your initial request for a consultation. You have fulfilled that duty. Second, you have rightfully left the decision to the primary physician as to whom is going to do the referring to other specialists based on your recommendations. Third, if you are going to make the referrals, you should clearly indicate to those specialists that the patient is a patient of the primary physician and both you and he should receive their reports. Fourth, you must take the time to fully apprise the patient and his family that his primary physician has requested that you request other consultations, that you will continue to consult with his primary physician as to his ischemic heart disease and that the other physicians who will examine him will report directly to his primary physician.

A major problem that is emerging nationally with the advent of DRGs, PPOs and multiple other federal and state mandated "cost cutting" programs is that consultant's often assume more of a duty than they should. In most cases they do so because they genuinely want to continue to assist the patient, in still other cases the level of competition for patients is such that some physicians only refer to certain other physicians without regard to the desires of the primary physician or the patient.

You must always involve the patient in decisions about whom to see. Remember, if the patients are part of the health care team and have some say about who will see and treat them, they are much less likely to sue you. You *must always* document carefully that the primary physician requested you to make the other referrals, that the patient and his family were fully advised that his primary physician concurs in the referrals and that he consents to be referred to whomever you propose.

One area where this is particularly important is where you practice with a group that has other specialists. Rather than assume that the patient wishes to see the neurologist in your group, ask the patient. He or some member of his family may have previously been seen by another neurologist and he may wish to be seen by that neurologist rather than your colleague just down the hall. Patients will often say, "They never even asked me about who I wanted to see, they just sent me down the hall." Whenever patients feel estranged from their physicians and participation in decisions in which they could have been consulted they are more likely to sue. If patients become estranged from their physicians in such situations, it is usually because physicians have become estranged from basic guidelines for referral that would have enabled them to avoid the problem. What are the most common liability problems raised by referrals and what precautionary practices will help you build a line of defense?

Knowing When to Refer

A decision to refer depends not only on the clinical facts of the case but on the qualifications and experience of the treating physician. Having reached the point where the diagnosis remains elusive or therapy has not been effective as expected, a physician should wisely refer to a colleague. Three other factors also generally govern whether you should refer. You may want the concurrence of another physician even though you have recommended a procedure, so you opt for the "second opinion." You may know exactly what to do next for the patient but lack the expertise to provide the service. On the other hand, you may have the expertise, but for a variety of reasons may be unable or unwilling to provide the service. For example, you may be abandoning the obstetric side of your practice and decide you do not want to handle additional OB cases.

How to Pave the Way for Referrals

In situations where you refer a patient to a specialist, and then withdraw from the case, you will not usually be held liable unless the patient can show that the specialist was unqualified or incompetent and that you should have known it. The problem that often arises is when two physicians begin treating a patient jointly— each seeing the patient on a continuing basis. Both will be liable for any negligence within the area in which both are involved. Confusion over responsibility for different aspects of care may be a central factor in triggering a claim. Negligence arises when physicians fail to specify what services they are requesting of each other.

Carefully Select a Consultant

An impressive curriculum vitae and a listing in a directory of specialists is not necessarily a guarantee of a doctor's value. You may have a friend in another city to whom you want to refer a patient but be unaware of his medical-legal track record. When making referrals, do not rely solely on a doctor's academic and professional qualifications or the fact that you knew him years ago. It's always wise to check on his competence with people who know him— knowledgeable physicians in the community. A call to local or state medical societies can also reveal if any disciplinary actions have been taken against his license.

Preparing the Consultant

Most doctors try to communicate relevant information to the consultant before the consultation, either directly or through office staff. Often a note is sent, or the referring physician talks with the consultant. This preparation is important for a number of reasons.

First, the consultant is made aware of unrelated medical problems and past medical history of the patient, all of which might influence recommendations. This is particularly important when the patient is unlikely to know or unable to describe such problems with specificity.

Second, the referring physician is in an excellent position to describe the patient's "history of present illness" (HPI), as he elicited it from the patient. Referral often is not made until well after the initial office visit, and most physicians document the HPI carefully at that time. Also, they are able to add to it over successive visits as the patient remembers different aspects of his problem.

Third, there is an opportunity to outline for the consultant the results of tests to date. This makes it less likely that the consultant will repeat tests unnecessarily. Some patients may know exactly what tests they have already had, but many do not. Thus, this notification is cost effective; moreover, since some tests are invasive— and therefore somewhat of a risk to the patient— the patient's exposure to risk is also reduced. Needless to say, this communication enhances the patient's confidence in his own physician. On the other hand, failure to convey this important information might detract from the relationship.

Fourth, the physician can describe to the consultant any treatment already rendered, as well as the patient's response. Having the consultant prescribe a medication already tried (appropriately, but unsuccessfully) doesn't reflect well on either physician.

Fifth, the referring doctor probably knows the patient's occupational history and exposure, and should pass on relevant information.

Sixth, the consultant should know of social factors that might influence his course of action. For example, he might be less inclined to consider a psychosomatic etiology in a depressed patient whose problem arose a month before the loss of a loved one.

Similarly, the consultant should be fully appraised of the possibility of secondary gain. The fact that the patient may be involved in a personal injury suit against a manufacturer, or has filed a disability claim, is relevant— even though the patient should still receive a completely thorough and objective consultation.

Finally, the referring physician is often on the right track; but right or wrong, it's useful to let the consultant know the working diagnosis.

Obviously, not every referral requires extensive preparatory communication with the consultant, but the outcome of some referrals clearly hinges on adequate preparation.

Don't Hold Back

Despite the clear need to refer when a physician is faced with a situation that goes beyond his expertise, many physicians hesitate. They fail to recognize that they cannot— and should not— be all things to all patients. They think they can handle the problem themselves or they are too insecure to let go. In either case, they may find themselves over their heads. Even if you are sure you are right, getting another opinion may be just the assurance— for your patient and from a medical-legal standpoint— that will make the difference in whether you are sued.

Take Charge: Schedule the Appointment Yourself

Once you have decided a referral is in order, all the arrangements can be made on your end to ensure that the patient is on his or her way within a reasonable amount of time. Whether an otolaryngologist needs to look at a patient's eustachian tube dysfunction or a child needs an allergy consult, your secretary can simply call ahead and schedule an appointment that is convenient for the patient and the doctor. Taking charge is especially crucial in emergencies such as in a case where you suspect endometrial cancer following a patient's D & C. In such circumstances you do not want a patient waiting three or four weeks before a surgeon finds time to see her or before the patient gets around to scheduling an appointment. In such cases the race belongs to the swift.

Pitfalls in the Referral Process

Beware of unnecessary delays that can worsen a patient's condition. Often the treating physician's office staff will call the consultant's office to schedule an appointment. Unless the physician has indicated clearly the maximum acceptable interval in the referral, the patient could be scheduled for the consultant's next available routine appointment. A patient's symptoms can worsen to the point where the consultant's appointment will serve little purpose in the face of a full-blown emergency or a developing crisis.

The referring physician continues to have a duty to treat the patient even though he has referred. This is critical in the acute care setting when primary care physicians often refer trauma patients to an emergency department. Unless the transferring physician has clearly outlined an arrangement whereby the accepting physician manages all aspects of the transfer, the referring physician could still have a duty to care for the patient during the transfer.

Defining the Scope of Referral

Consultants usually are careful not to go beyond the scope of the referral. Most consultants, unless the referring physician has requested otherwise, will assess the patient and report their recommendations back— except when it is obvious that the referring physician intends them to complete the diagnostic work-up and begin treatment. For example, a physician might refer his cardiac patient to a cardiologist for an evaluation, including a stress test. The patient should know which of the two doctors will be responsible for ongoing care of his cardiac condition.

It is not uncommon for a patient to "fall between the cracks" immediately after the consultation, waiting for his own physician to call him about the consultant's report, or assuming the consultant has "cleared" him inasmuch as no follow-up was advised. Ideally, the referring physician should schedule a follow-up visit, if that is appropriate, to take place shortly after the consultation appointment date, and indicate this to the consultant.

Another problem occurs when the consultant mistakenly "sends the patient back" to the referring physician who intended the consultant to take over care of the patient.

The referring physician can minimize the likelihood of these problems by defining the scope of the referral, including what problems he wants the consultant to deal with and what follow-up arrangements he intends.

Establish a System to Ensure Receipt of Reports

For some reason, the referring physician might not receive the consultant's recommendations. For example, office staff might have mistakenly filed the report, thinking the physician had seen it. Even if it is filed correctly, unless the physician has established a "tickler" system to ensure receipt and awareness of reports, the patient might suffer. This is particularly likely when the consultant chooses to recommend a course of therapy, but doesn't initiate it himself. Moreover, the consultant or his office staff simply might forget to send the report, or be very tardy in reporting. At any rate, the referring physician is at risk when he fails to receive or obtain the report; he can avoid this problem by implementing good practice management techniques.

Documenting Differences of Opinion

Disagreements on the interpretations of studies often set the stage for potential liability. In cases where the referring physician does not accept the consultant's recommendations, the rationale for choosing a different course should be documented. Carrying that line of thinking a step further, it may also be advisable to obtain another opinion— particularly when the correct choice among several options is crucial.

For example, a radiologist might suggest a bone scan to rule out an early osteomyelitis, a special view of the shoulder to rule out a posterior dislocation or a CT of L5/Sl to rule out a herniated disk in a patient with an Sl nerve compression syndrome. If the referring physician decides against this plan, he needs to document why he will not follow it.

Coordinating Follow-up Visits

If signals are crossed, patients may not be scheduled for follow-up and may wait for their own physician to call them about the consultant's report. On the other hand, they may assume that the consultant has not found anything wrong, since no follow-up was advised. That's why the referring physician should schedule a follow-up visit, if that is appropriate, shortly after the patient has seen the consultant. These problems can be minimized at the outset if the referring physician defines the scope of the referral and outlines what areas each physician will be responsible for.

Giving the Consultant Relevant Information

You do not need to photocopy the entire chart, because some of the information may be irrelevant or confidential. For example, a 16-year-old's pregnancy consult has nothing to do with her acute acne. To send the entire record to the dermatologist could add to your potential liability. If the consultant will not see the patient for another week, there is time to mail the material to him. On the other hand, if the appointment can be made sooner, ask the patient to stop back at the office later in the day, pick up the material and take it to the other doctor when he or she goes for the appointment.

Emergencies, of course, are another matter. The phone consultation is imperative at that point and the test results and other pertinent information should be sent directly to the doctor with the patient.

Involving the Patient

Accustomed to your care, a patient may grow apprehensive about the prospect of seeing a new physician whom he may not have heard of and who may practice in another community miles from his own. Discuss why the patient is being referred, where he is going and what will happen. If you are verifying your tentative diagnosis, make sure the patient is aware of that strategy. If the consultant's office is in another town, you may want to provide the patient with a rough map indicating a few landmarks and an easy route to follow.

The patient should be prepared for what will happen. For example, if you expect that he will need a lung biopsy or a myelogram or surgery of any kind, the patient should be ready for it. You may want to suggest that he pack a suitcase and that the consultant will make the decision concerning the need for tests or therapy. Explain to the patient that for a while, at least, his care will be in the hands of another physician. If it's an allergy problem, explain that the physician will be determining what course of therapy will be required and that after a regimen has been prepared, you will be administering the shots. It's also reassuring to the patient to know what the other physician is like— something about his credentials, expertise in this area and maybe even a few details about his personality. If the consultant, for example, is particularly reserved and does not generally volunteer a lot of information, you may suggest to the patient that he not hesitate in asking questions. Assure the patient that the consultant will be willing and able to answer all questions but that the patient has to initiate the conversation.

Tracking Referred Patients

All correspondence from the referral doctor should be logged in the chart as soon as it is received. Keep track of phone conversations that you have had with the consultant. Nothing can be more embarrassing— and revealing to the plaintiff's attorney— than if you cannot recall at deposition or trial what conversations you had with a consultant. If you receive a call from the consultant reporting that the patient did not appear for a scheduled appointment, this fact should also be documented. If the referral doctor is slow in sending you a report, call him to get a progress report. A "tickler" system that alerts you to the fact that you need a report from a referral doctor within a reasonable time can help you receive information when you need it.

So much attention is focused on a physician's need to refer that the responsibilities of the consultant are often overlooked. The consultant also needs to keep in mind basic principles of risk management that will help protect the referring physician. These include:

- **Remarks about other doctors.** Disparaging remarks about physicians who previously managed a patient can often set the stage for a malpractice suit. Comments in the chart for example, that suggest the referring doctor may have bungled certain aspects of care will constitute a gold mine for the plaintiff's attorney.

- **Do not assume care and become primary physician.** As competition heats up, it is inevitable that physicians will be tempted to assume the care of a patient rather than serve as a consultant. Consultants who preempt the responsibility of the referring physician, write conflicting orders or interfere with treatment decisions that should be left to the other doctor can also lead to confusion by the patient as to who is in charge. The decisions should be clearly delineated at the outset of care by the consultant.

- **Billing errors and overcharging.** Few mistakes seem to fuel a patient's anger as much as improper billing. A discussion about charges before a bill is sent can help defuse a potentially troublesome situation. Some physicians have an understanding about reciprocal charges for routine situations. They agree on a nominal fee for checking each other's patients in "non-momentous" cases, thus avoiding the problem of a patient's complaining about an exorbitant bill for the small amount of time that a consultant spent in examination. The judicious use of consultants through formal referrals or informal contacts can and should add greatly to the quality of care physicians provide, and the practice can enhance rather than decrease the patient's respect for the referring physician.

Moreover, referrals usually are thought of as a part of risk management—not only because the treating physician clearly has a duty to refer in some clinical situations, but also because a corroborating opinion can both defuse a patient's hostility and, in the event of suit, provide some favorable evidence of the standard of care. Nonetheless, and ironic though it may seem, the referral process itself creates numerous malpractice pitfalls. Avoiding the pitfalls results in better care for the patient and better legal risk management— for both the referring and the consulting physicians.

6
THE DO'S AND DON'TS
OF PRESCRIBING

MALPRACTICE CHECKLIST

- Note and prominently display allergies or interactions in the chart.
- Because of long half-lives, drug history should include all drugs taken during 30 days prior to patient's visit.
- Beware of medications that may not be absorbed properly in fasting or postprandial state or when taken with liquids other than water.
- Make sure patient understands what you mean by allergy— his or her sensitivity to a *drug*.
- Ask all new patients— and periodically confront regular ones— about medications they're taking and other doctors prescribing them.
- As long as you document in the patient record signs and symptoms consistent with continuing medication, there should be no liability problem.
- Print medication orders if you are prone to poor penmanship. Take special care with similarly spelled drugs (i.e. Digoxin, Digitoxin).
- Check with others to make sure your handwriting is clear.
- When covering for another physician, only prescribe enough of medication to last until the other doctor resumes care.
- Document every prescribing activity in the chart.
- Always record the pharmacist's name when you order or approve renewals by phone.
- On shelf, separate look-alike medications and separate medications from toxic chemicals.

DO'S AND DON'TS OF
PRESCRIBING

From risky oral medication orders to overdosages, from adverse reactions to addiction, drug-related negligence is one of the most common treatment situations that arises in malpractice litigation. Several surveys support that assessment. One recently published report from *Jury Verdict Research* found that medication orders are the most prevalent source of treatment error, reflecting an average award of more than $230,000. Other studies have demonstrated that 10 percent of all claims paid by your carrier are due to drug-related problems ranging from overprescribing to sloppy handwriting when prescribing. The biggest problem in prescribing are cases involving adverse reactions to certain drugs, ranging from nausea to anaphylactic shock and death. Some 45 percent of all claims filed against the Pennsylvania Medical Society Liability and Insurance Company are due to this drug-related error.

Although adverse reactions generally top the list of most frequently seen allegations, other commonly seen situations that trigger suits include: nerve/muscle injury during the administration of a drug, overdosages, patient addiction and mismanagement of anticoagulation therapy.

In addition to the frequency with which they appear as a source of malpractice trouble, drug-related errors are likely to be more of a concern for other reasons, too. In the era of Diagnosis Related Groups (DRGs)— when more efficient use of medications have become a focus— decisions on drug use raise new questions concerning liability problems. Will the incentive for early discharge— so essential to turning a profit under the DRG system— adversely affect the quality of patient care? If so, will the selection of certain medications and regimens, influenced by cost-containment considerations, loom as more of a factor in malpractice litigation? Consider, for example, that hospital inpatients receive, on the average, ten different drugs while hospitalized, according to recent epidemiological studies. Still another development that has made drug-related error more of a concern is the trend in the courts to expand a physician's liability in this area, especially concerning the need to recall patients because of newly discovered problems even years after a device was inserted or a drug prescribed.

What are the common errors that lead to litigation and how can you avoid them? How are courts expanding your liability for prescriptions and how can you stay alert to the potential for such exposure?

THE LEGAL BASIS FOR DRUG-RELATED LIABILITY

Physicians, pharmacists, and hospitals are not usually held accountable for injuries from drugs unless they have failed to "exercise due care." In other words, there must be proof of negligence. You will not be held liable as long as the drug-related problem arose from a "reasonable exercise of judgment." For example, if you prescribed a drug that was indicated and that, given the patient's history, would not be expected to produce an adverse reaction, you should not be found liable.

The area of law that imposes stricter obligations concerns your knowledge of certain risks and how you communicate them to the patient. The major reason underlying that obligation is that a physician is considered a "learned intermediary" between the drug manufacturer and the patient. Product warnings— which under other situations are required to go with the product to the consumer— are required instead to only reach the physician. It is your legal obligation to complete the information chain and inform the patient of certain risks as part of obtaining informed consent.

A key point to bear in mind is that physicians are not held liable merely for prescribing or administering a dangerous or defective drug. You have a valid defense as long as any injury that occurs is the result of an error in judgment and does not reflect negligence.

ADVERSE REACTIONS, INTERACTIONS
AND SIDE EFFECTS

The majority of adverse drug reactions are associated with the well-established classes of drugs— antibiotics, anticoagulants, vaccines, psychotropic agents, oral contraceptives, estrogens, diuretics, digitalis preparations and antihypertensives. In many cases, drugs are prescribed to patients with known and documented allergies to a medication. Physicians are charged with determining if allergies exist *prior* to drug prescription or administration. By noting and prominently displaying these allergies in the chart, you will alert yourself and other staff about the potential exposure from adverse reactions.

Many of these reactions from allergies or interactions with other agents can be nipped with a comprehensive drug history. The drug history is important for three reasons: (1) diagnostically it's a valuable tool, helping you to scout a patient's propensity for adverse reactions and identifying the drug or drugs involved; (2) it has therapeutic value because it permits prompt treatment and helps you quickly spot the need to adjust dosage or discontinue a drug; and (3) it averts dangerous multiple drug interactions for patients taking drugs prescribed by another physician or from over-the-counter drugs that may interact with the prescribed medication.

Physicians sometimes lose sight of the fact that many drugs have slow clearance from the body. Because of long half-lives, the drug history should include all drugs taken during the thirty days prior to the patient's visit. A previous history of adverse drug reactions is quite common and these patients are often predisposed to other drug-induced problems.

A good guide to follow is to determine if the patient is regularly taking any other medication that might adversely interact with or lessen the effectiveness of the drugs that you may want to prescribe. Despite the potential for exposure, you cannot guarantee that your treatment will be without complication. The law will not penalize you if a patient develops such a complication as long you satisfy certain criteria. These include: (1) an awareness of the possible adverse reaction; (2) proper warning to the patient about what symptoms to watch for; (3) careful observation; (4) prompt diagnosis of any drug-related complications; and (5) proper and timely treatment. The cardinal rule is that there must first have been an indication for administering the drug. The quickest way to be sued is for a bad result or complication to arise from a drug when no indication existed.

Inappropriate Route of Administration

Few errors are apt to nail a physician as quickly as using the wrong method to administer a drug. You might as well bring your checkbook to the deposition. In these cases, all the plaintiff has to prove is that a mistake occurred, and the only question remaining is the amount of damages that will be recovered.

These claims tend to be generated by inattentive staff who have been inadequately instructed, improperly supervised, or are preoccupied with other jobs or problems. The embarrassment is that it's so easy to check the proper administration for a drug. It's plainly indicated in the PDR, the manufacturer's brochure and usually on the package or bottle as well. The ill-conceived defenses that physicians often rely upon for lapses in supervision— that their staffs should have caught the error or that they didn't have time to oversee the administration— never withstand the test of litigation.

These errors often concern situations in which medications may not be absorbed properly in the fasting or the postprandial state or when taken with liquids other than water. Similarly, fruit juice, coffee or milk, for example, should be avoided when certain drugs are administered. Consider, for example, the consequences of administering a large dose of Lanoxin by injection. In these and other situations, it should be standard procedure for you and your staff to check instructions on administration. It is worthwhile to periodically remind your staff about how inappropriate administration can set the stage for a liability claim.

Allergic Reactions

The two most common substances that provoke serious allergic reactions are penicillin and tetanus antitoxin. As Angela Holder points out in her book, *Malpractice*, "Generally speaking, a physician is obliged to know exactly what the predicted adverse effects of any drug will be. Prescription of a drug in ignorance of its potential for harm is clear negligence. If there are warnings about the drugs in medical journals which the physician should read or if the manufacturer itself issues warnings, the physician is held to know them whether he actually does or not. He is also bound by any other knowledge which he may have received from any source, including his own experience, about the possibility of side effects." Some drugs are administered, however, in the face of calculated risks. And if the patient's condition warrants use of the drug and if no other drug is effective, a physician will not be held negligent even if side effects occur. Again, appropriate *indication* is the key. But if another drug would be as effective and less potentially hazardous, a doctor is legally obliged to prescribe it.

Generally, a physician cannot be held liable for allergic reactions if the patient has denied that he or she has an allergy and if the drug is indicated. But in some cases, a physician might still be considered negligent if following an allergic reaction, his office was not equipped to deal with it.

The rule to follow is to make sure that the patient understands what you mean by an allergy. Spell out the fact that you are referring to his or her sensitivity to a drug. Do not assume that the patient knows you are referring to a drug allergy. What's more, your office should be equipped to deal with sudden and unexpected emergencies by having on hand antidotes and emergency equipment.

Overprescribing and Potential Addiction

This area is a double-edged sword— civil and criminal. If you overprescribe certain drugs for a patient and fail to observe signs and symptoms that are consistent with prescribing the medication, you could expose yourself to a lawsuit from the patient who can claim you're responsible for his addiction. On the other hand, such practices can earn a physician a reputation as a prescription mill, and before long he may attract the attention of licensing authorities as he is monitored on the profiles that are routinely kept by state agencies on the number of prescriptions issued for narcotic substances.

Although overprescribing is more likely to lead to a potential for criminal prosecution, physicians should be aware of the possibility for malpractice. One of the factors that complicates this liability problem is that the patient may be considered "contributorily negligent." It's not easy to judge at what point a patient may be manipulating you to abuse a drug. In one North Carolina case, for example, a court considered a patient's claim against a physician who prescribed addicting drugs over a 12-year period.

The issue before the court was whether the patient contributed to his own addiction— as evidenced by his scheme to obtain prescriptions for narcotics. The court's opinion should serve as a warning: namely, that standard medical practice probably is not to regard addiction as necessary in the treatment of most diseases. Therefore, a physician will be judged on whether he knew (or should have known) that heavy and continuous doses of narcotics were not needed to control the patient's pain.

Physicians tend to hide behind the rationalization that patients embellish their symptoms and that there is nothing wrong with a little embellishing. As long as you document in the patient's record certain signs and symptoms that are consistent with the practice of continuing to prescribe a medication, there should be no problem with liability. The problem arises when there is no observation of an objective sign or symptom and where you have failed to justify yourself in the record.

Moreover, ask all new patients, and periodically confront your regular patients, about what medications they're taking and whether they're seeing other doctors who prescribe them. When appropriate, check a patient's drug history with other physicians and obtain records that will document that history.

In most U.S. jurisdictions, you must report any addicted person to a registry. The procedure is similar to the responsibility to report a gunshot wound and child abuse and neglect cases. Under such laws, confidentiality cannot be raised to shield an addict. In addition, in most states, you are not permitted to treat a person for addiction with a continuation of addictive drugs. An exception to this rule is made if you have been licensed for methadone treatment by the federal government and the patient has been appropriately registered. Giving opiates such as Percodan or Demerol or barbiturates such as Amytal or Seconal to maintain addiction constitutes illegal prescription of scheduled drugs and is against regulations.

Ethically, you have no right to do anything that continues to hurt a patient. Without question, the maintenance of addictive drugs may harm the patient. You should wean the patient as quickly as possible from dependency and then refer him or her to an appropriate counseling center for specific treatment of drug addiction. The average physician is not skilled in this area and lacks experience in dealing with the sociopathic drug abuser who expects the physician to provide tender, loving care and be an easy mark for scripts. Indeed, the street name for such a physician is a "croaker."

Illegible Prescriptions

A survey published recently by *American Druggist Magazine* says it all: More than half of the pharmacists who answered an inquiry reported that they had made errors in dispensing medication mostly because of sloppy handwriting by physicians. Mistakes in dispensing because of illegibility occurred at least three or four times in the careers of pharmacists who responded to another study reported by *American Medical News*.

Even more alarming is that one of every four pharmacists interviewed said that he had to phone for verification of unreadable prescriptions at least daily, with 14 percent saying that they went through this routine at least twice daily. Despite that warning, most physicians did not come to the phone immediately or failed to call back within hours.

The guidelines are simple but the consequences of not following them are devastating:

1. Print your medication orders if you are prone to poor penmanship.
2. Take special care with similarly spelled drugs like Digoxin and Digitoxin. Make sure that decimal points are inserted appropriately.
3. Maintain close contact with nurses and pharmacists on whether your handwriting is clear and with the hospital pharmacist to make sure you are using appropriate terms for all drugs in the formulary.

Duty to Recall a Defective Drug or Device

Within the last five years, courts have been expanding a physician's duty to recall patients and warn them of hazards newly discovered that were unknown when the drug was prescribed or when the device was inserted. The Dalkon Shield is the best example of an intrauterine device that was once one of the most popular and accepted IUDs on the market. Since 1974, however, serious questions have been raised about its safety, and physicians could be held liable in comparable situations for failing to warn patients about defective drugs or devices. This type of liability can transcend the limits ordinarily imposed on plaintiffs by the statute of limitations— the time within which a suit must be filed.

By ruling that physicians have "a separate duty" to warn, courts have extended the patient's time to file a claim. The lesson to be learned is that whether the device is an IUD or a pacemaker or a drug that later proves to be faulty or dangerous, you should notify your former patients of the hazards.

Physicians might argue that it is unfair to place the burden on them and that the drug manufacturer should share in the responsibility. To a certain extent, the drug manufacturer does share in that obligation, but only is required to warn the physician. The rationale of the court is this: It would be virtually impossible for a manufacturer to comply with the duty of direct warning since there is no sure way to reach the patient. The prescribing physician acts then as a "learned intermediary" between the drug manufacturer and the ultimate consumer— the patient.

It's not likely that courts will stop here at imposing a continuing obligation on physicians concerning various aspects of diagnosis and treatment. As your obligations grow and the malpractice net widens, the need for accurate and detailed record-keeping seems to expand too. If you have an efficient system for advising former patients in writing of any subsequent dangers from drugs or devices, you will have defused another time bomb ticking away in your records.

Oral Medication Orders and the Telephone

As indispensable as the telephone is to your practice, you pay a price for that convenience in its potential for exposing you to liability if you rely too heavily on oral medication orders. Consider these situations that could lead to liability problems:

• Phone conversations with a patient's relatives or friends too often provide incomplete information; often they do not provide enough information on which to diagnose and prescribe. They may exaggerate or underestimate the importance of the symptoms.

• Without consulting a patient's chart, you may be unaware of factors in the history that could be important in treating the immediate problem.

- If you don't instruct a nurse to repeat your orders to you, she may fail to provide what you want.

- Failing to tell a patient to report any changes in his condition after you have prescribed by phone could lead to trouble.

These problems and others are likely to arise particularly when a physician covers the practices of other doctors in his group or the practice of a colleague. Horror stories abound as to what can happen in situations when doctors rely too heavily on the phone.

A New Hampshire case is typical of what can happen when physicians receive and convey information over the phone. In this case, a Concord, N.H., clinic was sued for one million dollars by a woman who charged that doctors were negligent in their treatment and failed to evaluate her condition. Their alleged failure resulted in the patient being allowed to rebleed. As a result of the rebleed, she developed paralysis on the right side of her body and aphasia.

According to testimony, Walter Dwyer called the Concord Clinic in February 1974 and told a nurse that his wife, Jeanne, was suffering from a severe headache, nausea, and vomiting. During the previous year, she had been diagnosed at the clinic as having elevated blood pressure, bordering on hypertension.

When the nurse informed the doctor about the problem, he reportedly instructed her to tell the husband that a prescription would be phoned in to a drugstore. Compazine was prescribed by phone. The next day, the severe headache returned and Dwyer again called the clinic, speaking to the same nurse. The nurse relayed the information to a second doctor who— without talking with Dwyer or the patient— prescribed Empirin 3 (a compound containing codeine, a controlled narcotic) by telephone. The symptoms disappeared on the third day but returned more severely on the fourth, prompting Dwyer to visit the clinic and demand that his wife be examined as soon as possible and without having to wait.

Soon after he brought her to the clinic, a doctor diagnosed that she had suffered a subarachnoid hemorrhage. She was taken by her husband to a local hospital and later to a larger medical center. An aneurysm was clipped there about a month later.

The complaint filed in the trial court charged that the clinic was negligent in failing to properly evaluate and treat the plaintiff, and that the physician failed to advise her of the need for frequent monitoring of blood pressure. The complaint also accused the doctors of prescribing medication without seeing or talking to the plaintiff and without enough information. It charged the nurse with failing to provide the physicians with enough information to make an appropriate diagnosis, and claimed that she did not recognize the situation as an emergency. It further alleged that the nurse did not convey the husband's request for a house call to the physician or record these requests in the medical record.

Injuries listed by the complaint include: the subarachnoid hemorrhage, a ruptured aneurysm at the trifurcation of the dominant hemisphere middle cerebral artery on the left, with resultant intracranial vasospasm, severe expressive aphasia, monoparesis involving the right arm, hemiplegia, susceptibility to convulsions, and other related disability, all of which are permanent.

The New Hampshire case points up the obvious problems that can arise when clear, concise information is conveyed by telephone and a physician fails to evaluate the status of the patient before prescribing treatment. Liability-conscious physicians listen carefully for telltale signs when talking to patients by phone and before prescribing without first seeing them. If a patient does not seem to understand his or her own situation or the medication to be prescribed, you should be reluctant to prescribe via the phone. In most situations where a telephone prescription is required— or when one doctor is covering for another— a sound rule to follow is to prescribe only enough of the drug to last until the patient can see you or when the other physician comes on call.

Incomplete Medication Records

"Meticulous" is the buzzword for charting medications. Physicians should carefully document every prescribing activity on the patient's office chart: name of medication, dosage, date started, refills authorized by phone, each change in regimen, and date the patient was instructed to discontinue the medication. Lawsuits often allege that the physician has failed to adequately monitor the patient on medication. Thoroughness of documentation has the subtle effect of establishing the prescribing physician as a careful practitioner.

One area where documentation is crucial concerns when medication is intentionally prescribed for a therapeutic indication beyond the scope of FDA-approved uses— as is often the case with psychotropics— or beyond the suggested dosages as recommended in the PDR.

The chart should also reflect negative as well as positive responses that patients provide on drug-related areas. You can also protect yourself in other ways.

- Consider using prescription blanks with duplicates that can be kept in the medical record or a basic medication sheet attached to the file.

- Institute as part of office routine the recording of the pharmacist's name when you order or approve renewals by phone.

- Beware of situations in which an administering nurse initials an order on the hospital chart to indicate she has followed instructions. Such notations may obliterate or obscure parts of the order, including the dosage.

A Checklist for the Staff

Few physicians set aside the time to meet with their staffs and review risk management guidelines, but doing so serves two purposes: (1) it maintains a high awareness among the staff that the potential always exists for malpractice, and (2) institutes a protocol within the office or hospital that reflects risk management guidelines. Among the questions that staff need to ask themselves as part of a mental checklist before administering any medication are the following:

- Do you have the wrong drug? Similar drug names or side-by-side storage of drug look-alikes can lead to disaster.

- Are you preparing to give the drug by the wrong route? A medication that is quite safe by one route may, as you know, be hazardous by another.

- Have you neglected to review the patient's chart and the medication orders? Poor communication— written and spoken— is probably the leading cause of medication errors.

- Are you giving a drug you aren't familiar with? You don't have any defense if you harm a patient because you failed to read the manufacturer's warnings and directions in the package insert.

Safeguards to Avoid Giving the Wrong Drug

- *Avoid distractions.* Staff may become complacent in following procedures that have become routine. Nothing should become so routine that it is not checked and double checked. In addition, separate strong medications from weak ones on storage shelves to reduce the possibility of dangerous incidents.

- *Separate look-alike medications and separate medications from toxic chemicals.*

• *Discard out-of-date drugs.*

Safeguards to Avoid Inappropriate Route of Administration

• *Use accepted injection sites.*

• *Aspirate before giving an I.M. injection.* The chances are slim of hitting a blood vessel when you are supposed to inject medication into a muscle, but it's always wise to aspirate before you inject. Pull back on the syringe about ½ cc, and you can nearly always tell if you're into a blood vessel.

• *Use the right length needle.* The practice of many nurses on labor and delivery units is a good guide: Use spinal needles to give I.M. injections to obese patients. For your protection— and the physician's—ask the prescribing doctor to specify needle length in the drug order: "Use 3 to 3½-inch needle in thigh or hip."

AMA Prescribes a Trouble Shooter

Physicians looking for practice short cuts and ways to help them stay out of malpractice trouble when prescribing may want to explore the *Patient Medication Instruction* (PMI) Program offered by the AMA. During the last two years the AMA has expanded the program designed to inform patients on the indications for and use of a broad range of medications. The information sheets that a physician hands out to patients won't substitute for obtaining informed consent, but they will improve your communication with patients. The idea behind the program is to provide additional information to patients when it is likely to have the greatest impact— at the point of prescription.

Each PMI is a 5½ by 8½-inch sheet of paper with information on a particular drug class. It includes the name of the drug prescribed, directions for its use, what it is used for, dosage, precautions, side effects, and any special instructions. The information is meant to inform, not to alarm the patient. It is written in language that is easily understood.

PMIs are available for 100 of the most commonly prescribed drugs, covering 85 to 90 percent of all drugs prescribed. The AMA emphasizes that the information sheets are not intended as a substitute for instructions and information required to be given to patients, but they can improve effectiveness of drug use by increasing patient compliance, reducing the risk of improper drug use and curbing preventable and serious adverse reactions. The biggest factor in their favor is that they help build the physician–patient relationship.

7

AVOIDING RISK
IN
THE HOSPITAL

MALPRACTICE CHECKLIST

- Failure to properly investigate a physician's background and to grant privileges beyond the scope of his or her training can expose the entire staff.
- Transfer of a patient should not be done solely for the convenience of the emergency department and transferring hosptial.
- Alcohol ingestion, drug overdoses and child abuse often present in ER with deceptive signs, setting the stage for liability.
- In most states, you are required to file a written report within three days documenting suspected child abuse.
- If you are unable to obtain certified personnel in OR, document in the record that senior personnel were unavailable or already in surgery.
- Periodically and carefully review your nurse's progress notes to keep abreast of patient's response to treatment and possible errors in record that may need correction.
- A medication profile enables any pharmacist on duty to become quickly familiar with patient's total drug regimen.
- A DRG guideline can never be offered as a defense in a malpractice case.
- If you disagree with DRG guidelines, note them factually in writing; document your rationale.

86

- Do not postpone patient's discharge instructions until the day of discharge.

- Stay aware of late-breaking developments in a patient's condition prior to a short-stay admission.

- Discharge the patient yourself— do not delegate to others.

- If you are away on discharge day, spend extra time with the patient in advance, reviewing instructions, etc.

- Patients who leave against medical advice must sign appropriate forms and the decision should be recorded in the chart.

- If the patient threatens to sign out, check the nurse's notes of the two or three days before for possible causes of upset.

- Beware of July, August and September and the influx of new and inexperienced interns and residents.

- If writing discharge orders the evening before, make the discharge "conditional," indicating "ok if condition remains same or improved."

AVOIDING RISKS IN THE HOSPITAL

Hospitals pose one of the greatest risks to your being joined in a lawsuit! With the advent of DRGs and other so-called hospital and medical cost-cutting plans, physicians and all health care providers are becoming increasingly liable for actions over which they have no control. DRGs are not a legal defense— a fact that cannot be overemphasized. Hospital administrative directives are not a legal defense. The physician virtually stands alone to practice good medicine yet not perform tests that he feels are unnecessary. Juries have no idea about how DRGs limit the practice of good medicine. They are not concerned with the intricacies of cost-cutting formulas; what they are concerned about in any given case is the simple question, was everything done for this plaintiff that could and should have been done?

In the final analysis, cost-cutting is totally ineffective when compared with a single substantial jury verdict. Once the public becomes aware of what is happening as a result of DRGs, the lawsuits will begin to multiply. We are still in the incubation period for those lawsuits.

Let us analyze a prime example of the legal implications of DRGs as they simply relate to prescribing procedures. Let us suppose you are a general surgeon who has just performed intraabdominal surgery. You write an order for agent "A," which is not on the hospital formulary. The patient is given instead agent "B," which has been determined by the P&T Committee to be a theraputic equivalent. Agent "B" costs less than agent "A," and thus the profit margin is greater and the cost lower to the patient. You are never consulted about the efficacy of the use of agent "B"; however, that is what is given to your patient. Your patient develops complications, which after a prolonged hospital stay are cleared up with the administration of agent "A." You are just about assured of being sued— not because you did anything that fell below the standard of care, but because some hospital P&T Committee was more concerned about cutting costs than they were about the effectiveness of more expensive medications. A simple, but unquestionably real example. Certainly, the hopsital will be sued— but so will you.

Hospitals also create a litigious atmosphere. While you may have an excellent rapport with your patient and his or her family, a technician, nurse or even someone from the business office can create a bubbling cauldron for you. How? Lack of judgment, a perceived lack of concern, an attitude of "this bill is your responsibility" or idle Monday-morning quarterbacking, "Oh Dr. So-and-so would never have ordered that." All can cause very real problems and easily involve you in a lawsuit. Not because you did anything wrong, not because you breached any standard of care, but because of someone's attitude, lack of judgment or idle gratuitous opinions. Of course, the same applies to idle comments of other physicians.

DRGs and stray and inappropriate remarks in the hospital chart are part of a broad spectrum of liaiblity problems that could leave you exposed. One particularly insidious aspect of the malpractice risks associated with the hospital is that much of the exposure arises from situations over which you may have little control and from staff whom you cannot always monitor or supervise. Recent court cases have demonstrated how entire hospital staffs can be snared in a malpractice suit because the courts ruled that all physicians should have known about the incompetence of one of their colleagues.

CREDENTIALING: WHERE IT ALL STARTS

Credentialing is the building block of risk management in the hosptial, a first line of defense. The failure to properly investigate a physician's background and to grant privileges beyond the scope of his training are among the most common errors that can expose a staff to the errant actions of one physician. Even if a physician has presented proper training, the failure of a hospital committee to curb a physician's scope of activity when he has failed to keep pace with continuing medical education can also lead to big malpractice trouble. Impaired or incompetent physicians can no longer be protected: they make up the 3 percent of physicians who account for 48 percent of the malpractice settlements. Statistics show that one out of every 40 physicians has not had the proper training to qualify for a medical license. Part of the reason for that is the large number of doctors who have been admitted under special programs, especially those who are refugees from other countries. While they may be competent, they must present to credentials committees evidence that they have had requisite training. The failure of committees to thoroughly investigate the nature and scope of this training becomes even more critical when you consider how the Joint and Several Rule could be applied. This rule can hold a physician responsible for an entire judgment even if he is only marginally involved in a malpractice suit.

THE EMERGENCY ROOM

Few areas of the hospital represent as much of a pressure point for malpractice as the ER. This potential has become even more apparent with the advent of the DRG system. Multiple trauma cases, for example, which require stabilization and transfer to a trauma center are among the situations that raise the potential for liability. Transfer problems in the ER present themselves in a variety of ways. When should the ER staff transfer a head trauma patient who is precariously awaiting the arrival of the neurosurgeon in the ER? How should the ER staff deal with the cardiac patient who belongs in the coronary care unit but cannot be admitted because there are no beds available anywhere in the hospital? All too often the hospital is full. Patients are often discharged from the ER when they might otherwise have been admitted.

A general rule on which the emergency physician and the ER staff can rely is that the patient should not usually be transferred from one hospital emergency department to another unless the patient is clinically capable of sustaining the transfer without harm to his health as a result of the transfer. Another general rule of transfer can be stated in the negative— that is, when not to transfer. Transfer should not usually be conducted solely for the convenience of the emergency department and the transferring hospital. The most blatant example of such transfer reflects the "dumping syndrome," in which the private hospital emergency department transfers an indigent patient to the public hosptial. A new federal law has outlawed this practice.

Transfer of the cardiac patient raises special considerations. The emergency department staff is at least obligated to render initial diagnosis and treatment to this patient, according to Dr. James George in his book, *Law and Emergency Care*. If the patient's condition is stable, the ECG is normal and an intravenous line is available, it is usually acceptable to transfer the patient to another facility. But legal complications could develop if the patient sustains further damage through the transfer. The simple fact is that there will be no liability if the patient weathers the transfer without harm and there may be liability if the patient is injured as a result of the transfer. If the emergency staff is sufficiently concerned about the risk of injury through a transfer, it should err on the side of caution, says Dr. George, and not transfer the patient.

Patient transfer from one emergency department to another may be appropriate under the following circumstances: (1) if the transferring hospital is not clinically staffed to render the necessary care that the patient's condition requires; (2) if the transferring hospital is filled to capacity and, as a result, is physically incapable of accommodating the patient in the type of inpatient setting his condition requires; and (3) if the patient, after being informed of the consequences of his decision, requests to be transferred to another hospital.

Generally, however, the case that presents with the obvious problem is not the most troublesome, rather it is the patient whose symptoms are not obvious. A patient who fears he may be seriously ill, for example, may try to ease his apprehension by minimizing his condition. Should you admit for observation? Order a battery of tests? The ER is the place where one disease entity may masquerade for another, where the differential diagnosis for gastritis fans out into a wide array of conditions. The ovarian cyst could be acute appendicitis. Each possibility must be methodically ruled out as part of the triage. In ruling out the possibilities, the emergency room staff must work as a team and document that fact, because without a thorough record of their cooperation a jury could easily conclude that no one knew what he or she was doing and even worse, nobody cared.

Consider the case of a 20-year-old black female who appeared at the emergency room with complaints that could have been pelvic inflammatory disease, an ovarian cyst, acute appendicitis, urinary tract infection or ectopic pregnancy. She was referred to a surgeon who failed to order a flat plate and upright of the abdomen, which meant no one knew if there was free air under the diaphragm. Six hours later she was distended and her abdomen was rigid. She then developed adult respiratory distress syndrome and was hurriedly transferred to a major medical center, where she died. The diagnosis: septicemia and peritonitis. The first physician who saw her assumed that the second doctor would order the tests that would have ruled out the problem that his consult was called for. But the physician never ordered the appropriate flat plate and upright of the abdomen. The one weak link in the chain made it appear as if everyone on the emergency department staff had failed.

Alcohol ingestion, drug overdoses and child abuse may present in the emergency department with deceptive signs and symptoms that could set the stage for liability. Ingestion of alcohol, whether or not it results in intoxication, tends to make health care providers believe less in the plight of the people they treat. Patient complaints seem less significant, and the odor of alcohol generally detracts from the seriousness of the patient's apparent emergency in the mind of the person rendering care. Overlooked skull and cervical spine fractures are not uncommon in intoxicated patients who have been brought to the ER. Consider, for example, the patient who arrives at the hospital with a fracture and seems to be passing air adequately. The patient is given Demerol and may have an expanding intracranial mass lesion that goes undetected until brain damage occurs. The Demerol has had a masking effect on the underlying problem.

CHILD ABUSE

The ER is usually the place where a case of child abuse will appear and it may be among the most difficult judgment calls to make. This is a growing problem— especially for hospitals and physicians attending the ER— since all 50 states have now passed legislation requiring physicians to report cases of suspected child abuse. In most states, not only are physicians obligated to call a central hotline, they are also required to file a written medical report within three days that documents their suspicions. A physician may be sued and be held criminally liable for failure to report such abuse. There is not one uniform law about reporting or one way to report, since it varies from state to state. Few cases are blatant enough to eliminate all doubt from the physician's mind. Most fall into a gray area where parents and child give plausible excuses for the injuries.

The courts require that physicians have "reasonable cause" to report suspected child abuse, but "reasonable cause" is ill-defined. The suspicion must be supported by information. For example, does the history coincide with the physician's examinations? Is this syndrome being repeated? Is the patient doctor-shopping? Does this family have a history of abuse? Is the story told by the parents inconsistent with the nature of the injuries suffered? If you report suspected abuse "in good faith," you cannot be sued by the parents for slander or libel even if, upon investigation, the injury is found to be accidental.

OPERATING ROOM

With the doctrine of joint and several liability adding a new dimension to your responsiblity for other physicians, you need to be even more careful about the cases in which you serve as an assistant. The operating room is a prime example. Consider the first assistant who has adequate malpractice coverage but who scrubs in with someone who has decided to drop his policy. The first assistant may find himself in an untenable position if the primary surgeon is sued. If a jury finds the first assistant as little as one percent negligent, the plaintiff could collect the entire judgment from him because the other physician had "gone bare."

Although the "Captain of the Ship Doctrine" is no longer considered as applicable as it once was, there may be cases in which the surgeon is responsible for all negligence that occurs in the operating room at the time that he is performing surgery. While the negligent persons technically may be employees of the hospital, a court may still hold that they are— for purposes of performing surgery— "borrowed servants" and are under the total supervision and control of the operating surgeon. The "Captain of the Ship" doctrine comes into play when a certified registered nurse anesthetist is present, but would not apply if the anesthesia is administered by a board certified anesthesiologist. When the surgery is complicated and you are unable to obtain a board certified anesthesiologist, documentation becomes even more crucial. Records must reflect the fact that all senior personnel, for example, were in surgery and that you relied upon personnel with the most seniority. A few state courts have held that the latest hospital regulations in effect remove a nurse anesthetist from the direction and control of the surgeon, and thus the hospital, as her employer, and not the surgeon is liable for her negligence. But these cases are rare and the general rule is that the physician is liable for the negligence of a nurse anesthetist. Anesthesiologists, however, are considered to be "captains of the ship" in their sphere of activity.

NURSES

Physicians who take the time to read the RN's notes on the patient's hospital chart are probably aware of their medical-legal significance. Nurses do not just record routine medical data. They record what the patient says, whether or not the physician saw the patient, the time the doctor was called in an emergency and the time he arrived, the patient's toleration of treatment and much more. Physicians may be surprised at the level of detail in the nurse's notes and what is being said about them. So important are the nurse's notes that the plaintiff's attorney often examines them first when he is probing the hospital record for signs of weakness and other areas that deserve further exploration.

Nurses who have erred expect to be told off by a physician, but if they are treated with arrogance, your lack of respect for them as part of the treatment team could come back to haunt you at the deposition stage or later. Favorable remarks in the nurse's notes can help protect you. What's more, a nurse may help keep you out of court. She can calm an angry patient if you are late making rounds. She can alert you to angry feelings by the patient's family or a host of other medical-legal considerations that are as good as free malpractice insurance. A careful review of the nurse's progress notes not only can bring you up to date on the patient's response to treatment, it may also alert you to possible errors in the record that need to be corrected. Such changes in the hospital chart should be handled the same way that other changes in the record are implemented. Nothing should be erased. If a nurse's note needs to be corrected, simply make a new entry as near as possible to the one that is being corrected, and date and initial it.

INTERNS AND RESIDENTS

July, August and September are months in which the hospital atmosphere may be charged with an increased potential for liability. During these months, the hospital braces for an influx of new and inexperienced interns and residents who are beginning their training. They pose an extra risk when they have emerged from medical schools that have not provided them with much clinical experience. If that is the case, they pose a clear and present danger to everyone concerned with their care. They require extra supervision and overlapping coverage so that they are thoroughly briefed on all aspects of a patient's condition. Schedules should be carefully coordinated during these months until these new troops can become an effective part of the treatment team.

PHARMACY MALPRACTICE AND
STRICTER DRUG DISPENSATION

One survey attributes one out of every six malpractice suits to a drug-related error. According to *The Malpractice Reporter*, another recent survey of 23 insurance companies showed that the average drug product claim settlement in 1985 was $171,173— almost twice as costly as injury claims involving tractors and trucks, the next highest category. Most hospitals are saddled with a malpractice insurance policy deductible that commonly ranges from $250,000 to $1 million or more for the large medical centers, and a good part of that figure is attributable to drug misuse. The cases of drug-related error dramatically demonstrate the need for built-in checks and counterchecks, particularly for potentially toxic medications. Although incompetence and human error may be used as an explanation, a plaintiff's attorney is nevertheless presented with abundant opportunity to ply his skills, using a lack of administrative control and theories of corporate liability to anchor his arguments.

Consider the 43-year-old patient who received IV gentamicin after pancreatitis surgery for eight days, and neomycin 1 percent wound irrigation for 30 days. The patient became totally deaf, and the hospital pharmacist was charged with allowing excessive administration of aminoglycoside medications. If the pharmacy profile had been reviewed and the drug amounts ordered and used had been scrutinized, the neomycin would have been discontinued.

In another case recently brought to trial, podophyllum resin was inadvertently substituted for benzoin tincture during an orthopedic cast procedure for a 10-year-old boy in a city hospital clinic. The boy suffered necrosis, gangrene and subsequently had to have a leg amputated. The claim stressed that hospital personnel failed to follow proper guidelines for monitoring the medication. Similar horror stories dramatize the need for the hospital pharmacy to have a written procedure manual covering all drugs and a control policy that the pharmacists should thoroughly study during their job orientation and periodically review to refresh risk management guidelines.

The unit dose system, now widely used, has also helped to curb liability exposure. This requires that (1) each medication is contained in and administered from a single unit package; (2) the medication is dispensed in the most convenient, ready-to-administer form that is therapeutically feasible; (3) supplies are limited to a 24-hour doctor's written dispensation order; and (4) a patient medication profile is currently maintained with dispensation. If problems arise with any feature of the single dose system, a clinical pharmacologist with the assistance of the Pharmacy and Therapeutics Committee and the Department of Nursing should be consulted.

In the DRG era, when pharmacists are expected to recite chapter and verse on how to contain costs, it is essential that risk management guidelines are followed so that the efficacy of one regimen is not sacrificed for the sake of a cheaper drug or another form of the same medication. A medication profile enables any pharmacist on duty to become quickly familiar with a patient's total drug regimen. It enables rapid detection of potential interactions, unintended dosage alterations, substance duplications, overlapping therapies and contraindicated drugs.

Here's how it works in practice: All profile information, particularly the physician's medication order sheet, is reviewed by each pharmacist before he dispenses any prescription. It's important for him to review this information to avoid errors that could arise if drug orders are transcribed onto special forms for pharmacy use, according to Pharmacist James O'Connell, writing in *The Malpractice Reporter*. The pharmacist should, in turn, be supervised by a pharmacologist. In addition to maintaining drug profiles, an alert pharmacist should also inform a physician and patient about new, superior drugs, drug incompatibilities and known contraindications. Today's litigious atmosphere has reshaped the role of the hospital pharmacist. Not only is he expected to run a cost-effective operation, he is becoming an "inhouse drug surveillance agent," a vital cog in the hospital's line of defense against malpractice suits.

DRGs: HOW MUCH OF A LIABILITY THREAT?

It's probably too early to reliably assess whether the DRG system has been directly responsible for an increase in malpractice suits. No study has demonstrated that for a fact, but the potential for liability is inherent in the way the system operates. In 1984 the American Society of Internal Medicine surveyed its members regarding the impact of DRGs on patient-care activities and whether prospective payment had led to inappropriate decisions to limit care. Some of the replies were revealing in how the system could set you up for a claim. For example, one respondent indicated that one of his patients had complicated deep vein thrombosis and the other had severe pneumonia. The one with pneumonia had to be discharged on antibiotics, receiving the last dose of IM medication in the hospital and starting on oral medication after he went home. Both of these patients had to be readmitted within a few days and their relapses were predictable. Still another physician who answered the survey reported that the standard treatment for endocarditis is four weeks of intravenous antibiotic therapy, yet DRGs in his hospital recommended two weeks. Eight physicians indicated that there had been "an observable and a definite increase in morbidity and at least two possible fatalities, which they felt were attributable to premature discharge.

You may find yourselves on the horns of a dilemma when you are faced with decisions regarding DRGs. It's often a juggling act as you seek to balance standards of quality care with pressures to keep your hospital profitable. There is the potential for creating new areas of divisiveness— pitting the physician against the patient or the physicians against the hospital. There are no secrets for resolving such dilemmas that may arise over DRGs other than first to realize that a DRG can never be offered as a defense in a malpractice case. Your best defense begins with the rapport that you maintain with patients, making them and their families aware of the bind that you are placed in and the difficult choices you must make within the context of prospective payment. Secondly, if you are concerned about the fact that you need to disagree with the DRG guidelines of your hospital's Utilization Review Committee or PRO, note those disagreements in writing, documenting your rationale. Third, try to maintain an objective attitude when discussing these matters with the hospital administration. Despite their cost profiles and whether you conform to them, no one wins if you and the administration become adversaries rather than allies.

DISCHARGING A PATIENT

If DRGs have heightened the awareness of cost, they have also raised the consciousness of physicians concerning discharges— mostly regarding how soon to make them, because that is the factor that will affect their hospital's bottom line. Once that decision is made, however, a physician's guard may drop. As he loses interest in hospitalized patients ready for discharge, subtle factors can creep into patient care that may loom important after the patient is sent home. Too often physicians send a patient home with only a general idea of what is safe to do and what is not, how and when to take their medicine and what symptoms might be signs of trouble. Patients may harbor an assortment of fears about their discharge including whether they should be discharged at all.

Be specific. Going the extra yard to make sure that instructions are understood will pave the way for an uneventful recovery. Vague instructions like "take it easy" or "use your own judgment" could leave you vulnerable for liability, even from patients not considered at high risk. The biggest question on the minds of many patients is when they can return to work. By having them spell out their job duties in detail you will be better able to understand the stress to which they may be subjected. Along with instructions about the limits that seem appropriate, you need to spell out *why*— what could happen if they ignore your advice or do not follow it as closely as they should. Medication instructions demand that you be specific. In addition to explaining what the patient will be taking, and why, how and when to use the drug, it is always advisable to make sure he or she is not taking other medications.

Don't postpone discharge instructions. Leaving the going-home instructions until the day of discharge is unwise because there may be little time for a thorough review of all essentials. On the day of discharge, the patient may also be preoccupied with preparations so that much of what you say may not have the impact that it could have if it were discussed the previous evening in a more relaxed atmosphere. Home care services, if they are needed, should be arranged for well in advance.

Make it a "conditional discharge." If you are writing discharge orders into a patient's medical record the evening before the day when the patient will be released, take an extra precaution. In the interim, the patient may develop a fever that could be evidence of a wound infection. If the patient does not report a change in his condition prior to his being released or if it goes unnoticed by the nursing staff, you could be left with a liability because the patient would be sent home febrile. For that reason, view a discharge order written on a previous evening as a "conditional discharge"; i.e., the patient may be discharged the following day if his condition remains the same or is improved— a qualification that should be noted on the chart.

Dangers in short-stay admissions. Since short stays in the hospital are often booked well ahead, there may be late-breaking developments in a patient's condition that you need to know about before the patient is admitted. Some physicians routinely suggest that a patient visit the office a day or two before the scheduled admission. If the patient in for a short stay is scheduled for surgery, it is a good idea to see the patient before he or she is medicated because it enables you to review post-op discussions that occurred in the office.

Discharge the patient yourself.   Discharging the patient should not be delegated to house officers, nurses or anyone else if you can avoid it. Other staff unfamiliar with the patient's care could undo much of the discharge preparation that you have carefully made. Instructions that may not coincide with what you would have in mind could create difficulties for you later when you resume follow-up care. If you need to be away on the discharge day, plan to spend extra time with the patient in advance of his or her going home. By lingering in the patient's room on discharge day, you allow that extra time for questions and reassurances that may give you an added measure of rapport so necessary to good physician–patient relationships.

PATIENTS WHO LEAVE AGAINST MEDICAL ADVICE

It has been estimated that fewer than one out of every 100 hospital discharges reflects a patient who has decided to leave against medical advice. That number may seem small, but the problem is significant. Any patient who does leave against medical advice or threatens to defy medical opinion is not only asserting an independent spirit but is conveying how he feels about the physician and his confidence in the hospital. If this situation is mishandled, it can create liability problems in its own right. The reasons for leaving are as varied as the patients who exercise this option. A patient may have an addiction to drugs or alcohol that he is trying to avoid disclosing and the addiction could trigger withdrawal symptoms the longer he remains in the hospital. He decides to leave rather than risk exposing his problem. Nothing short of a commitment or an emergency situation can keep a patient in the hospital for treatment, but when a patient does leave against medical advice the appropriate forms must be signed and it is imperative that the patient's actions be recorded in the progress notes. Although some of these situations are regrettably unavoidable, the physician attuned to these patients may be able to spot a problem looming long before liability becomes a question.

Physicians experienced with the patient who talks about leaving against medical advice knows that he represents more of a *threat* to sign out. Most of these patients do not want to sign out. The message he is sending is that he is angry or frightened. The legal aspect is the last feature a physician should worry about. Instead of trying to figure out why the patient wants to leave, physicians often try to cover themselves legally, proferring another form that probably only serves to antagonize the patient more. "Yes, you can leave," says the physician, "but before you do, you have to sign this form that absolves us of all responsibility." The patient will think, "This doctor really doesn't give a damn about me." If you read the nurses' notes two or three days prior to the threat to sign out, you will usually find that these patients have been observed to be upset. If you can deal with these precipitating problems, the situation will never mushroom to the point of becoming a legal problem. A sick patient who threatens to sign out of the hospital against the advice of his doctor is behaving irrationally. It is the last desperate act of a patient to whom no other solution seems available to deal with his intense emotional distress.

As far as the malpractice implications are concerned, a physician may possibly be liable under two circumstances: (1) when the patient is not adequately informed of the consequences of his leaving the physician's care; and (2) when the physician fails to inform the patient who insists on leaving his care that he should contact another physician and that he will give that physician information on all studies already done and treatment that has been rendered. If the patient refuses to sign a form indicating he is leaving against medical advice, all that can be done is to fully document the fact.

8

THE
MEDICAL
RECORD

MALPRACTICE CHECKLIST

- Adopt the SOAP method of record keeping— Subjective, Objective, Assessment and Plan.
- Extraneous information on how a patient should be billed should not be in the medical record.
- A patient's failure to keep an appointment must be documented.
- Have consent forms signed and witnessed by office staff and filed in the record.
- Beware of changes: Make no obliterations, alterations or other changes of what has already been recorded.
- Draw a line through incorrect entries; date and initial it.
- Note in the margin that a crossed-out entry is in error.
- Add correct entry in chronological order, referring to incorrect entry being replaced.
- Maintain internal consistency-interrelationship of diagnosis, treatment, tests, etc.
- Justify diagnosis— differentiate rationale for one modality over its alternative.
- Avoid jousting in record— bickering, belittling, blaming of others.

The Verdict, a movie starring Paul Newman, dramatized how an attorney can devastate a physician by exposing how the doctor falsified the medical record. Your malpractice case could also hinge on how you maintained your records. The outcome could be decided long before deposition or trial by how well you kept the chart. The verdict for you will be related to matters of whether the record is complete and reflects an internal consistency that carefully documents the interrelationship of diagnosis, treatment, tests, medications, recommendations and follow-up care. The bottom line is that the medical record is the basic building block of your defense and plays a pivotal role in at least 25 percent of cases that are settled at trial.

Few aspects of medical care may seem as tedious and labor-intensive as good record keeping, but there is no substitute for the dividends of solid record keeping if a claim is filed. Similarly, there is no way to describe how devastated you will be— like the physician in *The Verdict*— if the plaintiff's attorney turns the record against you. Poorly maintained records are the soft underbelly that plaintiff's attorneys' explore and exploit.

What are the elements of good record keeping? How does completeness stand out as a factor that can work for your defense? How should the material in the patient's chart be organized to save you time and needless travail when an attorney asks to see it? Why is alteration of the record a legal minefield and how should it be handled? What do we mean by internal consistency? How can the tone of remarks in the record affect you? By addressing each of these questions and familiarizing yourself and your staff with the answers, you will have sealed off one of the main avenues that otherwise leave you exposed to liability claims.

HOW SHOULD YOU ORGANIZE THE CHART?

Because of the wealth of information that should be in the chart (and the potential that it has for harming or helping you), consider how it is organized. What happens when another physician is covering for you? Will essential information about your patient's condition loom immediately apparent? For example, allergies should be noted prominently on the front of the chart. Medications should also be prominently displayed— what the patient is on and in what amounts. Typing and signing are preferable to an illegible scrawled note. Typed notations should be read and initialed to ensure the accuracy of the transcription.

Many physicians have adopted the SOAP method of medical record keeping. This stands for Subjective, Objective, Assessment, and Plan. The first information noted in the record is subjective. This is not simply a clinical report of your observations, but what the patient tells you. Then the objective information is entered on the chart. It consists of the physical exam, lab findings, and the results of other relevant tests. Following this information is the assessment of the patient's condition, followed by the plan for treatment. Every entry in a patient's chart can be facilitated if the record is kept in a convenient place so that the office staff can easily update it when a patient calls. After the patient has been seen, the physician should review notations that have been made or need to be entered and initial the notations.

If portions of the record are kept in separate places, a physician could be vulnerable. This is critical when more than one physician becomes involved in the patient's care. For example, suppose someone is covering your practice for a week. That physician should be able to pick up the chart and after a cursory review of the record, be able to determine what medications the patient has been receiving, what allergies have been recorded, how many visits have been missed, and if there is a history of multiple somatic complaints without an organic basis. The physician should not have to check back to January 1983 to see what medications have been prescribed. The potential for malpractice could grow if information is not in the chart concerning referrals such as to a gastroenterologist. That physician may have prescribed a drug for the patient's ulcer problem or placed the patient on a restricted diet. The record must include that information.

Extraneous information, such as material on how the patient should be billed, should not be included with the medical record. Entries should always be to the point. References like, "Patient was seen for circulatory and other problems" are too vague, possibly paving the way for a plaintiff's attorney to accuse you of indifference. After phoning a patient concerning a diagnosis, you will want to follow up in writing. Copies of all correspondence should be tacked onto the record.

When writing to patients, beware of casual remarks that could mislead a patient into thinking a condition is less serious than it is, or that could raise false expectations of successful treatment. Similarly, beware of cavalier comments in letters to other physicians, copies of which should also be filed in the record. For example, indicating to a colleague that you or he should have performed other tests, or casually noting that you will do something differently next time may be all that an opposing attorney needs to slip a noose around your neck.

Why Completeness is Important

The attorney who properly analyzes the record uses the chart as if it were a road map. Will the attorney discover the signs that lead to the conclusion that you were negligent? An incomplete record virtually assures that conclusion. Attorneys look for what is absent from the record as much as for what has been entered. For example, take the common case of the patient who is advised to return to the office on a specific date and does not. A patient's failure to keep an appointment must be documented.

The same rule applies to any telephone calls coming into the office. These should be noted by the office staff because they may constitute building blocks for your defense. During such a phone conversation, your nurse may have informed the patient that you were willing and able to see her that afternoon and urged her to visit the office, particularly in view of the patient's complaints. Let's further assume that the calls were logged but something happened to the patient and he failed to show for an appointment. When your records are requested by the opposing attorney or subpoenaed, you have documented the fact that the patient was advised to come in and did not. Compare the security of being in that position as opposed to having the patient rail from the witness stand that she had called you on five different occasions with the same complaint and was unable to schedule a time to see you.

It is essential that such information and other material on compliance patterns be noted in the chart. If the patient has failed to comply with instructions for medication, your attorney will be able to use that fact in your defense. Have consent forms been signed and witnessed by office staff? Has a notation to this effect been entered in the record? These are the minutiae that can slip by during a busy day but crop up months later when you may be asked about them by an attorney.

As time-consuming as it may be, accurate and complete documentation is the fabric of your medical record. Don't overlook such situations as a notation in the office chart referring to a radiology report. Accompanying such references to these and other studies should be a notation reflecting the result of that report. The same holds true for any reference you make to a consultant. Again, adequate documentary evidence in their file must show what the results were.

A survey of selected cases illustrates how a lack of documentation can undermine a physician's defense. In one, a doctor performed a meatotomy, then dictated a report later in the week that contained the wrong date for the operation. The patient sued, claiming that he suffered complications that impaired sexual relations. The complaint accused the doctor of using an oversized French instrument on the patient's penis, an allegation denied by the doctor. In deposition, however, the physician conceded that the surgery notation was incorrectly dated. The opposing attorney was set to undermine the physician's credibility in court, asking pointedly, "If you can't even place the time of the operation accurately, how can we expect you to remember the size of the instrument you used?" This case was settled out of court for $2000 because the doctor's insurance company considered its case too shaky to test in court.

In another case a 56-year-old man came to an internist complaining of an upper respiratory ailment documented after a physical exam. Additional findings showed prostatic changes, which were also recorded in the chart. During the next year, the doctor treated the patient for emphysema, but he failed to note follow-up information on the changes in the prostate previously discovered. The patient died of prostatic cancer, and the family filed a claim. This time the case was settled for $67,000.

What to Record?

The first rule of adequate record-keeping is to record what the patient says about his medical problems. Quotes by the patient are particularly helpful if taken down verbatim at the time of the examination. For example, the patient's statement "I thought about coming to see you for two weeks before eventually making the appointment" can be very significant if the allegation in the case is delay in diagnosis. It could indicate that the patient's own delay in seeking appropriate medical treatment contributed to the problems.

Most often, a patient's recollection of the symptoms described to the doctor will be substantially different at the time of filing a malpractice suit. Thus, the physician's record becomes a significant means of protection against charges that the doctor failed to note symptoms. Patients are poor reporters of their own physical conditions, and many times they fail to mention the most important matter bothering them. If the doctor has accurately written down what was said about the problem, and the patient contends at the time of litigation that there were new or additional symptoms, the physician will have a record indicating what he was actually told.

The physician should also record any other relevant information provided from other sources regarding treatment of the patient. For example, a mother will often tell a physician more about a child's condition than the child himself will. The mother's statements should be documented.

In addition to recording what the patient has said and what you have done in the examination, make sure you record what you have told the patient. This is particularly important in a lawsuit involving informed consent. The patient says, "I was never told X," but your records says, "Patient told about X."

Obviously, the mere fact that you have made a purported record of some event does not mean you are going to be believed by the jury. A written record by itself is not proof that a particular event took place. The value of the record, however, is the added verification it provides for your testimony compared with the testimony of the patient. The patient will most likely not keep written records of what transpired. (A patient who does is so unusual as to be suspect.) The patient will be relying on his own recollection of something that happened a year or two before. If you have adequate and accurate records, you have the advantage in getting the jury to believe what really transpired at your office or in the hospital.

Many physicians fail to adequately document informed consent. A signed form may be useless if the patient suffers an adverse reaction and sues. A jury might believe the patient when he claims that he was disoriented and was unaware of what he was signing. A note in the chart concerning the patient's orientation and apparent ability to grasp what was going on may get the physician off the hook later.

Alterations in the Record: How Do You Make Changes?

False alteration of the medical record is lethal. Unfortunately, in an effort to improve their position in a lawsuit, physicians have attempted to alter their records. Foolishly, they forget that some errors in judgment do not necessarily constitute negligence and thus may not be subject to recovery of damages even if the patient has been harmed. If a correction has been made in a suspicious manner, it can devastate a doctor in court. It could trigger a charge that the physician tampered with the record— an accusation that in itself can lead to a malpractice claim and large awards. At trial, evidence of tampering can destroy a physician's credibility.

The irony behind many of these attempts is that the jury often awards larger sums than it would have if the physician had admitted negligence. Whenever such a change has been made, attorneys immediately focus on whether the changes were made to cover up something. An insurance company will almost always try to settle a case in spite of its merits if it believes that the physician could be accused of tampering with the record.

Any physician who is naive enough to think that he or she can alter the record when it is too late to make such changes will bring down the wrath of the jury. Document examination is a sophisticated science that can be used to determine the time entries were made. It is easy for an expert to determine who made the entries and even when. To avoid any question of tampering, the following procedure should be followed: Make no obliterations, alterations or other changes of what has been recorded. If something needs to be corrected, a line should be drawn through the incorrect entry. This should be initialed and dated. A note in the margin of the record should also indicate that the crossed-out entry is an error. Corrections should be made by an additional correct entry in chronological order, which will indicate the incorrect entry that is being replaced. If an entry is late, it should be noted as such.

Although Paul Newman's *The Verdict* did a masterful job of proving how a physician can hang himself on the record, case law contains equally vivid accounts of how other doctors have made similar errors. In a recent Florida case, for example, a patient was treated for what was thought to be an upper respiratory infection. No one performed a creatine count to monitor kidney function. For 16 days the patient was on nephrotoxic drugs until the staff finally found out he had a lesion in the colon. He never had a respiratory infection. The lesion was resected, but by this time he was in total renal failure. Someone on the staff had meanwhile added creatine counts into the record to give the impression that they were normal, but this entry was not stamped on a time clock as the other entries customarily were— indicating that the entry was false.

In her book, *Medical Malpractice Law*, attorney Angela Roddey Holder discusses a case in which a physician lost because of changes in the record. In a California case, *James v. Spear*, a woman had been treated for a stopped tear duct. An instrument used in the treatment brushed her cornea and abrasions resulted. After the incident, her daughter, a nurse, asked to inspect her mother's records at the physician's office. A liability claim was filed after the woman had examined the records. At the trial the nurse testified that the records that she had seen in the physician's office had been altered substantially by the time they were admitted into evidence. It was also established that a visit the patient had made after the accident had not been recorded. According to Holder, "The court held that the altered records created a presumption of negligence."

Why is Internal Consistency So Important?

In addition to incompleteness and improperly made changes, attorneys also look for the internal consistency of the record. This is the inter-relationship of the basis for making the diagnosis, the treatment, the tests, the medications administered, the recommendations and the follow-up care. These threads are intertwined. If attorneys see a lapse in one area they pursue it.

The plaintiff's legal counsel is attuned to what is not in the record. For example, consider the physician who had ruled out that the patient is suffering from an acute myocardial infarction versus a hiatal hernia. He had an upper GI series done, which showed no hiatal hernia, but nothing is in the record to indicate that tests were done to rule out the MI. If the physician is on the stand, he might be asked, "You had the tests, you knew she didn't have hiatal hernia with reflexive esophagitis, didn't you? Where are the tests to rule out the MI?"

Questions concerning patient complaints about the effect of medications are closely related to this line of investigation. What further analysis or tests were done following this notation in the record? Of particular importance in the medical chart are those situations involving two modalities of treatment. For what reasons did a physician consider giving X as opposed to Y? Whatever the choice and the reasons for doing so, the medical record must justify the diagnosis and treatment. That is, it must be internally consistent. If a patient is placed on an agent with known adverse effects compared with another that has fewer side effects, a physician has to justify it. For example, the following notation might be entered: "Mr. Jones was advised of both treatments available, but in view of his volatile hypertension we have elected to try . . ."

Internal consistency is critically important in prescribing. For example, a patient who has received prescriptions that should not be taken with other medications— including over-the-counter drugs— could be at risk if he or she is not given sufficient warning. I (Brooten) can recall one situation in which a patient was on a drug that thins the blood. The patient had a headache, took an aspirin, and suffered a stroke. You must document the fact that you advised the patient of that risk.

Moreover, everything in the medical record should serve a purpose. The medical record is no place for the physician to enter extraneous material, to editorialize. Most physicians recognize that statements such as, "In my opinion . . ." are self-serving and should be omitted. The patient's response should be described in factual terms.

Physicians who recognize that everything in the record serves a purpose have a better sense of the importance of the record in better patient care and, when necessary, their defense. They consider record keeping an integral part of rendering care. They do not make errors that come back to haunt them on the witness stand. Physicians who continue to make errors someday will be confronted by an attorney who can make their blood turn cold by asking those embarrassing questions that provoke long, pregnant silences before the jury. They have nothing to say in defense of themselves. It is all a matter of record.

How Can the Tone of Remarks in the Record Undercut Your Defense?

The potential for malpractice often provokes a defensive posture long before the plaintiff's attorney ever gets around to firing the first shot. Ironically, that defensive attitude may reveal itself in the record and can play a role in whether a plaintiff's attorney thinks he has a case. Unwittingly, through stray remarks in the record that allude to a lapse in care by other members of the health care team, physicians and nurses may be setting the stage for the filing of a claim. This sort of jousting in the medical record can be deadly and should be avoided because of the legal consequences. Yet it is surprising how many times such bickering, belittling and blaming of others occur in the chart, often in the nurse's notes.

Among the cases in which the records were a factor in disposition were these notations: "Dr. Smith paged at least four times to do arterial blood gases on the patient. Contacted after the fourth attempt." Closer scrutiny of records in the hospital, however, showed that this was not true. The blood gas order had been written by the doctor referred to in the nurse's note, so he was aware of the situation and the patient's needs. It was not urgent. But the nurse's statement that he had to be paged at least four times puts him in a bad light. Assuming that there had been a patient injury, a plaintiff's attorney would seize on such remarks to build a case for negligence.

Still other records reveal how smoldering animosities or even subtle differences of opinion can influence how information is recorded in the chart and can affect the outcome of a case. For example, another nurse's notation reads, "Dr. Black visited patient at 2:30 p.m. and refused to do arterial blood gases and restart patient's IV. Dr. White was called and restarted IV and did arterial blood gases . . ." It doesn't take much to read between these lines. The nurse felt that the physician should have done the blood gases and started the IV. A proper evaluation was soon done on this patient, so no harm was done. But consider the effect of such remarks on a jury that may easily be led to question the doctor's concern and medical judgment. The jury may even consider such comments as a sign of indifference toward the patient. Although this advice is seldom followed enough, there is sound legal basis to reviewing not only the progress notes and orders but also the nurse's notes.

You can imagine the surprise of still another doctor who responded to a page and upon reading the nurse's notes had discovered that he had not showed up. The notes had been signed off too early and he would have looked bad before a jury if a liability claim had developed and he had failed to review this portion of the chart.

Physicians often engage in their own battles through the medical record, but such quibbling with and belittling of colleagues or stray remarks that pass judgment about the care from peers can only backfire. Even when notes are technically correct, jousting may creep in. In one situation, for example, a doctor had ordered 100 mg of an antiemetic suppository. The recommended dosage is usually 200 mg, but the prescribing physician wanted to try a smaller amount. Before the prescribing physician checked on the patient, another doctor had bickered in the chart that 100 mg were given even though 200 mg is the usual dosage. This carping is needless and can only perk the index of suspicion of an attorney who may be scanning the record for irregularities and inconsistencies that will support a liability claim.

As these situations illustrate, one can never underestimate the importance of the record. It is comparable to a double-edged sword, capable of being your best defense or your worst enemy in a malpractice case. By monitoring your medical records as closely as you might follow the progress of a critically ill patient, you will have taken an important step toward keeping the chart in your favor.

9
HOW TO
DISCHARGE
A PATIENT
AND AVOID ABANDONMENT

MALPRACTICE CHECKLIST

- Under no circumstances should "financial reasons" ever be cited.
- The letter discharging the patient must be sent certified mail, return receipt requested.
- Avoid unilaterally discharging patients who need nursing care rather than hospitalization, involve colleagues, administration.
- Never indicate in the record that "the patient is unable to pay and continues to demand that he remain hospitalized."
- Never make a positive diagnosis that "patient has no medical problems."
- As long as your substitute is competent and requirements concerning notice and opportunity for patient to see are met, you will avoid liability for abandonment.
- Substitutes must be notified, available and reasonably easy for office staff and hospital to contact.
- It is not enough merely to arrange for a medical bureau or answering service to handle medical care of patients while you are on vacation.
- Those who want to reduce high risk profile should avoid all known high risk pregnancies.
- Terminating your relationship with a patient should be done during a nonemergency period.
- Twenty to thirty days warning is generally considered reasonable, depending on availability of alternative care.

There is an essential distinction between a negative wallet sign and a positive babinsky. Unfortunately, many good and skilled physicians have wreaked havoc upon themselves by discharging patients for all the wrong reasons.

The "art" of discharging patients is increasingly critical. Under no circumstances should "financial reasons" ever be cited. While financial considerations impose limitations on how you may care for a patient, the patient who does not pay also does not comply with a number of other things you may order. In other words if they are noncompliant relating to payment they will probably be noncompliant about taking medications, dieting, keeping appointments or following other orders that are necessary for their care and treatment.

Let's first examine how *not* to discharge a patient. The letter reprinted below is an actual letter received by the former wife of a client. It was sent by a physician who is competent in the practice of medicine; however, he could have exposed himself to litigation had he made the slightest mistake in treatment. As you read this letter, imagine that you are on a jury, and that the physician is being sued for medical malpractice for his failure to respond to a call when the child was critically ill and subsequently expired.

```
Ms.——,
    Due to the fact that there has been a financial dis-
agreement between us, I regret to inform you that I will
no longer be available to serve as your family's
pediatrician. If during the next 30 days, your child has a
bona fide emergency and you have not yet made arrangements
with another physician, I will see your child.
    In selecting another physician for your family, you
should know that I share call with Doctors——,——, and —
——. If you should transfer to one of them, I will not be
available to see your child when I am on call for them
(nights, weekends, afternoons off and holidays) as long as
your account with me is still deliquent. Should such a
situation arise, you would have to seek your pediatric
care from the emergency room physicians at —— or ——
Hospitals. I feel it only fair that I warn you well ahead
of time of the implications of your nonpayment to my of-
fice.
    Sincerely...
```

Consider also that the husband had made arrangements that all bills be processed through his insurance company. Consider further that there was an internal breakdown within the physician's office and when the letter was sent he was unaware that such arrangements had been made, and in fact that it was his office that had not processed the bills, which were less than $100.00. Consider further that the child's mother went to one of the other pediatricians and this particular physician refused to see the child because his office had not processed the insurance claim forms. The child died. What do you think a jury would do? None of us need reason either long or hard to determine that this letter would incense a jury. If the case got to the jury, the physician would stand virtually little if any chance of prevailing— not because he was negligent, but because of the method he used to discharge a patient. The following twelve points will help protect you:

1. An alternative letter should always be sent discharging a patient from an outpatient practice. The letter may read as follows:

CERTIFIED MAIL— RETURN RECEIPT REQUESTED

Dear Mrs. Doe:

As you know, you first came to my office in December of last year. At that time I advised you that you should lose a minimum of 20 pounds within the next year. I also advised you that you should walk 3 miles per day every other day.

I placed you on medication with strict instructions, which you acknowledged you understood in the presence of your husband. Since your initial visit, I have seen you on four occasions in the office and three occasions at the emergency room. The second time I saw you, I referred you for nutritional counselling to help you lose weight. On the first occasion when I saw you at the emergency room with a complaint of chest pain, you had not been taking your medication as directed, and you have gained instead of lost weight. Last Monday when I saw you, one year had passed and you are still not complying with the treatment I have recommended for you. I have discussed your noncomplaince with both you and your husband and unfortunately, you have persisted in failing to follow my instructions.

As I am sure you and your husband understand, I cannot continue to undertake the treatment of anyone who

does not wish to be treated. Accordingly, I will be
happy to send your complete records to the physician of
your choice. You should contact another physician to
treat you as soon as you receive this letter. If you,
your husband or any member of your immediate family
have any questions, I will be happy to discuss your
condition with them, of course with your permission.

Until you obtain the services of another physician, I
of course will follow you and see you in cases of emergency. I very much regret that this action is necessary; however, I am concerned about each of my patients
and cannot and will not attempt to treat those who do
not follow my advice.

Sincerely...

This is the type of letter that exhibits your concern not simply for this patient but for all your patients. It will help and not hurt you in court. You will note that the letter does not even mention failure to pay. That subject should be addressed by your business office. If "Past Due" notices fail, consider turning the collection over to an attorney. A letter discharging or "firing" a patient must be sent by Certified Mail, Return Receipt Requested. If they fail to claim the Certified letter, you should retain the envelope unopened and send a copy by regular mail. You should note on the unopened Certified Letter "copy sent by regular mail" and month-day-year and the name of the office person sending the copy of the letter. First and foremost you must protect yourself. Diplomatic, formal notification is your best protection, and when another physician takes over care of the patient, a copy of the letter should be included in the medical records.

2. Be sure to recommend two or three other physicians in the community when you are discharging a patient.
3. Be sure and follow up a patient when you are discharging her to be sure that your records follow the patient to the new physician.
4. Be sure to send the patient's records to the new physician regardless of whether a formal request is made and be sure to chart the fact that a copy of the records were sent to the new physician.
5. Confirm that the records have been received.
6. Be certain that more than one physician knows the history and status of your patients with potential complications or risks.

7. Be certain that you are present physically with high risk or problem patients (among those still under your care) when the onset of labor occurs and through the delivery process.

8. Send patients who are being discharged or are discharging themselves an informed consent-type document advising them of the need to discuss their history with their new physician. They should also be told to discuss in particular their history with respect to that treatment that you have rendered.

9. The letter mentioned in (8) should be carbon copied to the husband or father of the patient.

10. Never couch an AMA letter or chart entry regarding the discharge of a patient in a negative or hostile fashion. The reason given for discharge should be phrased "in the interest of patient care," especially when you are discharging her because of inability to get along or inability to communicate your wishes. No physician should abandon a patient because of money.

11. High risk situations should always be outlined to the new physician with excruciating care. When cancer is involved or suspected, particularly in gynecological care, strong warnings should be issued and the patient followed closely by the new health care team.

12. The key to all of this is to not leave an image that the patient was discharged or discharged herself without some effort on the doctor's part and the part of the doctor's staff to be certain that the patient was cared for. This must be true despite the patient's poor judgment or inability to handle the realities of a given situation.

Timing

Although these are basic precautions to minimize risk, some fine distinctions among the 12 points and additional elements to keep in mind when winding up the relationship are also important. Concluding your obstetric care should be done during a nonemergency period. As the AMA's *Current Opinion* states, "Physicians are free to choose whom they will serve. The physician should, however, respond to the best of his ability in cases of emergency where first aid treatment is essential."

There is slight disagreement among medical legal experts on how much notice you need to provide before phasing a patient out of your obstetric care, but thirty days warning is generally considered reasonable, depending on the availability of alternative care. Courts look at the amount of notice given a patient on a case-by-case basis. There are no magic numbers. Moreover, the amount of time should be based on the severity of the patient's condition and how readily available is the referral.

HOSPITAL TRANSFERS

"Nesting" is a term I (Brooten) began to utilize a number of years ago when I was an administrative officer of a 480 bed Veterans Administration Hospital in Florida. Various and sundry patients migrate south with the snows of winter. They would have admissions to rule out various nonexistent conditions at various hospitals down the Eastern seaboard. They would present with a series of complaints that virtually mandated an admission to rule out metastatic carcinoma or some other equally devastating condition. The more ingenious patients would go to a private hospital, knowing that they had no insurance and were eligible for VA benefits. An emergency room physician would carefully document each complaint and then call to transfer the patient. After my second year in the business, I would determine where they spent their summers and determine which route they took south. Then I would methodically call various VA Hospitals along that route and "surprisingly" discover they had those same symptoms at the last seven VA Hospitals. When confronted, some would simply leave. The hard core ones always maintained they were getting the shuffle and had finally arrived in the promised land where they could get help. How do you "lead" an unwilling patient out of the hospital when they are intent on "nesting"? Lead a patient out of the hospital— don't kick them out!

All of us tend to be cynical about patients who only want to "nest." The "nester" is perhaps the most litigation-prone bird of the species. The problem is determining whether something is genuinely wrong with the patient. Beware of the nester; they are not the blue bird of happiness, they will swoop down with an attorney and sue you if you give them even a slight excuse.

Nesters are probably best treated by a rapid but methodical series of tests, all most carefully documented. Unless you are practicing in a major medical center, or even if you are, there is someone somewhere who is the national expert on whatever anomaly they are complaining of. When all else fails, your final recommendation must be to transfer them to a facility that has the capacity to totally diagnose and treat their condition. In all fairness to your colleagues, you should always advise them of your suspicions about the patient.

Those patients who do not require hospitalization anywhere are harder to place. They may require nursing care but not hospitalization. They may become threatening or their families may become threatening. They will be more likely than not the type of patient who will be demanding and demeaning to the hospital staff. Such patients must be discharged or transferred to an appropriate nursing facility. In such cases, turn to your colleagues on the medical staff. Have them make a complete review of the necessity for continued hospitalization. You should have at least three colleagues concur; then contact the hospital attorney. Once you determine that hospitalization is not necessary, the patient becomes an administrative or legal problem. Let them handle the matter - in some cases even instituting legal action for a declaratory judgment. Remember, once there is no need for hospitalization the patient becomes a social or administrative problem. There are people in virtually every hospital who have the responsibility to handle those problems. "Nester" medical records must be carefully documented. For example, when the nurse checks on the patient and innocuously asks, "How are you doing today Mr. Jones?" The patient may say "Fine." The nurse should document exactly what the patient said. If the patient defecates in the bed when he or she is fully capable of using the facilities, consider ordering a psychiatric consult. A psychiatrist can accomplish a great deal and perhaps find where the real problem exists.

Under no circumstances should the medical records contain any entries about "patient unable to pay, continues to demand that he remain hospitalized." In the progress note section you may consider notes as follows:

```
All tests completed, patient fully advised of results. Ad-
vised further hospitalization was no longer necessary.
Refused to be discharged. Stated he would "sue" if I dis-
charged him. Drs. 1, 2 and 3, requested to review entire
record and examine patient to determine if continued
hospitalization is necessary. Dr. — requested to do a
psychiatric consultation.
```

Your colleagues may not like to become involved, but it is imperative that they do so. Similarly, a psychiatric consultation is necessary if you suspect the patient may have some underlying psychiatric problems. A psychiatric consultation may also establish that the patient may have *no* problem, which is important if legal action is to be taken. Fortunately, these cases do not occur that frequently; however, when they arise they must be handled with the greatest of caution.

One final word of caution: never make a positive diagnosis that "patient has no medical problems." As each of us know, many conditions may be asymptomatic. If that entry is made and something manifests itself after discharge, it could cause serious legal problems.

AVOIDING ABANDONMENT

Circumstances surrounding the discharge raise the potential for a charge of abandonment if the release of the patient from your care has not been handled properly. Unfortunately, few physicians have a grasp of the legal significance of the term "abandonment" and the precautions that they need to take to avoid it.

Although the term "abandonment" usually denotes deliberate, premature termination of the physician–patient relationship, it may have a much broader application. In connotations, it can be applied to a variety of situations in which physicians or other health care providers negligently fail to adequately or completely attend or observe the patient. This is termed "constructive" abandonment. There are four essential elements to abandonment:

- There must be an established physician–patient relationship. This can sometimes be created with minimal contact: giving an appointment over the telephone, telling the patient to wait for the doctor, or giving a referred patient an appointment for consultation knowing the important basis for the appointment.

- The patient must have a reasonable reliance that care will be provided.

- The patient must have a medical need such that lack of care will cause injury.

- There must be a lack of care that actually causes injury. Lack of care may take the form of total premature discontinuation of treatment or an insufficient, inadequate, or infrequent attendance by the physician.

How Does It Happen?

Let's consider how the act of abandonment may occur. Abandonment can be alleged if a patient was not observed often enough to recognize potentially harmful developments in time to treat them safely. Exactly what constitutes "often enough" depends on how quickly foreseeable complications are likely to develop. For example, if a complication develops and if untreated produces injury in as short a time as several minutes, then the minimum safe interval between observations is less than several minutes. The attending physician is expected either to appropriately attend the patient at safe intervals or to delegate this responsiblity to an appropriate health care provider, including a nurse or house officer who is *competent* to recognize and treat the problem. Proper delegation requires that the attending physician instruct the delegatee so that he or she is capable of managing the patient.

Abandonment may also occur if a physician refuses to see or give an established patient an appointment. In this situation, he or she may be liable for abandonment despite the fact that the patient has not paid a bill, failed to keep an appointment, has gone to another physician temporarily or unilaterally sought consultation from another physician, or has not followed orders. In all these instances, the physician is liable unless he or she has properly and adequately notified the patient as already discussed.

Abandonment may also be charged in cases of premature discharge or failure to appropriately designate a qualified substitute. In addition, a patient may claim abandonment if the physician does not give notice ahead of time that he or she does not make house calls or fails to provide care if hospitalization is needed.

Hospital Care

Discharge from the hospital before it is medically indicated may be considered abandonment if the decision to discharge is in any way based on the patient's inability to pay or on lack of sufficient insurance coverage. This may be a particularly hazardous area. Under diagnosis related groups (DRGs), the attending physician may be tempted, coerced, or intimidated to discharge the patient prematurely, or to transfer an unstable patient to a charity or county hospital. If injury results from discharge or transfer, liability for abandonment can conceivably be established.

In addition, the patient is entitled to the assurance that if a hospital maintains an emergency department, he or she will be treated or appropriately transferred in a true emergency, i.e., an immediate threat to health or life. If the patient with an emergency is refused for any reason, particularly an economic one, liability for abandonment is likely. Further, any physician on a hospital emergency call roster who refuses to provide emergency care may also be liable in abandonment for injuries caused by the resulting delay in treatment.

Substitute Physicians

What happens if illness, excessive patient load, personality conflict, or any other factor prevents the attending physician from being regularly available for patient care? In this case, the patient should be promptly and properly notified and a competent replacement secured. If the patient is hospitalized and the attending physician is unable to secure a competent replacement, this responsibility may rest with the hospital administrative staff, such as the department chief or the chief of the medical staff. Whether or not there are house staff or consultants available, there must always be an attending staff physician to take primary responsibility for the patient's care.

If you are ill and unable to attend to your patient, you can avoid liability for abandonment by providing a competent substitute, adequate notice of this substitution and a reasonable opportunity to choose a different practitioner. As long as the substitute is competent and the requirements concerning notice and opportunity are met, you will avoid liability for abandonment. If you will be temporarily absent, perhaps on vacation or attending a professional meeting, you must identify a substitute who is competent to handle foreseeable problems for office and hospitalized patients.

A substitute physician must be of equal competence to the regular physician. The substitute need not necessarily be in the same specialty, but must be skilled in the care required by the patient. The substitute must be notified, available and reasonably easy for the office or hospital staff to contact whenever necessary. Also, the substitute must be informed of pending patient problems, particularly if a patient is likely to require urgent attention. The substitute must, of course, be given any additional information useful for the patient's care and it is best to have a backup for the substitute.

When planning for a vacation, you are well advised to make the following arrangements:

* Advise the patient of known vacations prior to undertaking his or her care.

* Appropriately notify and arrange for patients requiring regular care during your absence.

Staff should be available in the office to help patients secure appropriate care. It is not enough merely to arrange for the medical bureau or answering service to handle medical care of patients during a vacation. This could bring about legal and medical repercussions. Patients seen on a regular basis require assistance only to the best of the staff's ability, but the staff must make every effort to be as helpful as possible.

Document, Document

Abandonment can prove to be legally devastating, particularly when something goes wrong in the care of a patient and malpractice litigation is threatened. Adequate documentation is therefore essential. It usually takes the form of progress notes to establish a good attendance record on the part of the physician and the health care team. Without such evidence, effective malpractice defense may be impossible.

Abandonment constitutes particularly effective grounds for liability. The absence of a physician when one is needed is generally viewed with very little tolerance by the courts. Abandonment is sometimes so outrageous that jurors need no medical expert to explain that it is negligence and are unlikely to believe anyone who tries to disagree.

DISCHARGING THE OBSTETRIC PATIENT

From genetic counseling to diabetic pregnancies and other circumstances that may suggest an uncertain outcome, more physicians are abandoning the obstetric sides of their practices. By shedding the high-risk portion of their practices, they hope to save in malpractice insurance premiums what they are sacrificing in income. The trend is growing. New figures from a survey recently compiled by the American College of Obstetricians and Gynecologists (*Professional Liability and Its Effect, Report of Survey of ACOG's Membership, November 1985*) revealed that 12.3 percent of obstetricians have now abandoned the OB side of their practices, compared to 9 percent in 1983. The survey also documents that the number of physicians who are performing less "high risk" OB is also on the rise. The percentage of doctors who are doing fewer of these high-risk procedures has gone up from 17.7 percent in 1983 to 23 percent. Although no figures are available, the same trend is apparent among family practitioners.

The changing profile of practices in some areas threatens the availability of OB services. In states considered high risk areas in which to practice, such as New York and Florida, where premiums have shot upwards to more than $80,000 per year, the trend has stirred fears that some sections of these states may be left with a scarcity of practicing obstetricians. With the number of liability claims continuing to rise nationally and the size of awards growing, more physicians are likely to consider abandoning the OB side of practice or at least discontinuing some aspects of care that will help lower liability costs.

If you decide to discharge patients from obstetric care, how can you pave the way for a smooth transition that does not leave you exposed to charges of abandoning the patient? If you choose to eliminate some aspects of practice, which pregnancies are the ones to avoid? What consultations with patients are generally advised from a medical legal point of view? What paper work is required between physicians to iron out the transition between you and the doctor who will resume obstetric care?

Targeting High Risk Areas

Those who want to reduce their high-risk profile should bow out of all known high-risk pregnancies. These situations would include fertility counseling and the use of fertility drugs, diabetic pregnancies and genetic counseling and all pregnancies with known prior genetic deficiencies such as transchromosomal spina bifida, Down's syndrome or Tay Sach's disease.

Physicians should avoid all deliveries in which herpes or communicable diseases such as lupus may be present or suspected because of the threat that these deliveries represent for an untoward result. Women who have a history of having excessively large babies— even though they may not have a diabetic history— raise special problems because of the dysplasia that may result from the use of forceps. We might add to this list all deliveries where there will be an obvious difficulty anticipated with natural childbirth. This is especially true of those in which pelvic blockages or malformations loom apparent.

You would also be wise to bow out of pregnancies in which there are indications of placentus interruptus, deficiencies in the uterus or uterine walls or those preceded by an excessive number of abortions known by or reported to the physician. Genetic counseling has become a lightning rod for malpractice suits for one primary reason: It's impossible for you to review all 900 genetically related problems that patients may later say they should have known about before they became pregnant or before the fetus became viable.

How to Make the Break

Having eliminated these aspects of your practice, you are ready to move on to other phases of disengaging yourself from OB while still protecting yourself from abandonment. Eliminating obstetrics, however, may not be the only reason for discharging a patient. A variety of other factors—such as nonpayment or a lack of compliance with your instructions—may also lead you to that decision. Whatever the case, you need to carefully follow a series of steps to avoid charges of abandonment. The 12 points already covered here will help to protect you.

ANTI-DUMPING LAW

A new federal law is having a sharp impact on whether you can admit or reject a patient and also has broad malpractice implications that relate to many of the discharge questions previously discussed. The newest enactment of the Congress makes mandatory the admission of critically ill patients in an effort to protect the indigent. Under the provisions of the new federal law, you are told how long you may keep these patients, how you may treat them and that you must accept them. Unless you can demonstrate that you do not have adequate facilities to treat these indigent patients, you could be held personally liable for your failure to admit them.

The warning shot was fired years ago by the federal government with the enactment in 1964 of the Medicare and Medicaid laws. Since then the ever growing and pervasive hand of the federal government reaches all aspects of the health care profession. It is a sad commentary that decisions to admit to a facility are no longer based on medical judgment but upon pronouncements of Congress that have been translated into law. Thus, it matters not whether your emergency room is full, whether you are critically understaffed or whether you have no beds available in your intensive care unit. If the patient requires admission, you are required to admit him. The legal fact of admission coupled with the duty-of-care laws relating to the nonremoval of artificial life-support systems have created a legal conundrum that is inextricably intertwined with the delivery of health care.

The day is rapidly approaching when a physician will have little to say about whom he sees and the procedures that he performs. We will have reformed ourselves as have the Soviets and adopted assembly line medicine. The scenario might unfold this way: The patient arrives at your hospital with an acute myocardial infarction and your ICU may already be full. You may have two other MIs ahead of this one. There may be a hospital across the street that has room but it is illegal to transfer that patient. Under the anti-dumping legislation recently passed, that patient must be admitted. Similarly, the same rule applies to the multiple trauma case that arrives at your overcrowded emergency room. The patient deserves to be transferred to a level 4 trauma center but they will not allow him to be transferred under the anti-dumping law. It not only gives the trauma center a perfect excuse for refusing the transfer, but far worse, it could condemn the patient to death— not because the physicians didn't try but because the facilities are overcrowded.

The Malpractice Implications of Anti-dumping

The only way you can protect yourself in these situations is to document not only the patient's condition but the status of the hospital. You need to chart the fact, for example, that there were no available beds in intensive care, no private rooms or nurses who could tend to the patient at that point, that there were two other MIs in the ER and that you did not have the proper facilities to treat the patient.

In the final analysis, the jury will not fully understand what DRG means or its implications any more than it will understand what the anti-dumping law means. But hopefully they will understand what an overcrowded facility is and what the law has mandated that you do under the circumstances.

10

SERVICE
OF
SUMMONS

You are in the office. It is 8 a.m. Your receptionist bursts in and exclaims, "There's a little green man out there."

"A little green man?"

"Yes, a man in green and he's got a badge, and he says he has something for you. He wants to give it to you personally, but doesn't have an appointment." Should you: (A) set an appointment for him, (B) run out the back door, or (C) see him on an emergency basis? Answer: (C) Do not attempt to evade the service of process. Have him escorted back to your office, accept the papers graciously, and let him leave. Then:

1. Do not discuss anything with anyone.
2. Cancel your entire schedule and arrange with someone to cover your practice for at least 24 and preferably 72 hours.
3. Immediately impound all records relating to the case. Number the pages carefully, yourself. Make copies for your insurance carrier, yourself and your personal malpractice defense attorney. Put the original records in a fire safe. Check everything yourself. Never delegate this task to anyone.
4. Notify your personal attorney and schedule an appointment with him immediately or as soon as possible.
5. Notify your malpractice carrier and send the carrier a copy of the complaint and the medical records either by certified mail (return receipt requested), by Federal Express or a similar method, and with a short

letter indicating the name of your personal attorney and all the telephone numbers where you can be reached.

6. Do not speak to the press. Simply say it would be inappropriate to comment on pending litigation instead of replying with a curt "no comment" or worse, something about the merits of the case.

7. Schedule time off. You must have sufficient time to catch your emotional breath. The office or the operating room are not the places in which to keep your mind off of a malpractice suit.

8 Cooperate with your attorney.

9. Make all requests to your malpractice carrier and attorney in writing.

10. Be prepared to commit time to this matter. This is your lawsuit and it won't go away.

11. Do not blow the suit out of proportion. It is not the end of the world.

12. Be candid with your attorney.

13. Learn how to fight, outwork and outthink the plaintiff. Learn courtroom manners, how to dress, to sit, to act, and to maintain the proper attitude.

14. Your full legal name does not begin with "Doctor." Even the appearance of arrogance or a manner that suggests you are talking down to the jury could be lethal.

Once you are sued, your discussions with others— especially your colleagues— could set the stage for bringing them into the suit as witnesses. If, for example, you bemoan to your colleagues that you have been sued, you may say something damaging about which they may later be asked during the deposition. For example, you may expect to be asked at a deposition, "Doctor, with whom have you discussed this lawsuit?" To truthfully answer that question you should indicate the names of everyone with whom you have discussed the lawsuit. However, the best answer you can provide at that point is "With no one, except my attorney." Physicians often undermine their cases with glib and unthinking remarks made to colleagues. They may inadvertently say to a colleague, "Well, I cut the vegas nerve but it really didn't do him any harm." Later, however, while that may not be an issue in the case, a plaintiff's attorney could take the deposition of the physician if you have named him (having discussed the lawsuit with him). Since your conversation with him is not privileged, the attorney may wring from that physician the fact that you also cut the vegas nerve, which may even demonstrate further negligence on your part, albeit harmless.

Anyone who asks you about the case should be informed that you have
been told by your personal attorney not to discuss the matter with anyone
because doing so could unwittingly involve them in the case.

GENERAL RULES

Cancel your schedule. Service of a lawsuit against you should be considered in the same light as you would any medical emergency. It is imperative to have someone cover your entire schedule for a minimum of 24
and preferably for 72 hours immediately after the summons has been served. There are several practical reasons for this: First, you must impound
the records and personally handle the work associated with making the
copies. This is necessary so that you can maintain the integrity of the
records and be able to state unequivocally under oath that you personally
numbered and copied the records. This procedure becomes important in
view of the fact that states are enacting criminal statutes for the tampering,
altering or removal of medical records.

You must also spend time with your family. You have suffered what
may be regarded as one of the most damaging emotional blows in your entire medical career. They must know that you have everything under control. Furthermore, if you do not arrange for someone to cover for you, the
fact that news concerning the lawsuit has appeared in the paper will
probably mean that you will be asked about it. Your colleagues, other
hospital personnel, and administrators may all express curiosity about your
involvement, and in speaking with them you may unwittingly say something that could haunt you. Generally, it is advisable for a physician to set
aside at least 72 hours away from the office, and certainly away from the
operating room, to regain his emotional breath and to avoid further errors
that could be committed in the wake of a service of summons. The emotional disturbance that you may be experiencing immediately following the
service of summons can be distracting enough that it leaves your practice
vulnerable to other errors. There are numerous cases in which competent
physicians preoccupied with lawsuits have committed even greater errors in
judgment while being sued over a relatively simple and minor matter. Distracted by the impending case, they have missed critical diagnoses or performed unnecessary surgery because they failed to retain the focus and
concentration necessary in daily practice.

From the moment you receive the summons, you should consider yourself an impaired physician— at least temporarily. Just as you would not

consider performing surgery while intoxicated, you must consider yourself similarly impaired by a lawsuit. The emotional trauma generated by the filing of a liability claim is no less devastating than an alcohol or drug-related problem. If it requires longer than 72 hours for you to recover from the trauma of having been sued, then it is imperative that you take all of the time that you feel you need.

Impounding the Records

Another reason for personally impounding the records is that you can testify under oath that as soon as you received the summons, you followed certain instructions of your attorney. Upon his instructions, you should carefully and sequentially number each page in the patient's chart and personally make copies of the entire record. Thus, you have preserved a chain of custody over the chart and you have demonstrated— when you are asked questions about the record— the gravity with which you consider the lawsuit. This task cannot be delegated to anyone. A loyal or well meaning nurse may be tempted either to add or remove something from the record. The fact that the record may be tampered with could be lethal to your case.

Meeting with the Attorney

The original records should then be sealed in an envelope and placed in a fire safe. Next, notify your personal attorney and schedule an appointment as soon as possible. This is a medical-legal emergency and it requires the immediate attention of your personal counsel who is a specialist in matters of health-care law. The malpractice insurance carrier will turn the matter over to a claims adjustor. At this stage, you do not need to be speaking with a claims adjustor, but instead need the experience and the singular dedication to your cause of a personal attorney. You will discover that he will always make himself available to you. It is crucial that you meet with the personal attorney wherever he may be, even if it means that you travel out of state, which in itself, can be helpful for the change in environment. It removes you from the hospital or group practice setting that will seem like a fishbowl in the aftermath of being sued. By meeting as soon as possible with your attorney, you can avoid questions about the case until you have thoroughly discussed it with a legal counsel. It keeps you away from the press and it allows you to place the suit in proper perspective by jointly determining its gravity, your culpability, if any, and offers you the perspective of someone who has been counsel in many other liability actions.

Notification of the Carrier

After the records have been impounded and the pages numbered and copies made, you should notify your malpractice carrier first by telephone. Make a notation of the date and time and the individual with whom you spoke— preferably a claims manager or risk management officer— and send a copy of the summons and the complaint to the carrier. This should be sent by certified mail, return receipt requested, Express Mail, Federal Express or similar method which verifies for you that the carrier has received the packet and provides you with the name of the person who received it. Time is critical. Since some summons require answers to be filed within 20 days, on the day you receive the summons a copy of it, the medical record and a short cover letter should be sent to the carrier. The transmittal letter should read:

```
Dear Mr._____
   In accordance with our phone conversation at 10:30 a.m.
today, I am enclosing a copy of the summons served upon me
at 8:05 a.m., a complaint consisting of 14 (or whatever
number) typewritten, legal size pages, bearing case no.
_____ and my office medical records, consisting of
_____ sequentially numbered pages.
   My personal attorney in this matter is
_____, address _____ telephone
_____. During the next week, I may be reached at the
following telephone numbers _____. Thank you for
your prompt attention to this matter...
```

It is not necessary to write a long letter regarding your opinion about the case or your analysis of the allegations. What is needed is for you to ensure that your malpractice carrier can never say it never received a copy of the complaint.

Do Not Speak to the Press

Even a fish gets caught when it opens its mouth. Similarly, you can trigger a series of problems by speaking with the media. A curt "no comment" may be interpreted as a sign of arrogance. On the other hand, an elaborate discussion of the merits of the case can be fatal. If you are contacted by the press, simply tell them that you have been advised by your attorney that it would be inappropriate for you to comment in any manner on litigation to which you are a party and which is pending.

If there is any doubt about it, type your reply on a piece of office stationery with your letterhead, make copies of it and distribute it to the media if they ask for your comment. This is not the time to be saying, "There is no case, he was a paraplegic when he came in and I did the best I could." The newspaper or radio station may blow your comments out of proportion and may convey the impression that you showed little concern for the patient. Depending on your state, the newspapers may be allowed to publish the amount of money for which you are being sued. This is known as the *ad damnum* clause in the complaint and enables newspapers to publish the information because it is a matter of public record.

Scheduling Time Off

After your preliminary work or meeting with your personal attorney is out of the way, it is important to make time for a medical meeting or convention that you may not have planned to attend to remove yourself from the environment in which you practice. You must also set aside time for your family. You may feel a sense of embarassment, fear or insecurity because of reports in the newspaper. Your family may feel some of the heat from this publicity in their social contacts.

You must explain to them that the case is under control and that you do not want to discuss it with them. They should also refrain from commenting on the litigation to their friends other than to say that their father or mother has told them it would not be discussed in the home and that it is in the hands of an attorney. The family needs reassurance and you are the only one who can supply it.

Time with Your Attorney

Who knows the medical facts better than you? Because of your familiarity with all aspects of care, you must be prepared to educate your attorney. He may be able to read the medical records and may have a sophisticated understanding of medical science compared to your patients, but he may be unable to understand the significance of the particular issues. That's why it is up to you to interpret the record for him and become an active member of the defense team. You have a duty and a right not just to cooperate but to let your attorney know of your willingness to do so and of your committment of time to the case. You should also volunteer to obtain background information on the plaintiff's expert witness or witnesses by consulting with your colleagues. Advise your attorney that you can also research the literature for material that could help in your defense.

You must also assure your attorney that you will provide him with an objective analysis of the expert's opinion and that you will work closely with counsel to secure expert witnesses in your defense. You can be instrumental in this regard, providing the entree by saying, for example, "John, as you know, I am being sued. My attorney will be calling you and I would very much appreciate your setting aside some time to meet with him."

Similarly, you can serve as the liaison with out-of-town expert witnesses. When you call, identify yourself and indicate that you have been sued. You may want to mention that you consider this physician to be one of the leading authorities on the subject and that you have read a number of articles that he has published. At that point, you should ask if he would be interested in speaking to your attorney about the possibility of his serving as an expert witness. The prospective expert witness will be less likely to turn you down as a colleague than he would an attorney who is calling him and who may be 3000 miles away.

Making All Requests to the Malpractice Carrier in Writing

To a physician, it may seem strange to write a formal letter to an attorney, simply to transmit a piece of information or make a routine request. For example, you may indicate that you intend to conduct a literature search on a topic or plan to contact various physicians to determine if they are interested in serving as expert witnesses. Attorneys are accustomed to having matters presented to them in writing, and by communicating with them in this way you have ensured that there is no misunderstanding about what you plan to do as part of the defense team. Beware of an attorney who discourages you from making requests or reports in writing. Their files are privileged and they should welcome a written confirmation of a conference scheduled for your office.

Committing Time to Your Defense

When you allocate time for your defense, you will need to schedule intensive preparation. For example, the preparation for the deposition may take at least 6–12 hours. As a matter of practice, you should arrange for a colleague to take calls when you need to spend time with your attorney so that you are not distracted by your obligations for delivery of health care to your patients while you are trying to prepare for a critical deposition. For example, your attorneys may want to conduct a series of drills with you about what to expect during direct and cross examination and they will need your uninterrupted attention at such times. They may want to instruct you on how to sit and talk and to familiarize you with certain idiosyncracies of the plaintiff's attorney or a host of issues that are likely to arise when a physician's deposition is being taken. It is a good idea to confirm in writing that you have set aside the day before the deposition so that your attorney knows that you have allocated this time.

Do Not Blow the Case Out of Proportion

Physicians frequently make the mistake of assuming that a liability claim with no merit represents a potential windfall for the plaintiff. You may become exceptionally upset about the possibility that a meritless case can ruin your reputation. Although you may lose sight of the fact, the quality of care that you rendered is the standard by which you will be judged. Contrary to popular belief, the fact that you have been sued and that this fact was heavily publicized in a local newspaper will pale during the next week, overshadowed by the next aircraft hijacking. One way to reassure yourself in this respect is that your personal attorney has handled numerous cases such as yours and will help guide you. He will be as tolerant of your mistakes as you are about your patient's problems; but he needs your time, your candor and your committment to being an essential part, perhaps the most valuable member, of the defense team.

How to Fight

You must outwork the plaintiff in every respect, anticipating what will arise and how to counter it. Involve yourself in the case. Ask to be taken to the courthouse. Instead of an afternoon of golf, go to the courthouse alone and watch a trial or a portion of it. Familiarize yourself with where you will be sitting and what happens at different stages. After several visits to a courtroom, you will feel more comfortable. The apprehension that you are feeling is somewhat akin to what a patient feels when he or she is wheeled into an operating room for the first time. But in the final analysis, you exercise more control over a lawsuit than you imagined, but to do so you must participate actively, ask questions, and seize the opportunities to contribute to your defense.

Doctor versus Doctor

Apart from the reasons already mentioned, there are other reasons for not speaking with your colleagues about the service of summons. It may seem to you at first blush that they will want to help you and will want to stand united against the plaintiff. But if two physicians are defendants, and one can win by making the other lose, the desire for self-preservation is likely to prevail. The friend you thought you could count on could become an adversary if he, too, is named in the case for whatever reason. The instinct for self-preservation looms even more important when a hospital and a physician are named as defendants. Administrators and staff who did not think about taking issue with a physician's quality of care will give the hospital attorney a different story when the only way to exonerate the hospital is by attacking the physician's orders. Additionally, if a physician's attorney believes that the only way he can defend his client is by attacking a co-defendant physician, he will do so in the hopes an assessment of damages will be shared rather than be borne solely by his client. It is up to your personal attorney to spot these potential problems with other defendants and to devise a strategy for defusing them.

11

EVALUATING YOUR MALPRACTICE DEFENSE ATTORNEYS

MALPRACTICE CHECKLIST

- Retain a personal attorney in addition to the one supplied by your insurance carrier.
- Talk to the carrier's attorney in medical terms. If his knowledge is deficient on basic questions, you will find out at an early stage.
- Beware of the attorney who believes it is unnecessary for you to appear at a deposition that relates to the course or effect of treatment.
- Your personal attorney may step in and direct the carrier's lawyer if he disagrees with the tactics used.
- A good preparation requires four to six hours out of court for every hour spent in court.
- You should rehearse until you know 95 percent of what to expect on entering the courtroom.
- You may need someone beyond your immediate area as your medical legal specialist.
- Participate in the decision to settle your case.
- Never discuss the case with anyone on the "other" side.
- Never contact the other party's lawyer.
- Never alter medical records or files after the fact.
- Don't discuss your case with your colleagues.

Shipwrecked and marooned on an island surrounded by sharks, a physician, a lawyer, and a priest pondered their fate. Each considered the odds of swimming to the next island, where they could summon help. The physician, watching the shark fins cutting the surface, concluded that the effort was too risky. The priest heartily agreed and suggested that they pray for someone to rescue them. The attorney disagreed. "I'll go, I'll go," he shouted. He jumped into the water and began stroking toward the next island. Like the Red Sea parting, the great sharks separated and escorted the attorney as he swam to the next shore. Wide-eyed, the priest cried, "Look at that! Our prayers were answered. That is divine intervention." The physician scoffed. "Hardly, that's professional courtesy."

Widely circulated jokes such as this one have created a long-standing myth that physicians harbor a deep-seated dislike of attorneys. Many physicians, stung by a malpractice claim or threatened with an action, may nurture a distrust of the legal system. On the contrary, it is in a physician's best interests to get along with his attorney as well as he does with his professional colleagues. A doctor should have the highest degree of faith and confidence in his personal attorney and the one supplied by the insurance carrier to guide him through the legal maze.

How well you get along with your attorneys depends on a number of factors. How well your personalities mesh is one of the most important. Apart from chemistry, the nuts and bolts of your agreement and how well each abides by it could determine the length of the professional relationship. Considering your high insurance premiums, you may hope the carrier will supply an attorney with the charisma of Clarence Darrow and the tenacity of Perry Mason. Think again. The reality could fall short of the expectation. Your insurance carrier's attorney might bear more resemblance to Caspar Milquetoast, capable of mustering no more legal firepower than a popgun. Many carriers provide legal counsel, and some of the best defense attorneys and trial attorneys come from the ranks of insurance carriers. But as malpractice pressures have mounted and carriers have been forced to cope with larger caseloads, their legal staffs are often torn between conflicting loyalties. That's why, long before you walk into the courtroom, you should assess the attorney's strengths and weaknesses, and feel comfortable about investing as much confidence in him as a patient could in the hands of a skilled surgeon.

A carrier's attorney must be skilled at juggling his loyalty to the insurance company and the ethical duty owed to you, his client. But those loyalties can catch him in a crossfire, and complicate and threaten your chances of winning the case. That's the first reason for retaining a personal attorney over and above the one furnished by the carrier. If necessary, he can intervene on your behalf and direct the carrier's attorney to stay more in line with your interests.

In evaluating how well an insurance carrier's attorney is likely to defend a claim, physicians need to examine:

- the extent of his medical knowledge and his ability to comprehend the clinical aspects of the case;
- the nature and quality of his preparation, and the extent to which he prepares the doctor for various pretrial conferences, depositions, and the trial;
- his receptivity to working with a personal attorney; and
- the methodology he follows in analyzing the case.

ETHICS

An attorney's ethics is an important consideration, because his ethics may determine whether he is looking out for the physician or the insurance company. The lawyer may walk a razor's edge, especially if the carrier pressures him to settle a case and you believe he should pursue your defense. In spelling out his role, he should indicate that he represents you, but is nevertheless employed by the carrier. He should acknowledge there are certain matters he cannot handle because of conflicts of interest.

For example, you may have purchased a malpractice insurance policy that covers you for damages up to $500,000. But if a plaintiff is asking for $1 million, you will not be covered for the excess amount. You need a personal attorney for your potential liability beyond the policy's limits.

There are nuances here that need to be kept in mind. In many states, the plaintiff does not need to ask for a specific amount, only to indicate that he seeks damages in excess of $5000. If your coverage is for $100,000, you may still be personally responsible for any damages awarded over $100,000.

MEDICAL KNOWLEDGE

In the lair of the lawyer, a physician may feel mystified by the maze of conferences, depositions, and other procedures required before trial.

However, a physician is on firm ground when it comes to testing an attorney's medical knowledge.

Talk to the carrier's attorney in medical terms. If his knowledge is deficient on basic questions, you will flush him out at an early stage. The malpractice defense attorney should have a broad base of medical information to aid him in understanding the problem raised by your case. Also, how far does his knowledge of medicine extend? Does he know, for instance, that you ought to attempt intubation on a pulmonary arrest patient before you try an invasive procedure? In other words, how well does he know standard procedures?

Watch for the types of questions he asks. Before he asks you to explain why, if the patient has bronchial asthma, you gave her a medication that is admittedly contraindicated, he should be perceptive enough to discover whether you were able to prove with certainty a diagnosis of bronchial asthma.

FIRST MEETING

The first meeting should be arranged immediately after you have contacted your carrier concerning the filing of a claim. This initial encounter is crucial and should take place at the lawyer's office, so you have an excellent opportunity to examine the attorney's credentials. The scope of his medical knowledge should be revealed at this time.

At the meeting, probe into the attorney's background and determine the percentage of his total practice time devoted to handling medical-legal issues. Then, inquire as to how he handles office procedures pertaining to your case. For example, how will he maintain a record of the pleadings, documents, and other writings in the case? Will he provide you with complete copies so you can maintain your own files? You should also receive an absolute guarantee of confidentiality between the two of you, and be advised of who else in his office will have access to your file. A malpractice claim is such a sensitive issue for physicians that strict confidentiality cannot be taken for granted and must be ensured.

PREPARATION

One way you can judge an attorney's preparation is by reviewing his attitude toward your attendance at depositions. For example, beware of the attorney who believes it is unnecessary for you to appear at a deposition that relates to what occurred, the course or effect of treatment. When an attorney doesn't want a physician around, or discourages him from attending a deposition, that should raise a red flag. It indicates that the carrier's attorney feels uncomfortable about his client's presence. If that's the case, the attorney should provide a reasonable explanation for his reluctance.

For example, it may be a tactical maneuver. Perhaps, in the physician's absence, the plaintiff will so exaggerate matters that the doctor's attorney will later be able to capitalize on the statements. But in most situations, especially when an expert witness gives a deposition, it's critical for a physician to attend.

ATTITUDE AND STRATEGY

The insurance company's attorney and your personally retained attorney both represent you in the malpractice case. It's imperative that they agree on strategy. But your personal attorney may in some cases step in and direct the carrier's lawyer if he disagrees with the tactics used.

If a carrier's attorney is competent and confident, he will look forward to working with a personal attorney. Rather than posing a threat, the personal attorney is a valuable asset, a partner in the doctor's defense. But if the carrier's attorney feels he owes a greater loyalty to the insurance company, he will not want a personal attorney meddling in the case.

SIGNS OF INCOMPETENCE

Although it is rare, you may discover the carrier's attorney is blatantly incompetent to defend you. If you believe that to be the case, instruct your personal attorney to contact the carrier and inform the legal department that it has not provided competent counsel and that they have breached their contract to defend you.

A telltale sign of incompetence is when the carrier's attorney is ill-prepared to ask questions of a physician during a predeposition conference. Some carrier attorneys go into these conferences without any knowledge of what the physician is going to testify to. In their ignorance, every question they ask serves only to enlighten the plaintiff's attorney.

A defense attorney who is obnoxious to witnesses or litigants should never be tolerated. Jurors have a collective sense of fairness and propriety. The "gunslinger" without class may be perceived as a fighter, but he will ultimately hurt you if he offends the jury.

Preparing a physician for conferences and trial is a painstaking art. It should cover every feature of the doctor's testimony. The hallmark of a trial lawyer is that he will take the time to review the minutiae that, piece by piece, build credibility. A good preparation requires 4–6 hours out of court for every hour spent in court. Clients should be told how to dress, how to sit and how to address the jury. A physician and his attorney should rehearse their presentations until they have reached the point where they know 95 percent of what to expect on entering the courtroom.

If it looks as if the case may be settled before trial, how well does the attorney explain the strategy of negotiation? Your criteria for settling are usually complex. If there is also the likelihood of a large award, it may be a time for you to be magnanimous and settle. But this is not the time to discover you have basic philosophical differences with the carrier's attorney. Long before it's time to settle, as early as the first conference, you should test your carrier's attorney to gauge how well you can work together.

Regardless of how well your carrier's attorney measures up, think about hiring a personal attorney to monitor your case, for extra measure. Your choice of personal malpractice defense attorney will have a bearing not only on the disposition of your case but ultimately on your risk management on a day-to-day basis. Your personal attorney can sometimes serve as an extra "partner" in your practice, advising you at certain junctures in patient care and medical-legal "turning points" where your skill in handling a situation and avoiding a claim may hinge on your attorney's advice.

MAKING THE SELECTION

Selecting a personal attorney, hammering out an agreement, and evaluating his representation of you are activities that should be undertaken with the same care that you use to develop a protocol for managing your patients.

You probably have a general practice attorney who helped you in buying a home, reviewing a lease for your medical office, or defending you if you were invovled in an auto accident. But few generalists have the background and skill to handle a physician's case when it requires a specialist. A physician should turn to a specialist for real estate transactions, divorce proceedings, tax matters, the drafting of a will, and most importantly, malpractice defense. A physician should not look to one attorney to handle all legal affairs, any more than he would look to one physician to treat all his ills.

If you need an attorney to handle business matters, look for one with broad-based knowledge in corporate, estate, and tax-related matters. For medical-legal concerns, you should retain a personal attorney in addition to the one provided by your insurance carrier. For a medical-legal specialist, you may have to look beyond your immediate area to find someone conversant in medicine— someone who understands the relationship between medicine and the law. You may well have to find one out of the state.

Although experience and reputation among other physicians are good indicators of how an attorney practices, you may want to check the *Martindale Hubbell Law Directory*, published by Martindale Hubbell, Inc., to find a rating of your attorney. The directory should be available at a local law library. It contains ratings of attorneys who have been confidentially evaluated by their peers and judges. At a minimum, your attorney should score a 'bv' rating.

If an attorney is rated well in *Martindale Hubbell*, he has earned considerable respect in the legal community. If you are satisfied with his reputation and credentials, ask yourself whether you feel comfortable discussing your legal problems with him. Look for familiarity with terminology and in-depth understanding of the area of law in which you need representation. Moreover, you must be able to confer candidly and confidentially with your attorney, rely on his judgment and advice, and trust him fully. If you have any doubt about your ability to do so, even if it is a feeling that you cannot explain, find and retain another attorney.

Among the questions that should be asked are these: Does the attorney have good rapport with doctors? Does he have an understanding attitude toward physicians? Do not enter the lair of the lawyer unprepared. Leave nothing unexplored, in much the same way you would explore every avenue to determine the etiology of a complex problem.

THE FIRST MEETING

What to Ask

Among the first questions to ask before the meeting is how you should prepare and what you should bring. The attorney's answer will give you an idea of how thoroughly he will conduct the meeting.

Most likely, the attorney you have chosen will view the meeting as a new business opportunity. He may have a vague understanding of your malpractice problem after your telephone call, but if you have prepared well for discussing it he will more quickly determine whether he can provide the service and what ought to be done.

As part of your preparation, you should present a written chronology of the events leading to your seeking his help. Include names, addresses, and telephone numbers of persons who may be a party to or a witness to the dispute. Also bring written material concerning dates, transactions, diagnoses, or treatment. These are all essential to the attorney's understanding of your problem.

You should also take time beforehand to write down all your questions regarding the attorney's background: his age, where he lives, how long he has lived in the community, his marital status, and other questions about his education, experience, former clients, the percentage of practice time spent in your problem area, and his estimate of the time and fees required to resolve the problem. Look at the credentials in his office.

The key to that first meeting is ironing out potential problems that could crop up later to undermine your relationship. For example, if another attorney in his office will be doing part of the work, when will you meet him? Who will supervise his work? Do not be misled into thinking that an experienced lawyer will be representing you, when an inexperienced assistant will be doing most of the work.

You should also ask how the attorney expects to approach your problem, his expectations of the probable outcome, and in what sequence legal services will be provided. An attorney should not, however, guarantee an outcome, any more than a physician should guarantee the result of treatment. Any attorney who guarantees a result should be avoided.

Although it is extremely hard to estimate, the attorney should approximate the amount of time required to handle your case. But remember, this is is only an estimate and should be tempered with your understanding that unforseeable events can revise his estimate.

Expect A Confirmation

After the first meeting, you should receive a letter from the attorney confirming your fee arrangement or have a signed retainer agreement. Too often, physicians casually hire a lawyer on the basis of an oral agreement, and if the relationship begins to deteriorate, no record exists to hold the attorney to their understanding.

By obtaining a written agreement that outlines why you hired the attorney, you will be protected later if a dispute arises over his obligations. Make sure that the attorney has already signed this agreement and has provided a signed copy for your files before he submits it to you for your signature. Do not sign it unless you completely understand it.

Be Clear on Fees

In every case, the physician and attorney should reach a firm understanding of the billing procedures and the rates for services. Without this understanding, an attorney and his physician-client will be headed down a rocky road. You can expect to pay different rates for different attorney services.

For example, some attorneys bill on an hourly basis, whereas others may require an annual retainer. If the representation relates to trial matters, it may be billed on a monthly basis. There are also contingent fees and flat fees. Remember that fees for some legal services are negotiable. They are unlike the usual and customary fees that are paid for hospitals or physician services or the fee-for-service arrangement that you have with patients.

If properly prepared, the lawyer's bill is a good yardstick for judging his activity. As the client, you have the right to insist that an attorney submit his billing statement to you in a way that is easy to understand, and the right to ensure that you are paying only for those services actually provided. Whatever the format, it should provide an itemized and detailed accounting of services rendered, the amount of time spent, and when it was provided.

The basis for this accounting is the fee arrangement: the written agreement that outlines the understanding that you have reached concerning how fees will be computed and the manner in which they are to be paid. Without such an agreement, the billing statements from your attorney may spark a dispute and could lead you to distrust your attorney in related business dealings. If you remain skeptical about the agreement after the attorney has submitted it to you for approval, review it with a friend whose judgment you respect or a business consultant. Do not sign it unless you are satisfied.

Excessive fees and unnecessary legal services can lead to an explosive situation between attorney and physician. If a doctor continually pays for such services while harboring resentment toward his lawyer, he may unjustifiably find other shortcomings in his attorney's performance. This resentment could lead to growing mistrust and an impasse.

You should not pay for unnecessary research or for research into matters that the attorney should already have known. If you need an explanation of a bill, your attorney should provide it.

Double billing is another trouble spot. For example, a partner or associate may also be assigned to a case. If that is true, the client should not be required to pay for the training of an associate to assist, but this requirement should be discussed with you before trial.

Beware of an attorney handling matters that he is not competent to handle and thereby doing research, and billing you, for services that could be done more efficiently by someone else. For example, it is extremely rare to find an attorney, competent in corporate and business matters, who would also be qualified to handle a medical-legal matter, in court or even on a preliminary basis. Each matter requires a different specialty of attorney.

YOUR RIGHTS

A frequent complaint about lawyers is that they fail to keep their clients advised about the progress of the case. You should insist that you receive monthly itemized billing statements, regular status reports, and copies of all correspondence, documents and pleadings prepared or received by your lawyer. You also have a right to confidentiality concerning information you disclose to your attorney, just as a patient does in his relationship with you. If you are concerned about how the attorney preserves that confidentiality, discuss how he keeps his records and who has access to the files. Always be suspect of an attorney who seems unwilling to provide a written explanation of what he has done or advised.

Depending on your malpractice insurance policy, your carrier may or may not have the option of settling a case without your permission. Whenever possible, you should participate in the decision to settle your case or in other decisions affecting the outcome of your case. Your insurance carrier's attorney may ill-advisedly want to settle a claim that you think should be defended. On the other hand, you may find it advantageous to settle when the carrier wants to pursue it, thus exposing you to liability beyond the limits of your policy. To protect your rights in the defense of a malpractice claim, you should retain your own attorney to follow the progress of a case and intercede when needed.

Cases that are defensible should never be settled for the convenience and economy of the insurance company. That is the reason why you need an attorney who is a medical-legal trial expert and can provide you with independent counsel.

EVALUATING PERFORMANCE

A client monitoring the performance of an attorney is somewhat analogous to a patient's following the progress of his own open-heart surgery. It may be difficult for a physician to assess how well the case is proceeding; for the most part, you invest blind faith in your personal lawyer. Nevertheless, yardsticks are available, including client contact. You should assess how well your attorney keeps you abreast of developments in the matter. Does he provide detailed letters on request, or is most of the contact hurried and over the phone?

As stated earlier, if you are involved in a malpractice case and are represented by your carrier's legal counsel, you must have a personal attorney to apprise you of your options and give you his independent advice. How prepared does your attorney appear when matters pertaining to your case arise? How does the work done compare with what he initially outlined to you?

Appearing unfamiliar with facts that you previously called to his attention or failing to perform required or requested duties constitute danger signals. Whenever you become dissatisfied with an attorney, do not waste time before raising the issue. Allowing your discontent to simmer and failing to notify him of alleged shortcomings will only imperil your chances for success. Most of these problems are unlikely to arise if you know your attorney well and like him as much as some of your professional colleagues. If you strive for that goal, you can openly and candidily discuss your differences and defuse them before they jeopardize your case.

An open-door policy is equally important for your attorney. He, too, should feel as free to probe your defenses and weaknesses as you would in exploring the symptoms of a patient's illness during a physical examination. Perhaps both can benefit from the advice contained in a proverb that instructs, "Deceive not thy physician, confessor, nor lawyer."

Defending a malpractice suit is a team effort and requires the skills of both the physician and his personal and malpractice lawyer to succeed. How can a physician help his defense lawyers? Following are nine ways to ensure that the lawsuit, trial, and subsequent results are as favorable to the physician as the facts and the circumstances allow:

1. *Never discuss the case with anyone on the "other" side.* Often a doctor served with legal papers feels the need to get in touch with the patient, or patient's family, and "straighten them out." This natural tendency is often coupled with indignation and anger, both of which preclude calm judgment in such a situation. Contacting the "opposition" can have disastrous effects on the outcome of the lawsuit. No matter how unjust you feel the suit is, how much you need immediate feedback to reassure yourself, or how angry and upset you become, *never* contact the other party directly.

2. *Never contact the other party's lawyer.* Under no circumstances should you call or write to the lawyer acting for the plaintiff. Never list your grievances against his client or all the reasons why the lawsuit is ridiculous and can't be won, or attempt to justify your actions regarding your treatment of that patient. Your call will only show the opposing attorney that you can be easily "rattled" and are ruled by emotion not calm, good judgment. He will use this to his advantage during the course of the lawsuit. Worse than calling is writing a letter to the plaintiff's attorney. Such a document might be offered as evidence and, again, can only work against you. So, fight your natural inclination to respond to the lawsuit and to try to vindicate your actions. Discuss the case only with your own attorney.

3. *Never skimp on "practice" time with your attorney.* Failure to properly prepare with counsel is almost always a costly mistake. Granted, both the physician and attorney are busy professionals, and the physician may feel that this particular action is just a frivolous bid for attention by a dissatified patient, but the fact remains that the physician's head is on the legal block. It is the physician's responsibility to make sure his lawyer understands all the medical aspects of the case. The physician should explain his records and demonstrate the treatment, if possible. He should familiarize his attorney with every medical term pertinent to that particular case.

4. *Listen to your defense attorney— he does know best.* Doctors are well trained in giving advice and instructions, but do not always receive advice well. The fact is that a trial is nothing like a patient treatment, and a court of law is nothing like a physician's examining room. Here, the physician is in alien territory and must bow to the expertise and judgment of his legal advisers. Therefore, a physician should take careful notes during all meetings with his attorney. He should list the tips his attorney gives him about his deportment in deposition and in court. He should carefully follow his lawyer's advice about how his answers should be phrased, and even what he should wear on his day in court.

5. *Never alter medical records or files after the fact.* Perhaps a physician's single most self-destructive act is to alter, adjust or add to the medical records in a case that is already in some stage of litigation. Perhaps the physician didn't have enough time to fill in the record with as much detail as he would have liked or forgot to add certain notes. Even if he feels that a small addendum to explain a certain treatment might improve his chances of winning the action, the unanimous

recommendation is not to touch medical records at all. It is far better to be seen as a physician with lax or sloppy record-keeping skills than to be seen as one who deliberately attempts to alter evidence in his own favor. In this case, an honest mistake or omission in the records is better than a series of erasures and additions, which put the physician in a self-serving light.

6. *Don't discuss your case with your colleagues.* Even though the temptation is great to discuss your malpractice case with your peers, it is necessary that you fight that temptation and keep silent. A lawsuit is a lonely and isolating event. However, involving your friends, even casually, can be damaging not only to your own case, but to your friendship. The rules in a lawsuit are different from the rules of medicine. You invariably will be asked, under oath, "With whom did you discuss the case?" If you reply, as you will have to, listing the names of your peers and colleagues, it is not unlikely that they will be served and will find themselves in the witness chair, testifying. Remember, the only person you can safely discuss the case with is your own attorney. So if you have the urge to call someone and talk, that's who to call.

7. *Resist the urge to get specialized information from your former professor.* What harm can there be in calling or writing to your old professor, an authority in the area in which you are being sued, and pouring out your situation or asking for his opinion? On the surface, there is none. This is a normal response to the pressure of a lawsuit, finding corroboration for one's actions. However, again, don't do it without the consent of your attorney. This seemingly innocent call can result in your concerned professor sending you a written opinion. And this document can be admitted into evidence and used against you, particularly if your trusted professor suggested that you did have other alternatives or other treatment channels available.

8. *Have the right attitude in court.* It is not just the predeposition or pretrial preparation that is important to the favorable outcome of a case, but also the attitude of the physician-attorney team in court. A case can be lost because of improper attitude. Arrogance, boredom, or a conceited demeanor will "turn off" a jury that might otherwise have been sympathetic. For the same reason, ostentatious clothing or jewelry should not be worn. The way in which the physician answers questions can also have a negative effect on the jury in a malpractice case. If the doctor appears overly nervous, anxious, and unsure of himself, he can

undo all of his attorney's preparations. Similarly, if the physician seems too cocky and volunteers unnecessary information, he may harm his own case.

9. *The physician must trust his personal attorney 100 percent.* From the attorney's point of view, every malpractice case presents one unique problem, exactly how much information to share with the physician/client. There are instances when the attorney, during the course of the pretrial research, interviews several expert witnesses and discovers that his client has not met the standards of practice. If the physician is told what these expert witnesses are saying about his skill and judgment, he might create such a sense of despair that he destroys the entire case. It is critical that the physician believes that the course of action he took at the time was the best under the circumstances. To undermine the physician's confidence is to undermine the defense. On the other hand, it is essential for the physician to refrain from pressing for too many details. The key word in this team, as in all others, is trust. If you have a personal attorney, then you should be able to trust him, because his sole allegiance is to you.

12

THE PLAINTIFF'S ATTORNEY
MALPRACTICE
CHECKLIST

- Innocent and seemingly innocuous requests for charts by the plaintiff's attorney are often the most dangerous.
- Before releasing any information, immediately review your legal obligations.
- If you suspect a claim, number pages of the record, impound it and immediately contact your personal defense attorney.
- A simple cover letter should accompany records you send to the plaintiff's attorney. No comment should be made.
- Beware of phone calls from a plaintiff's attorney who may call before making a request for medical records.
- Discovery tools are not available to an attorney before a lawsuit is filed.
- Unless your personal attorney is bird-dogging the carrier, the case could be settled without your permission.
- On receiving a summons, immediately notify your personal attorney and insurance carrier.
- Beware of plaintiff's attorney's attempts to pin you down on "authoritative texts."
- When in doubt, ask to see the record when testifying.
- Don't speculate, don't guess.
- Leave the impression of being courteous yet in control because if you lose your cool, you have played into the hands of the plaintiff's attorney.

- Your attorney should set a time limit of no more than four hours at a stretch during deposition.
- It's important that you set the pace of questioning during the deposition.
- Three areas are under attack: your credibility as a physician, the validity of your evidence, and the logic of your conclusions.
- As the trial date approaches, coordinate your schedule with one or more of your colleagues.

THE PLAINTIFF'S ATTORNEY: BEWARE!

A letter from the plaintiff's attorney will be the first of many close encounters with the plaintiff's attorney. How you handle that first encounter and subsequent meetings with the plaintiff's attorney will play a major role in deciding the outcome of a malpractice case. Dealing with the plaintiff's attorney is as much art and science as any other aspect of building your defense. The hallmark of your defense against him, as with all aspects of litigation, is preparation. You must be prepared for whatever comes along, including the gamesmanship with which he is likely to try to trip you into damaging revelations to undermine your case. From that first phone call or letter on up through your testimony, the war is likely to whipsaw. Trial attorneys on both sides are apt to play a dazzling array of games. They will play bait-the-judge, bait-the-other-lawyer, the innocence game and the outrage game. Chances are they are applying a few of the lessons from the last workshop at the convention of the Association of Trial Lawyers, which focused on "Psychological Aspects of Trial Technique."

The innocent and seemingly innocuous requests for charts are often the most dangerous. Consider an action that started when a plaintiff's attorney wrote a physician a polite letter requesting a chart summary on a patient whom he said he was representing in an auto accident, "so that I may more readily assess the value of her claim." The doctor dictated a three-page letter that thoroughly outlined the state of his patient's past and present health. Within a month, the physician was served with a summons in a lawsuit, not as a witness in the imaginary accident case, but as a defendant in a malpractice claim.

FIRST SALVO

The letter from the plaintiff's attorney requesting a copy of the patient's medical records is often the first salvo. It may come as a surprise to you, depending on whether you suspected that a malpractice claim was ticking away in the patient's file.

Before releasing any information, immediately review your legal obligations. Assuming the letter is accompanied by a signed consent form from the patient, most state laws require that you must provide the attorney with the records. But under some circumstances, you aren't obligated to release the information. This is particularly true of medical records that contain information from other physicians. Release of such information is the prerogative of the other physician.

Release of information relating to drug or alcohol treatment programs funded even indirectly by a federal agency may be a potential source of trouble for you. An attorney who requests this information must have specific written consent from the patient that complies with the appropriate provisions of the United States Code. Similarly, a request for psychiatric information requires a specific consent from the patient, because the information is privileged in most states.

CONTACT YOUR ATTORNEY

Whenever you receive a written request for the medical record, you need to analyze the request. Are you the target of a malpractice case, or are you receiving the request because you're the treating physician in a personal injury case? If you suspect that a malpractice claim might be brewing, carefully number the pages of the record, impound the record, and immediately contact your personal malpractice defense attorney, as well as your insurance carrier's attorney.

You will have several days within which to comply with the plaintiff's attorney's request for information. During that time, a methodical review of the record and the quality of care rendered should suggest whether the patient is likely to sue. For example, was the patient hospitalized for an unusually long stay after surgery? Was the patient unhappy with the results? Before releasing the medical record to the plaintiff's attorney, you may want to send a copy of the complete chart to your personal attorney for his or her evaluation.

A simple cover letter should accompany the medical records that you release to the plaintiff's attorney. No comment is required or should be made.

TRICKY PHONE CALLS

Beware of telephone calls from a plaintiff's attorney. An attorney may call you even before a request for medical records is made. He may sound informal and congenial, but you're not obligated to answer any questions over the phone, nor should you. Simply inform him that you will not release any information without the patient's written consent, and that you will be happy to do so once you have received such authorization.

Situations develop, particularly involving young and inexperienced physicians, in which an attorney will call after the doctor has ill-advisedly spoken about matters that may have affected the patient's care. These remarks or premature judgments based on half-baked assumptions can return to haunt you when they are improvidently passed on to family members. Comments like "a machine malfunctioned" could lead to a phone call from an attorney who is eager to question you about the remark that a family member has attributed to you during a difficult moment, perhaps at a time when you strained for an explanation.

Some attorneys follow up with a phone call, like Columbo, the television detective played by Peter Falk, who was noted for his casual and seemingly harmless line of questioning that nevertheless struck the jugular: "Just a couple of things, Doctor." Or "Oh, by the way, Doctor."

Telephone calls from an attorney representing someone in a personal injury case are another matter. These calls are different from the call you may receive from an attorney who is representing someone in a malpractice case. Once you receive a request from a personal injury lawyer, along with the patient's consent, you can usually sense that you aren't the target. Here, the attorney might call and inquire straightforwardly about certain aspects of care, and he is justified in doing so. It's not a fishing expedition, and you should not regard it as such. For example, he might ask, "Doctor, how long will it be before the pin comes out?" In these situations, there is nothing wrong with your giving the attorney a definite answer.

One mistake that will trigger trouble in a personal injury case is to stop talking to an attorney. The attorney will simply have you served with a subpoena for your deposition. When your care isn't at issue, and your patient has been injured, be helpful to the attorney. It can save you considerable time in the future.

RELATED PRELIMINARY GAMES

Aside from these straightforward phone calls, there are other versions, opening gambits by the plaintiff's attorney that should put you on notice that he is on a fishing expedition. For example, he may call you in a congenial manner, informing you that he has a client who thinks he or she has a malpractice case against you. He may sound extremely accommodating, trying to reassure you that he does not intend to sue you but that he has an ethical obligation to check out his client's allegations: "A meeting would be useful to resolve this little problem." If the doctor accepts, he will discover that the attorney has brought along a stenographer who will take notes because "facts are facts and are not likely to change."

The danger is that it is unlikely that you have had a chance to review your records or the hospital records carefully, and you are not under oath as at a formal deposition. But anything you say could be used against you. The meeting with the attorney is tempting, especially if a physician is gullible enough to take the attorney's carrot. The line of reasoning usually followed by the physician is that he will be able to talk the attorney out of the case without ever having to inform his insurance company and have an incident report filed and a possible premium increase levied against him. Think again. The physician is instead locked into an off-the-cuff account before he has been able to discuss his case with his attorney or insurer. It's surprising how many physicians walk into this trap which could easily be avoided by one phone call to the defense attorney. The plaintiff's attorney has obtained information that he wanted without even having to subpoena the medical records.

The Let's-Settle-It-Now Ploy

The plaintiff's attorney may try another route, ostensibly on the grounds that "I hate to put you through the ordeal and aggravation of a trial." He will suggest, "Let's just settle it now without the publicity." This is an unethical move on the attorney's part, but when a physician is naive enough to succumb, the attorney will take advantage of it.

The attorney who is not permitted to obtain the physician's records has few options. He may tell the client that he does not have information to file a complaint and decline to accept the case. That is unlikely, if it looks like there is substance to the plaintiff's remarks. Once he does find merit, he may file the complaint and seek your medical records through discovery.

There are three major tools of discovery: interrogatories, depositions and subpoena.

Interrogatories are written questions directed at a defendant that must be answered by him, under oath, within a specified time. In a typical personal injury action, these questions usually concern insurance limits, proof as to who was at fault and proof of negligence. In a medical malpractice case, these questions may be expanded to include references to others who also may be liable. The lawyer may ask, for example, "Who else was in the operating room?" In answering interrogatories, you should understand that attorneys do not yet know what caused the injury and must rely on documentation from other physicians or medical records to substantiate or deny a client's claim.

Depositions are statements given under oath by any witness or potential witness or defendant, usually in an informal setting such as the physician's or attorney's office but in the presence of a court reporter.

Subpoenas are court orders directing specific action. Under various state court rules, a judge may order any party or witness to produce any documentary evidence relevant to a suit.

These three discovery techniques play an important role in preparing a personal injury case. You should be aware, however, that with few exceptions the discovery tools are not available to an attorney until a lawsuit is filed. The attorney cannot take statements under oath, either by deposition or interrogatories, and cannot subpoena documents without filing a lawsuit. As a result, a decision on whether to proceed with a formal complaint is usually made on the basis of information the attorney gets from talking with potential witnesses and reviewing medical records.

Attorneys sometimes find that if they can document their position with medical records before filing suit, they can settle with a potential defendant or his insurance company. Of course, this involves obtaining records informally, by simply requesting them. By responding callously to the request for records, physicians frequently precipitate a suit. An attorney may find that it is cheaper to file the lawsuit and engage in formal discovery rather than pay exorbitant fees for photocopying of records or the preparation of a medical report. This attitude only hardens feelings between attorneys and physicians and clogs already crowded courts.

Attorneys do not object to paying reasonable costs for reproducing medical records. Some physicians, however, have used this as a license to charge outrageous fees for photocopying several pages.

If an attorney asks for a written report and a copy of the medical records, the physician should charge for the report based on the time spent in preparing it, as well as office and secretarial time. A reasonable fee for a report may run from $50 to $250, depending on its complexity and length. A charge of $100 for each response to a request from an attorney, even if only for a photocopy of a three-page medical record, only inflames ill feelings between attorneys and doctors.

After you send a copy of a patient's medical record to an attorney and suspect that a claim is brewing, prepare yourself for either of two developments: (1) the attorney may call you, informing you that his firm has determined that you are guilty of medical negligence and that he would like to talk with your insurance carrier; or (2) you may receive a letter, stating something to this effect: "You have committed a breach in the standard of care due and owing to John Doe, who is our client. We would like to discuss the matter before the necessity of our filing suit."

When the plaintiff's attorney puts you on notice that the filing of a claim is imminent, you should begin to mobilize your defense by contacting your malpractice carrier and your personal attorney. Your personal attorney will ensure that the malpractice carrier will not allow time to elapse without taking action. The failure of an insurance carrier's attorney to respond to such a letter can provoke a malpractice suit. No action in these circumstances may be misinterpreted as a tacit admission of guilt. Remember, most often, insurance carriers represent their interests, not yours.

Conflict of Interest

An appropriate response from your defense counsel at this point is critical to your defense strategy. For example, after having the strength of your case independently reviewed by your personal attorney and some of your colleagues, you may decide that you weren't negligent, and therefore refuse to negotiate a settlement. However, without your personal attorney taking charge, your defense may hinge on whether the malpractice carrier judges that it's worth taking a stand. The carrier may fold up its tent too soon, concluding that since the plaintiff's attorney plans to sue, they will offer him $5000 to settle. Unless your personal attorney is bird-dogging the carrier, the case could be settled without your permission.

Inflated *Ad Damnum*

Some states have abolished the amount of an *ad damnum*, but in others it is still permitted. Attorneys will file for outrageous sums, i.e., $10 million. They know that while your defense is asking the court to strike it, the newspapers will have seized it and publicized it. When the doctor sees his name in the papers alongside that amount of damages, he frequently runs scared and pressures his attorney to settle the case. In most cases, even if a verdict goes over policy limits, the plaintiffs are satisfied with the results most of the time.

Interrogatories

You may receive interrogatories, a series of written questions to which you must also reply in writing.

The plaintiff's attorney may try to snare you with innocuous questions that call for simple answers. For example, "How many cholecystectomies similar to this one have you performed?" The danger in providing a precise answer is that the cholecystectomy in question might have had a complication, perhaps an anatomic anomaly or some extremely large stones. In this case, your answer should be "None. This case was unique." On the other hand, if it was not, you should only approximate how many you have performed, always making sure to qualify your answers.

If you assert that a specific procedure was similar to 240 cholecystectomies, you have given the plaintiff's attorney a shot at you. At trial, he can claim that you said it was similar to 240 other procedures, and any distinction you try to make on the witness stand will then undermine your credibility.

But innocuous questions are only part of a wider scheme that the plaintiff's attorney has in mind concerning interrogatories. For example, a laundry list of questions is a potential danger because you may be tempted to complete it hurriedly without showing it to your attorney. It may be that a bombshell is lurking among the seemingly innocuous questions, such as, "Do you contend that anyone other than yourself was responsible for the complications in this case?" It's a double-edged question because if you say yes, you are then obligated to name one or more colleagues later. On the other hand, if you deny that anyone else accepts responsibility, then you have admitted that you alone are responsible for the complications. The best answer: "I do not contend that anyone, including myself, is responsible for the complications."

Loaded questions may be hidden amid interrogatories that are concerned with how much insurance coverage you have and what carrier underwrites your policy. These may seem like routine questions, but if you assume that anything is routine in the course of malpractice litigation, you could be setting yourself up for a large verdict against you.

Textbook Testimony

Beware of the plaintiff's attorney's attempts to pin you down on "authoritative texts." This is an area fraught with danger. An attorney may be skilled at trapping a physician, setting him up by getting him to admit that a text is authoritative and then demonstrating by the same text that the treatment didn't conform to the standard of care described in the text.

When you're asked questions about so-called authoritative texts, field them this way: "Medicine is a dynamic science. Our knowledge this week is more advanced than it was a week ago." With that as an introductory remark, you may acknowledge texts that are relied on, common references and guides, but steer clear from classifying them as the authority.

Depositions

This phase is so crucial that attorneys should spend a minimum of 4–6 hours preparing a physician for every hour of a deposition. The deposition can be a minefield for the physician ill-prepared for the traps that await him. As in the interrogatory stage, seemingly innocuous questions are potential time bombs.

Consider this question by the plaintiff's attorney: "Doctor, have you read the entire record in this case?" If he says no, the attorney may raise questions about why he hasn't reviewed all the details. If he replies that indeed he has, he exposes himself to further questions that might leave him suspect in the eyes of the judge or jury, since he may not be as conversant with the record as he purports to be.

A better method of deflecting this line of questioning is to acknowledge that you don't know whether you've reviewed the entire medical record. In qualifying that reply, you may point out that portions of the record stem from treatment by another physician or may be on tape and not yet transcribed, in which case you may not have had the opportunity to review certain aspects of patient care.

By remembering that you can only reply to questions that are directed at what you have read, you can avoid another potential trap during the deposition. Always ask to see the record when testifying. Don't speculate. Don't guess.

Psychological Warfare

Plaintiff's attorneys are skilled at intimidating games, as well. For example, the conference room of their office where your deposition is taken may be festooned with copies of newspaper articles headlining gigantic malpractice verdicts. It's all part of a well calculated strategy to set your teeth on edge in the hope that a nervous doctor is a defeated one.

One of the most unsettling attacks may be the openly hostile attorney who seeks to rile a physician with comments like, "Doctor, you may be a little tin god in your office but you're just another witness around here." At all times you must leave the impression of being courteous yet in control because if you lose your cool you have played into the attorney's hands. The plaintiff's attorney may have researched a number of articles by superb physicians and may have talked to them prior to the deposition. The impression that the attorney wants to convey is that these experts are ready to testify for his side and that if you don't settle now, you are sure to be humiliated by a barrage of distinguished testimony at trial. The fact is, however, the academics have not agreed to appear and even if they did, the defense attorney could depose them in advance and pin them down to exactly what they plan to say.

Convoluted Questions

The plaintiff's attorney may try to erode your credibility in still other ways. Convoluted questions are sometimes designed to befuddle you, but don't be deterred from breaking up his game plan by setting your own ground rules for a reply. A blunt but tactful reply will serve notice on the plaintiff's attorney that you will not be rattled by questions too involved for you to tackle without addressing them as separate queries. It's sufficient to say: "Sir, you have asked me not one but four questions. To which question do you want me to respond first?" Or "Please rephrase your compound question, and I will try to answer it."

If you maintain a presence of mind throughout the deposition, it's not likely that you will commit errors. If you have prepared well, virtually nothing during the deposition or trial should surprise you. In fact, you should know 95 percent of what to expect by the time you enter the courtroom. If you don't, your attorney hasn't properly prepared you and you may well be surprised. It is the unknown 5 percent that will spike your hypertension. But whoever said everything in law or medicine is predictable?

If the convoluted questions do not trip you up, the plaintiff's attorney may resort to an assortment of other tactics during a deposition, ranging from playing Mr. Nice Guy to keeping the deposition going indefinitely. He may be profuse in his praise for the physician, crediting him with being the "finest surgeon in the community." But the physician may not realize that he is using the same line on other doctors during their deposition, hoping to convince at least one of them to accuse one of the others, thereby improving his case against virtually everybody. Other attorneys seek to discredit the physician's attorney, hoping to shake the doctor's confidence in his own defense. But perhaps the most obnoxious tactic is the information search that drags on for 10–12 hours as the plaintiff's attorney seeks to wear down the doctor and catch him with his guard down. It's up to your attorney to set a time limit of no more than four hours at a stretch during deposition.

Set Your Own Pace

Often it may not be the tone or the line of questioning but the pace. One of the most common traps to avoid in responding to an attorney's questions is thinking that you have to keep up with the pace being set. It's important that you set the pace for the deposition and the pace of questioning.

Don't let an attorney take off like "Marvelous" Marvin Hagler against Thomas "Hitman" Hearnes. If the plaintiff's attorney launches into a rapid-fire line of questioning that sets your teeth on edge because of the pressure to match his speed, slow your response; reflect on each question to accommodate your style rather than that of the plaintiff's attorney.

Although the style of questioning is important, so is the substance, and you need to be aware of the "Doctor, can you and I agree?" type of questions. What is it you are agreeing to? Is the plaintiff's attorney leading you down the primrose path? Such questions should be immediately suspect, because the attorney is setting the stage for a follow-up. And the next question could be the "left hook" that leaves you suddenly staggering to maintain the advantage you had carefully built.

Similarly, beware of the "over-the-shoulder" question, often asked at the end of the deposition or trial: "One final question, Doctor; it was iatrogenic, wasn't it, Doctor?" A physician blew apart his defense by answering "yes" to that question. He simply wasn't thinking, and the sudden lapse may have cost him the case.

THE TRIAL

The deposition should have prepared you for 95 percent of what to expect at trial, but that does not mean that the plaintiff's attorney will not shift gears to throw you off guard. You will need to fight to keep your composure on the witness stand. The opposing attorney may try to attack your professional competence and integrity with a barrage of sarcasm, pointless questioning and insinuations. Before you appear in court, you should have prepared at least four hours for every hour you expect to be on the stand. Since the patient's chart will be a key exhibit, your notes must be thorough. Any errors or inconsistencies will surely result in a charge by the attorney that the entire record is unreliable.

Three areas are generally under attack: (1) your credibility as a physician, (2) the validity of your evidence, and (3) the logic of your conclusions. The line of attack varies considerably. It may be openly hostile or an almost friendly, seemingly objective line of questioning. The tactics at the trial stage are not limited to the courtroom, either. As the date approaches, for example, the plaintiff's attorney may try to postpone the date, and this could create havoc with your appointment schedule. Make sure that as the trial date approaches you have coordinated your schedule with one or more of your colleagues so that you are covered for such contingencies. Many plaintiff's attorneys surmise, and correctly, that if they can postpone the trial enough times they will encourage the physician to settle so that he can resume his normal schedule.

The Excess Judgment Threat

At the outset of the trial, you might expect a scenario comparable to this: The plaintiff's attorney requests a meeting in the judge's chambers with the defense attorney, ostensibly to inform him that the plaintiff will accept the doctor's policy limits in settlement of the case. But then he switches gears, asking the judge to call in the doctor. When the doctor is on hand, he tells him that if an excess judgment is rendered by the jury, the amount that exceeds his policy limits will have to be borne by the physician. The implication is there that the judge can oversee settlement of the case at that point. It is a scary tactic and has rattled more than a few physicians who have not stood their ground or had a personal attorney.

Personal Attack

Since so much of the examination of witnesses will focus on attempts to undermine their credibility, the personal attack, probing a physician's background and training, is often the linchpin of the examination. The attack is usually concentrated on your credentials, especially if you are an expert witness. The objective is to convey the impression to the jury that you are testy, defensive and arrogant. Once again, composure is the key. Refrain from playing the attorney's game, and take to high ground as you stick to a strict review of the facts and a cool and objective assessment of how they relate to points in your case.

Amending the Complaint at the Last Minute

For the physician who is a novice to litigation, the tactic of amending the complaint can throw him off stride and may even panic him into a premature settlement. This is usually done after the attorney has filed a suit for less than $100,000. Since the physician has more than ample insurance to cover damages that may amount to $25,000, the insurance carrier may have assigned its least experienced attorney to the matter. That is when the plaintiff's attorney suddenly amends the complaint, asking for another $2 million in damages, an amount that far exceeds the coverage limits of the policy. The physician, rattled about the amended complaint, may be concerned that the attorney has discovered something that even he is unaware of and in view of the unknown, may pressure his attorney to settle.

Seeking Punitive Damages

Seeking punitive damages is a strategy designed to drive a wedge between the physician, his carrier and his attorney. Punitive damages are generally sought because the physician showed "complete indifference or conscious disregard for the welfare of his patient." Filing for punitive damages creates tension between the parties because judges have ruled that insurance carriers would be acting in bad faith if they did not protect the plaintiff from these damages when the plaintiff has agreed to settle within the basic limits. Few insurance policies are written to cover a physician for punitive damages. The plaintiff's attorney is seeking to make an example of the physician by asking for punitive damages. Compensatory damages cover the damages accrued from negligence, but punitive damages are designed to punish the physician for what is considered outrageous behavior. Rather than pay the punitive damages, an insurance carrier may become skittish enough to settle a case and abandon the defense.

The latest trend on the part of plaintiff's attorneys is to routinely file for punitive damages. Previously, punitive damages were generally sought for some outrageous act of negligence, i.e., the physician who failed to respond in an emergency, the psychiatrist who had a sexual relationship with a patient. But plaintiff's attorneys now use punitive damages as a threat during interrogatories and depositions, badgering the physician into believing that unless he settles, he will personally be responsible for the award unless he lets the carrier settle the case for his policy limits. Despite the increasing tendency to file suits for punitive damages, physicians might keep in mind that such awards are still rare. Juries are not so eager to punish physicians, especially those who have thoughtfully prepared their cases, presented excellent documentation and expert testimony that they practiced according to the appropriate standard of care. Another point to bear in mind is that even if punitive damages are awarded, these judgments are frequently reduced or overturned on appeal.

Punitive damages are also difficult to collect even if the award is upheld. Assets that are held jointly are especially difficult to reach, so it often remains to be seen how vigorously the plaintiff's attorney wants to pursue assets that could be vulnerable to this type of an award. It may be that a jury will never consider the question of punitive damages if the judge considers it without merit. Because of these factors, physicians should not let themselves be herded toward a settlement because of the specter of punitive damages. Like so many other fears raised prior to trial, this one may have little substance.

Courtroom Antics and Skullduggery

You may think that the deposition will have prepared you for whatever sneak attacks the plaintiff's attorney is ready to use. But the presence of a jury and his ability to grandstand may help the plaintiff's attorney become more inventive during trial. For example, you may find yourself beseiged with a rapidfire series of questions, all designed to fluster you and leave you puzzled about how to respond. Your reply is simple and the strategy is thereby easily foiled if you address the attorney and say: "Sir, you have asked me a number of questions. Which one would you like me to answer first."

Long, vague and misleading questions may be sprung to create an atmosphere of uncertainty about your knowledge in a specific area. Chances are, if the attorney is trying that tact, there is little use in asking for the question to be rephrased. If he does, you will get an equally involved variation that will be just as hard to tackle. The most disarming technique you can use is to rephrase the question. You may reply by saying: "As I interpret your question, you are asking me to address whether . . . . "

Although asking the same question more than once is forbidden when a witness is being directly examined, the prohibition is largely removed when a lawyer is crossexamining. When it is, the stage is set for the attorney to hammer away with the same set of questions but slightly rephrased. When you are under this barrage, it may seem that no matter how well you address the question, it never seems to hit the mark. The method in the attorney's madness is simple: He is trying to make it appear as if you are not answering the question, and if he achieves his end, to exasperate or confuse you. Break the attorney's stride by confronting him with what you would construe a satisfactory answer and add that you thought you had answered the question adequately several times. By noting that "If you'll explain why you're not satisfied with my response, I'll try to do better," you will take the edge off of his attack.

13

PRE-TRIAL PROCEDURES

The most critical stage in any lawsuit is the taking of your deposition. There have been numerous cases in which ill-prepared physicians "lost" their cases by violating basic instructions of their attorneys or failing to spend enough time with their attorneys before confronting the plaintiff's counsel. The deposition is a pretrial testimony but it's much more than that. Since most malpractice cases never proceed to trial, the deposition could be your chance to present the kind of evidence that will be presented in the courtroom— x-rays, records, charts, etc., which will be brought to the deposition as part of the discovery process. Prior to the deposition, you should:

1. Spend a minimum of 6–12 hours with your personal attorney, reviewing all aspects of procedures and related aspects of care about which you may be questioned. Conduct drills during which the attorney will ask you the kinds of questions the opposing attorney might ask.
2. Review all the medical records and scrutinize them for any areas that could be probed by the plaintiff's attorney. Be particularly mindful of consistency in the record and a logical sequence in documenting care.
3 Review all the available medical literature on the subject, particularly articles that reflect the latest standards of care. You may want to conduct a computer search of this literature by using data bases at the National Library of Medicine.
4. Be totally familiar with how lawyers ask questions.
5. Strictly follow the instructions of your attorneys. If they direct you not to answer a question, do not answer it. A physician should never decide

whether he wants to answer a question when his attorney may have doubts about the wisdom of his doing so.

6. Listen carefully to the question and answer only the one that is being asked.
7. Beware of questions that begin "Doctor, would you agree..." Such queries are designed to lead you into entrapment.
8. Remember that there are no "authoritative" texts.

Your attorney should also make you aware of a number of other factors that can influence the outcome of the deposition. Distracted by what the case means to you on a personal and professional level, you may be unaware of matters such as dress, demeanor and attitude. In addition to reviewing the factual matters at hand, your attorney should also discuss the impact of how you dress (it must be conservatively) and your demeanor (never arrogant, always concerned and respectful).

Beware of friendly banter before the deposition with the plaintiff's attorney. The attorney may appear cordial and eager to engage you in conversation, but remember at all times that there is also a method to this madness and he may be on a fishing expedition for something that can be used against you. That is not to say that you should ignore him, but he should not find out anything more about you than the fact that you are cordial.

Some defense attorneys may overlook that the deposition should never be held in the physician's office. Preferably, it should be in a court reporter's office. Wherever it is held, and despite the fact that you are not in a courtroom, what you say in a deposition can and will be used against you at trial. Above all, you must learn how to be a witness.

You may have been an expert witness in a personal injury case and think that your experience will fortify you for what to expect in your malpractice case. Think again. In a malpractice case, you are on trial and what you say, the demeanor with which you say it and the attitude you have may cast the die that changes the outcome. Never exhibit anger because to do so only spurs you to make reckless statements that may be read into evidence at the trial. The physician's deposition is the single most critical element of all pretrial procedures. It eclipses the interrogatories and all of the negotiations before the trial. Cases can be won or lost by what you say. A physician who is properly prepared by his personal attorney and the insurance carrier's counsel may be dropped from a case if he is a confident and formidable witness. Keep in mind that the plaintiff's attorney is not only seeking information on how to proceed with his strategy, he is also determining how you will perform before the jury, and how believable and sincere you will appear. What compassion and concern do you show for the plaintiff? How do you adjust to changes in the line of questioning? Are you easily irritated? What are your weaknesses?

"I think what happened to Mr. Jones is very tragic. However, it is one of the well recognized complications of the procedure," is a simple statement that demonstrates a sincere concern for the plaintiff but does not create the impression that you were negligent.

ANSWERING THE QUESTION

In most cases, your attorney will direct you to answer questions that you hesitate to answer. However, before you answer, it is critical that you listen closely to what has been asked. Determine whether more than one question is being asked and then divide your answer so that you address each point. For example, you may be asked, "Did you perform a physical examination and what were the results of that exam?" Your response should be, "Sir, you have asked me not one but two questions. I did a complete physical exam and if I may refer to the record, I will review all of the aspects of that examination. The second question you asked me is about what I found on that examination..." This type of prepared response is not likely to be given unless you review beforehand with your attorney how such double-pronged questions need to be handled. As a result of your finesse in such situations, the plaintiff's attorney will soon discover that you are not a witness who is easily intimidated. He will probably have noted that you are confident in your position, that you can recognize and dissect his compound question, that you are not an argumentative or arrogant witness and that you will be a formidable opponent at trial, perhaps the most formidable opponent on the defense team.

AUTHORITATIVE TEXTS

There are no authoritative texts. If you agree with the attorney that something is authoritative, you will have helped him set the stage for a dangerous line of questioning. This is a basic trap that plaintiff's attorneys are fond of springing. And if your attorney fails to warn you about it, it's a good sign that his advice in other areas may also be lacking. There are some well-recognized texts that are often referred to, but medicine is a dynamic science and what represents a treatment of choice may be subject to question in the light of fresh data that suggests a new and more effective alternative. When you consider the amount of literature that is published during the 6–9 months after a medical book is completed, edited and indexed, it is easy to understand why no text can be considered authoritative.

Even the newest medical textbook was completed about a year prior to its becoming available to the profession. By that time, numerous studies have appeared in the peer review literature that could render some of the material in the text obsolete or at least open to question. During your deposition you may acknowledge that a text is recognized as a resource often consulted by physicians in your specialty, but not the only one, and new data must always be considered.

As modalities of treatment change and as the profession learns more, it is critical that you not be bound to call anything authoritative even if you wrote the material yourself. The best illustration of that principle can be found in a case involving a professor of law who was testifying as an expert witness in a case. The opposing lawyer approached him on the witness stand and asked, "Professor, you are the author of this text?" The professor paused and said, "Indeed I am." The lawyer then circled and came back to the professor, following up with, "You have testified directly the opposite of what you have written in this section of the book." The professor carefully read the portion he had been handed by the attorney. Without hesitating, he tore the page out of the book, handed the text back to the lawyer and said, "Now, counsel, you have Anderson's revised edition..."

Moreover, when replying to questions at a deposition, confine your answers only to the question that has been asked. Many physicians mistakenly believe that the more knowledge they display, the more credible they become. But this is not the time for verbal incontinence, or your opinion about the plaintiff's attorney or the attorney's parentage. If you need to refer to the medical record, do so as often as you feel it is needed. It is much better to refer often to the record during deposition than at trial, because during the trial it will appear to the jury that you are not familiar with the facts of the case. Frequently the plaintiff's attorney will have you read portions of the record aloud, an obvious attempt to decipher elements that may not be clear to him. Anticipating that tactic, you should carefully review your records and become familiar with handwriting that may not be clear at first glance.

ATTITUDE AND DRESS

One of the dangers of attending a deposition casually dressed is that a smart plaintiff's attorney will assume from your attire that you will have a casual attitude toward the charges. Casual dress detracts from your image as an authoritative figure. But other aspects of your presentation may also detract from your credibility. Displays of temper, for example, may be particularly damaging and can be read back to the jury at trial. In any case, do not argue or correct the plaintiff's attorney. If he is wrong, that's his problem.

Another danger zone is the introductory remark that a plaintiff's attorney may use, such as, "Doctor, isn't it fair to say that... am I to understand that..." Your reply needs to be phrased carefully so that you do not create the impression that you have unilaterally agreed with the attorney and will be trapped into a response later in the questioning. You may want to reply to such questions with a remark that states, "As a general statement 'yes', but not as applied to this case, because Mrs. Jones did not have a rigid abdomen when she presented." In other words, beware of questions that are general in nature and do not apply to the specific facts of the case.

MAINTAINING CONTROL, EXPRESSING CONCERN

One of the ways that you can keep control is to confine your remarks strictly to what has been included in the complaint. Resist the temptation to stray from that agenda and address questions posed by the plaintiff's attorney that concern material not having to do with the case. It is your right to refuse to speak about material that is not relevant to the matter at hand.

Always show the greatest amount of respect and courtesy for the opposing counsel. Your composure may be the barometer by which your negligence is judged. It may be difficult to do so, but it is far better to have the response "Yes, sir" or "No, sir" typed into the record than "Hell, no." It's all part of avoiding any remark or attitude that can be construed as arrogance. If the attorney tries to goad you about the unfortunate nature of a patient's condition, it is preferable that you gauge your response, replying in words to this effect: "Of course, I feel terrible about Mrs. Jones. I'm careful about every patient I treat. Unfortunately, Mrs. Jones suffered a well known complication of which both she and her husband were well aware. It was a complication I could not have prevented and even today I feel sorry that she will have to live the rest of her life with a partially paralyzed right leg." In doing that you are expressing concern about the plaintiff and all of your patients while denying liability of any kind because of a complication that could not have been avoided.

Physicians have undermined their cases with blatant outbursts of temper at the deposition, losing sight of the fact that everything is admissible at trial. The private nature of the proceeding may, for the moment, obscure the fact that the material gathered during it is admissible during trial. As a result, physicians may blurt, "The patient is a neurotic and has no business suing me. She deserves nothing and you had better well understand that." If remarks with that tone are read back at trial, the jury will not think twice about nailing the physician.

ANSWER THE QUESTION— PERIOD!

It is typical for many malpractice carrier attorneys to schedule an appointment with you 30 minutes or an hour before the deposition to brief you on how you should answer the plaintiff's attorney's questions. The physician who relies on his malpractice carrier's attorney is taking a chance. In many cases they are conscientious counsel, among the best defense attorneys in the country. But the bottom line is that they represent the insurance company and often do not invest the amount of time needed to prepare you adequately for a deposition.

There is an adage in law, "plead not what you need not or you may have to defend that which you cannot." A deposition is not the place for you to educate the plaintiff's attorney concerning all of the recent literature. It is neither the place nor the time for you to expound on how wrong they are in bringing this suit against you. If physicians would realize that they should limit their remarks to the question being asked, they would not pave the way for other questions that enable the plaintiff's attorney to continue his fishing expedition. Consider this exchange:

```
Q. Did you consider an alternative modality of treat-
   ment?
A. I did.
Q. You didn't write it down.
A. Of course not. I don't write everything down. But I
   did consider other modalities as part of the treat-
   ment plan.
Q. You did. Isn't this procedure totally inappropriate?
A. I wouldn't say that in view of what the current
   literature suggests about treatment.
```

Such an exchange will give the attorney the opportunity to further explore the defense, branching off on collateral discussions that will not help your case. Similarly, never answer a question that you do not fully understand. Ask the attorney to rephrase the question, and if you still cannot answer it, candidly acknowledge that you are unable to. In response to questions that you could answer with more information, you may want to add that you cannot do so without a great deal of study, which you would normally do if such a problem were presented to you. You might add that you would also consult with your colleagues and recent journal updates concerning that medical problem. There is no shame in replying that you do not know and that it is not within your field of medicine.

WHERE THE DEPOSITION SHOULD BE HELD

Depositions should never be held in the physician's office. The reason is that this location would offer the plaintiff's attorney a prime opportunity to see your medical library— the abundance of it or lack thereof— and question you about certain books, how thoroughly you have read them and what journals you regularly receive and read. The deposition should be held in a court reporter's office. The ambiance of your office can be used against you. Consider, for example, if the plaques in you office indicate that you were board certified in 1982 and that you completed your residency in 1976. It may provoke a question from the plaintiff's attorney about how many times you took the board examinations before you were certified. Without seeing such information, the attorney may not think about asking such questions. Your office is a virtual minefield that can blow up in your face. For example, in one case involving a neurosurgeon who testified that a lumbar myelogram was negative, the physician's library came back to haunt him. The attorney noticed a 1974 issue of the *Journal of Neurological Surgery* in the physician's office, a copy of which the attorney had studied prior to the deposition. The attorney asked the physician to retrieve the copy from the shelf and refer to a discussion on a specific page. He asked the physician for the title of the article—"The predictive value of lumbar myelography." "Doctor," he asked. "Isn't it the conclusion of that article that there is a 20 percent false negative rate for herniated disk?" The physician was forced to agree, thus undermining his finding of a negative lumbar myelogram. If the myelogram is negative for a herniated disk, contended the attorney, it does not mean that the condition is not there. The attorney had extensively researched the subject and had hoped the volume would be in the physician's office when he arrived for the deposition. When he found it in the library, the trap was ready to be sprung.

TAKE ALL THE TIME YOU NEED TO RESPOND

Part of the strategy of the plaintiff's attorney may be to hurry your responses so that you do not adequately answer a question. Refer to the chart whenever you need to. By referring repeatedly to the chart you may even upset his strategy, making him impatient. Whenever you refer to the record, however, indicate what progress note you are reading from, citing page numbers. Read the entire note into the record so that it will be placed in proper context. At various points, the plaintiff's attorney may ask you if that is all there is to your answer. Never indicate that you have nothing to add, but that at the moment it is all you can remember.

EXPECTING THE UNEXPECTED

If you are properly prepared, you should know 95 percent of what will transpire during the deposition. It's the other 5 percent that worries defense attorneys, and there is no predicting what that may be. Generally, however, the 5 percent falls into three categories. There may be new literature relating to your case that casts doubt on what you have said. Surprises also occur when a physician has been less than candid with his attorney. Tampered records and undisclosed information may be revealed during the deposition and the effect is devastating on a physician's case. Another area where surprises may occur concerns changes in the patient's condition. If you are questioned about such changes or new information about which you are unaware, it is best not to comment before you have had a chance to evaluate its impact on your testimony.

14

THE
EXPERT
WITNESS

MALPRACTICE CHECKLIST

- The best initial contact with an expert witness is made by the physician being sued.
- Experts should be selected based on their qualifications and how convincing they will be to a jury in your locale.
- Obtain a copy of the expert's curriculum vitae and articles pertaining to your defense.
- Make sure the physician has not always testified for the defense or plaintiff.
- Don't let the expert get trapped into calling any texts "authoritative."
- Set aside uninterrupted time with the expert and attorney to review all aspects of the case, what will be asked of him and what role the expert's opinion and report will play in the case.
- The expert should not give an opinion until he has examined pertinent records and all other information.
- The expert should prepare a written report before meeting with your attorney.
- At least four hours of preparation are required of any witness for every hour spent in deposition or court.

- Your attorney should be wary of areas where the expert's testimony may contradict his previously written material.
- If you are an expert, insist that scheduling of court appearances be as tight and accurate as possible.
- The expert should know how to address the jury in simple English.
- The jury is likely to make its decision based on its impression of the medical witness rather than the actual testimony.
- Encourage an attorney to go through the expert's qualifications in detail before the jury rather than have the expert presented to the jury as a stipulated expert.
- The expert should address his answers to the jury, not the attorney or judge.
- Aim at aspects of opposing expert's professional background that raise doubts about the reliability of his testimony.
- You may discredit an opposing expert by demonstrating he does not practice in a similar environment.
- Review an opposing expert's previous depositions and courtroom testimony for contradictory information.

The appearance of the expert witness conjures up a moment of high drama in a malpractice case, a time when attorneys and witnesses match wits in an examination that could prove pivotal to the outcome of the case. But this drama, like virtually every other aspect of the deposition or trial, has been carefully rehearsed, with each side painstakingly preparing its witnesses. Preparation is the most important factor in whether your expert witness scores enough points with the jury to help swing the case in your favor. But numerous related factors need to be considered long before the expert witness is retained.

In today's medical-legal climate, more physicians are testing their mettle as expert witnesses and you, too, may choose to do so or be called upon by a colleague because of your special competence in a particular discipline or your familiarity with the details of the case. Except in circumstances that are self-evident, as with the doctrine of *res ipsa loquitor* (the fact speaks for itself), expert witnesses are required to define proper standards of care. Expert witnesses testify as to how a physician's actions conformed to or deviated from these standards. The expert's opinion should be based on an informed, professional belief that the accused physician's actions were or were not negligent and should include all aspects of diagnosis and management.

EXPECTATIONS

Writing in the *Annals of Internal Medicine* (1984; 100:139-143), Dr. Calvin Kunin suggests that the expert witness is not expected to testify about points of law or his personal judgment of the merits of the case. He should not be concerned with the amount of damages asked by the plaintiff nor should he be an advocate for either side. He adds, "Because all expert witnesses are human, by nature they will eventually arrive at an opinion based in part on factors outside the case. They will also develop sympathies for one party. These considerations should determine whether one agrees to work for the defendant or plaintiff, but should not bias the physician's expert opinion given during the depositions or trials. The test of a good attorney is that he not only accepts but strives for such behavior from the experts he selects. The merits of a case often depend less on the patient's outcome than on how well the diagnosis and management proceeded at the time. The expert witness should place himself in the position of the accused physician under the circumstances and in relation to the state of medical knowledge at that time. A physician is not expected to be a master of all medical knowledge but to be responsible for providing care within his qualifications and commensurate with community standards."

SELECTING THE EXPERT WITNESS

The best initial contact with an expert witness is made by the physician who is being sued. Assuming that you are the defendant, you should contact an expert witness based on your review of current medical literature, your awareness of the expertise exhibited by speakers you have heard at medical conventions or who are prominent in their respective fields. Experts should be selected with two things in minds: (1) their qualifications, and (2) how convincing they will be to the jury in your locale.

Two schools of thought prevail on where the expert witness should come from. Some attorneys suggest that the expert witness should be the physician who espouses your view and is the best known in his field. For example, if you have used a procedure that was first established by a physician, some attorneys suggest that you retain that doctor to evaluate the efficacy of the technique in the situation where you used it. The second school of thought on expert witnesses suggests that in a small urban area or a rural area, it is anathema to bring in the out-of-town gun or the expert who is the nationally known authority. The thinking that best applies to the small urban area or town is that the expert witness should be someone from the same community who is well known and respected. If you cannot find someone within your immediate area, then choose the chairman of the appropriate medical department at the state medical school. In any case, you do not want to range too far afield because of the hostile reaction that may be triggered in a jury by the outsider who is perceived as a "hired gun."

Even if a physician from the outside has earned a glowing reputation, he may not appear as impressive or convincing to the jury as someone locally who has also published on the subject. Thus, "extralegal" factors need to be weighed and should not be considered lightly. Remember, credentials make more of a difference in a metropolitan area but may be a drawback in others.

PRECLUDING THE OTHER SIDE FROM SELECTING THE EXPERT

An anecdote from a Florida physician illustrates a common practice used by attorneys to win the upper hand in signing up an expert witness. Several times an attorney had called him to retain him as an expert witness in a malpractice case. After banking another check for $300, the physician began to realize how he was being played for a fool. Each time the same attorney had called him to retain him as an expert witness in a malpractice case, he had unhesitatingly accepted. Invariably, the check for $300 followed and he had deposited it. But he never heard from the attorney concerning his role in the case. Nobody ever asked him to review a record. That was when it occurred to him what was happening. By being retained this way, he was precluded from joining the other side as an expert witness. The attorney who repeatedly retained him never intended to call him for further assistance in the case. He was being used as a pawn and if he continued to accept the checks he would never realize his potential as an expert witness.

For their pivotal role, expert witnesses are well paid— up to $300 an hour and $2500 a day, depending on geography and the scope of a physician's knowledge. It is not, however, a role that everyone can readily play. It may mean braving the conspiracy of silence that often cloaks a medical community and tends to smother testimony against one's peers. In testifying against a colleague, no matter how righteous it may seem at the time, a physician may be regarded as a hired gun. He may lose his privileged status in the brotherhood.

STRINGS OF BOOBY TRAPS

There are other pitfalls lurking for the expert witness. As soon as a physician answers the phone and begins talking to an attorney who needs the doctor's services, a physician should beware of a string of booby traps that extend all they way to the witness chair. In failing to adopt precautions, a physician may leave himself exposed to embarrassing and damaging conflicts in schedule between patients and mandated court appearances, poorly negotiated fees that are virtually uncollectible, and ill-prepared testimony in court that an opposing attorney could easily torpedo.

As likable as an attorney may sound when he or she calls you to enlist your help as an expert witness, maintain your guard. You need to question whether you want to become a witness in this case. The problem is, when the attorney calls, you will not know much about it. The best approach is not to commit yourself. In refusing to commit yourself, you reserve your right to determine whether a report should be rendered and whether it should be made to the attorney orally or in writing. This report, for which you should be paid at your usual and customary fee, will discuss your thoughts on the case after you have reviewed the records.

RELATED AREAS TO CONSIDER IN
THE SELECTION OF EXPERTS

Obtain a copy of the physician's curriculum vitae and a copy of all of his articles that might pertain to your defense. In reviewing the material, make sure that the physician has not always testified for either the defense or the plaintiff in malpractice cases. Regardless of whether you are being retained as an expert or you have paved the way for one to testify in your defense, your attorney should draft a letter that spells out the terms of the agreement and that stipulates the *attorney* is engaging the physician. Once the attorney has become obligated for payment, ensure that the terms are specified. This closes another loophole.

A letter should indicate that you expect to be paid within 30 days of rendering the bill. In addition, the attorney should indicate whether he or she wants you to itemize your charges. If not, the attorney may wriggle off the hook, since he or she may not understand how you have spent your time. How much time was spent clinically? How much time reviewing the records? Because of these potential snags, it is often a sound idea for you to hire your own attorney to iron out the details of this letter, at least for the first time you are called as an expert witness. It can become a form for other agreements the next time an attorney wants to contract for your services.

PREPARATION: REVIEW OF RECORDS

Preparing for deposition or trial is as important as the appearance of an expert witness. The witness needs to review all of the medical records, particularly when the physician will be addressing questions on the advisability of treatment or diagnosis. Bear in mind that a physician can be challenged for lack of professional conduct or poor practice if he renders an opinion without knowing enough about the history and background and the procedures that followed. Before testifying, the expert witness should familiarize himself also with x-rays, statements of other witnesses (if available), and any other pertinent material. Rechecking basic textbooks or journal articles will also give that additional and sometimes needed perspective as long as no text is considered "authoritative." Expert witnesses sometimes become trapped when they call a text "authoritative," only to discover that a new standard of care has been introduced in a later publication that may render the "authoritative" text obsolete.

After the expert has reviewed the records, he, the defendant and his attorneys should set aside some uninterrupted time to review all aspects of the case, what your attorney will ask him, what the plaintiff's counsel will ask and what role the expert's opinion and report will play in the case. A report is not always required, but in some states it is important. For example, in states with medical malpractice screening panels, an attorney must produce a report to justify proceeding with a case. In still others— Pennsylvania, for example— depositions of experts are not allowed if there is a written report. In that case an expert witness might not want to write a "complete report," because it will pin him down to an opinion and he will not have a chance to expand on it until the case goes to trial.

Preparing a report is a critical step, because it will serve as the basis for subsequent testimony in depositions or the trial. It will be examined by the opposing side. Because many months may pass before a case proceeds to trial or settlement, a fairly complete record should be prepared to avoid having to review all of the material again. The report should contain the following information: (1) listings of the materials reviewed; (2) synopsis of the case (preferably problem-oriented); (3) assessment of each of the problems; (4) a request for more information, if needed; (5) a response to questions; (6) a statement of willingness to testify; (7) pertinent references and copies of key papers; and (8) a curriculum vitae. All materials should be kept until completion of the case.

ASSESSING AND DISCUSSING THE CASE

The attorney defines the scope of the work to be done by the expert witness, and a contract is drafted based upon that definition. The physician who agrees to review a case should state clearly that he is not obligated to testify until he has assessed the case's merits, and he should not give an opinion until he has examined the pertinent records and all other information.

Customarily, an attorney will prefer to discuss the case either on the telephone or personally because a written opinion may be discovered by the other side. The attorney also reserves the right not to use the physician as expert witness if the expert's opinion could harm the defendant's chances. Despite that, it's a good idea, at least from the expert witnesses point of view, that a written report be prepared before he meets with the attorney. The reason is that it sets boundaries on the testimony he may want to provide.

If the report looks favorable, the attorney will have a series of questions ready for the expert witness when they meet. These discussions with attorneys will help to identify the key issues of the case and help in examining their merit. These meetings should resemble an in-depth case discussion with peers and an experienced attorney. The defendant will not try to influence the physician's views other than by providing new information or asking specific questions for clarification. It's also a good idea to hold these meetings with attorneys away from the physician's office. A lunch or dinner meeting frees you from job-related responsibilities and pressures and contributes to an open-ended and uninterrupted discussion.

As a rule, at least four hours of preparation are required of any witness for every one hour to be spent in deposition or court. In critical cases as much as six hours of preparation is advisable. As part of that preparation, your attorney and you should emphasize that you have called him for a limited purpose and that you will not be asking him to address questions outside of his area of expertise. Your attorney should also be wary of areas where the expert's testimony may contradict something that he has previously written. In these situations, the expert should point out that medicine is a dynamic science and that modalities of treatment and diagnosis may change. As a result, the expert's opinion may take a different direction from what appeared under his name in the literature.

Assuming that you have agreed to testify, beware of pitfalls if the attorney has not adequately prepared you. Insist that you and the attorney meet beforehand, rehearsing what to expect on the witness stand. In reviewing the upcoming testimony, three areas are crucial:

1. You must be sure that your attorney knows everything about the case, from a clinical and factual standpoint.
2. You must have the attorney prepare you for a difficult cross examination. As a physician, you can play a key role in helping the attorney do that because you know what another physician should say to defend a doctor's actions.
3. The attorney should also instruct you in responding to inane questions and others that make no medical sense.

SCHEDULE CONFLICTS ARE LETHAL

The best prepared witness will be useless to an attorney if schedules have not been coordinated well in advance: Conflicts in schedule that leave a physician torn between patient commitments and the court docket can be lethal to a case. The problem in most large cities is (1) you cannot predict when the trial will be held and (2) you cannot predict when you will be called as a witness. You may not realize it, but you have the power to control, within a reasonable period, when the testimony will be given. To accommodate schedules, an attorney can call a witness sooner or later than initially arranged.

A physician should insist that scheduling of a court appearance be as tight and accurate as possible. This is often a problem. In Los Angeles County, for example, a case may not be called for trial as much as a month or two after the date on which it has been set. When it is finally called, the plaintiff may take two weeks to present his or her case when you only expected one. That could deep-six your vacation schedule, not to mention what it could do to your appointment calendar. There are two ways to avoid scheduling conflicts:

1. Make it clear in your contract that the attorney must be specific and

give you at least two weeks notice of when he or she expects you to be
called as a witness. It must also be clear to the attorney that you intend
to block out your calendar for that day and expect to be compensated
for it even if you do not testify.

2. You must insist that, when appropriate, the attorney will call you
   sooner or later than anticipated to meet scheduling commitments.

Meanwhile, you should notify other professionals of your expected appearance in court so that they, too, will not be inconvenienced. Physicians
on staff at hospitals, for example, need to advise their colleagues of their
commitment.

THE DEPOSITION

Before the deposition the expert witness will confer with the attorney to
review the material that will be covered. Rather than being a coaching session, this meeting is designed to refresh the expert's memory about the
ground that will be covered. One question always asked of the expert by the
opposing attorney is his prior experience in malpractice cases. The question
is aimed at finding out whether the witness is a "professional" expert whose
opinion can be bought. A physician should keep a record of previous cases
to indicate how he has testified— for a defendant or plaintiff.

In preparing for the deposition, the expert witness should encourage the
attorney to discuss his answers with him until he thoroughly understands
what's being said and that the expert knows how to answer questions in
simple English. Phrases such as "periorbital echymosis" become "black
eye," "psychosis" becomes "insanity," and "fracture of the fifth phalanx"
becomes "broken little finger."

Once he has prepared a carefully written report and formed an opinion,
an expert witness should be confident about facing a deposition. The witness should be as responsive as possible to the questions (provided they are
not objected to by the attorney for whom he has been retained). An experienced lawyer will not let the witness expand on a point detrimental to
his argument. Physicians are most frustrated when asked to respond yes or
no to complex medical questions. When they are asked, the expert witness
should try to qualify such simplistic replies but not overdo it.

Physicians often forget that a deposition is testimony taken outside court
under oath and bearing the same pain of perjury as if given in court. The
deposition phase permits the gathering of information by parties involved
in the lawsuit. It also provides material to impeach the reliability or

credibility of the witness when he is testifying before the jury. Responses in a deposition must be as carefully weighed and thoughtfully phrased as if they were given in court, and they must coincide with the answers later given in court or the discrepancy will be seized upon by the opposing attorney and pointed up to the jury.

Consider the situation in which a physician, during deposition, was asked if the main concern of a surgeon following a hysterectomy was infection. He replied, "A main concern after any operation is infection." At the trial, the physician was asked the same question, but this time he replied, "No." Seizing his deposition the lawyer read to the jury his earlier answer, providing his own emphasis: "A *main* concern after *any* operation is infection." The physician then asked if he could accent the statement the way it had been delivered. When permission was granted, he read: "A main concern after any operation is infection." The physician may not have succeeded but he wanted to at least impress on the jury that he had not changed his mind.

The medical expert is relatively free to rely on any information that the members of his specialty consider significant and relevant to the issue in question. It might include the review of records and depositions, conversations with the plaintiff or the plaintiff's family, consultations with other specialists or published articles. The normal "hearsay rule," which in essence does not allow the introduction of spoken statements made outside the courtroom, is broadened considerably to allow the expert witness to form his opinion. A fact does not have to be in evidence for him to testify to it. For example, the attorney might ask, "Do you have an opinion within a reasonable degree of medical probability that Mr. Jones had asthma?"

During deposition, a few additional precautions are in order. The expert witness, or any physician for that matter, should be careful not to say what is best unsaid. Don't go out of your way to provide information for the opposing lawyers. What's more, an intemperate remark or a crudity read into the record at trial can undermine your testimony. For example, at a deposition relating to a plaintiff's complaint of priapism, the lawyers engaged in coarse humor. The expert, a urologist, gave his deposition. He first explained that priapism occurs in some cases of lymphatic and myelogenous leukemia and with some spinal cord diseases or injuries. But then, sensing a light mood that had been established by the lawyers, he wisecracked about the plaintiff: "Maybe the guy is just horny." In court, evidence was presented that the patient was unable to urinate satisfactorily, that he needed catheter drainage and that cystostomy was being considered. The remark came back to haunt the urologist in court.

QUALIFYING THE EXPERT

The initial qualification of the expert witness figures most in whether the jury will believe his testimony. If they think you're an expert, your testimony will be credible. That's because jurors are not medically knowledgeable and often don't understand what the physician has said. Unfortunately, the jury is likely to make its decision based on its impressions of the medical witness rather than actual testimony.

Many lawyers, especially the young and inexperienced, do not grasp this situation. They do not understand the need to make their expert witness stand out in the minds of the jury as the most important expert witness. For example, if the qualifications of all the witnesses are presented to the jury in much the same way, then the witnesses are placed on the same level regardless of training, experience, and competence. For that reason, you should encourage an attorney to go through your qualifications in detail rather than have them presented to the court as facts mutually agreed to by the opposing attorney. This "qualification of the witness" is done by asking a series of questions so that the jurors get a complete resume of your training and background. This helps ensure that they will remember you and your testimony when they retire to the jury room to deliberate.

Physicians feel extremely uncomfortable when simply asked, "Doctor, will you state your qualifications?" When discussing training, experience, awards, and other pertinent information, physicians may become uncomfortable and even embarrassed, because doing so seems to violate the ethical sanction against advertising or bragging about accomplishments. That's why the expert witness should be qualified with questions that will bring out his qualifications one at a time, presenting a more complete picture. Otherwise, if the witness becomes embarrassed in discussing his qualificiations, he tends to cut the matter short, leaving the jury without everything it should know to evaluate his qualifications. As a guide, here's a checklist of information that should be asked of expert witnesses:

- Your name, residence and place of business. While seemingly self-explanatory, this question may have to be changed if the witness comes from out of state. For example, if the case is tried in the Deep South and the witness is from New York, the lawyer might simply ask for the witness's name.

- Your profession.

- How long you have practiced. (Juries weigh experience heavily.)

- Where you received premedical education.

- Where you received your medical degree and internship training.

- Whether you have had military service and, if so, when. What was your rank and what were your duties? This may be a loaded question. If your jury contains members who have had prior service, they will be familiar with rank and duties and they will better understand the qualifications of the expert witness. But if you feel that the jury is anti-military, you should advise that this question be omitted.

- Whether your license to practice is on record in a particular state. This question is to inform the jury that the requirements of the statutes pertaining to medical practice have been met.

- Whether you practice full time. Lawyers often are not aware that there are many part-time physicians and others who do not practice. The jury is apt to consider them dilettantes who have been called to testify about something not currently important to them.

- Whether you are associated with any clinic or medical group. Its name and your duties should be stated. This question should only be asked if the clinic is locally prestigious or well known nationally.

- Your membership in professional societies or organizations. It indicates interest in the current status of medical practice.

- Whether you have a specialty.

- Whether you have specialized medical training. If so, state what it was and where you took it. Most juries don't know what sort of training is required to become a qualified medical specialist. This will educate them about the effort. It will point out that a physician becomes a specialist through years of study rather than by his own declaration.

- Whether you have ever taught medicine.

- Whether you are a board-certified specialist. If so, by which board? Describe the procedure for getting certified. This is one of the most important questions, because board-certified specialists must be examined by panels of their peers prior to certification. If the process of certification is adequately described to the jury, the board-certified specialist's opinions will be taken more seriously by the jury than those of a specialist who is not so qualified.

- Your age and the number of years you have practiced your specialty. (In these days of plastic surgery and youthful hairstyling and clothes, the jury may find it hard to distinguish between the experienced physician and the younger, less experienced one.)

- Whether you have written articles in your field, lectured, or received any awards for service in your field. Laymen are impressed by published articles or affiliations as a teacher with a medical school. The lingering myth that medical school professors are smarter than practitioners is widespread enough to use the question if you have a teaching affiliation.
- Any consulting positions you hold and your duties. The word "consultant" implies above average knowledge and experience.

Converting from an expert into an expert witness requires close cooperation between yourself and the attorney. A careful pretrial interview will reveal your strengths and weaknesses as an expert witness and allow you and the attorney to become comfortable with each other and the testimony. The adage "forewarned is forearmed" is nowhere more appropriate. Attorneys should remember that their expert must be relaxed, comfortable and familiar with the proceedings to testify effectively and understandably.

Trial lawyers have a rule: "Never ask a question unless you know what the answer will be." As an expert witness, you should make it a rule to know what the questions will be before you take the stand. Of course, you and the attorney who is calling you as an expert witness may not be able to anticipate all the questions you'll be asked on cross examination. But on the basis of your pretrial discussions, you should be confident that few, if any, surprises await you on the witness stand.

CREDIBILITY UNDERMINED

Despite the days of painstaking preparation for their moment on the witness stand, many physicians undermine their credibiilty by failing to observe a few simple rules:

1. Keep your answers short and simple.
2. Refer to records whenever they are available. Never try to testify from sheer memory. You can only be wrong.
3. You are not obligated to answer a question that is not clear to you as an expert. If necessary, force the opposing attorney to rephrase the question so that you can answer it accurately and succinctly.

FIELDING LOADED QUESTIONS

Bear in mind that attorneys have the right to argue inferences. Beware that if they ask you a loaded, general and nonspecific question and you try to answer it, they may read into it anything they wish in further cross examination or in closing arguments. In replying to the opposing attorney, address your answers to the jury. Look toward the jury, not at the attorney or the judge. By speaking to the jury, you evidence sincerity. These are the people in the courtroom whom you must convince. And there are subtle factors that may influence your credibility. For example, when an attorney sizes up prospective witnesses, he checks their dress habits. He does not want his witness to appear in a bright plaid sport jacket and green pants. He will probably bypass that physician as a witness because he realizes how hard it is to change a person's dress habits.

On the stand, be alert to defusing potentially explosive exchanges between you and the opposing attorney. Never be argumentative, no matter how much the attorney baits you. View your testimony in a wider context, as just one part of the case. Even if you are convinced that you know more than your attorney and want to volunteer information, refrain from offering it unless asked. Allow your attorney to serve as your guide.

By maintaining a smooth and consistent tone to your testimony, you will convince the jury of your reliability as a witness. Unfortunate situations often develop in which a physician blows his cool. For example, he may not understand a question and reply to an attorney, "I'm sorry I don't understand your question as worded." At that point, an attorney may try to trigger an argument. He may goad the doctor by asking, "Well, what is it that you don't understand about the question?" That is an invitation to argument. The reply should be delicately worded, something like, "It doesn't make any sense from a medical point of view. All I'm asking sir, is that you rephrase the question so that I can understand it." Responding this way keeps the ball in play. The attorney will soon learn that it will not be as easy as he had thought to ruffle the witness.

BE PREPARED

You must anticipate how to react in a variety of situations. One must not improvise while on the stand. Under scrutiny by the judge, jury and others in the courtroom and feeling the pressure cooker-like atmosphere that may prevail during a crucial stage of testimony, a physician must be prepared for battle. If you are prepared well for taking the stand, your testimony will be seamless. But your preparation, whether it is for testifying or consulting, should begin long before a case is scheduled for trial.

THE OPPOSING EXPERT

Since any expert witness's stock in trade is his credibility, your attorney should aim at aspects of his professional background that raise doubts about the reliability of his testimony. Many physicians hire themselves out as "professional witnesses," and if testifying as an expert witness provides a substantial part of their income, it will offer evidence that this physician is a "hired gun." This is an especially useful tool to use in a small urban or rural area where the "hired gun" is resented and a jury is more apt to view the testimony from local physicians in a favorable light compared to the big city consultant. By quizzing the expert on his background, practice and partiality, your attorney may raise doubts about the strength of testimony.

DID HE EXAMINE THE PATIENT?

One way to discredit the opposing expert is to question how familiar he is with the patient's condition through a personal examination. It is highly unlikely that the expert had examined the patient around the same time when the alleged negligence occurred. There may be features of the patient's care in the past that may be used to raise doubts about the expert's assessment of the patient's current condition.

EXPERT MUST BE SIMILIAR IN TRAINING

One of the best ways to discredit the opposing expert is to demonstrate that this physician does not practice in a similar environment or that he has access to more sophisticated equipment. For example, if he suggests that a CT scan should have been done on a patient, he may be unfamiliiar with the fact that CT scanning can only be done when a mobile unit visits the area where the accused physician practices. The lack of familiarity with the conditions in the community should be pointed out to the jury.

INVESTIGATE BACKGROUND AND PREVIOUS TESTIMONY

Some expert witnesses have undermined their credibility by offering a different view in other trials. If the expert has testified in previous cases, your attorney should review previous depositions and courtroom testimony for contradictory information. The expert's fees are also open for discussion, and he should be asked how much he is receiving to testify. If it appears to be excessive and if this type of work is the chief source of his income, the jury may begin to think that he is not as impartial a witness as he claims to be be, especially if he consistently testifies for one side.

Other weaknesses may be found in the expert's testimony if he does not practice in the area of medicine in which he claims expertise or if his knowledge on the standard of care has not led him to publish much on this problem. Your attorney might ask, "Doctor, how many cases similar to the one at hand have you personally managed in the last year?" or "how many times have you managed the same problem under the circumstances that have been described here?"

15

ANATOMY
OF A
TRIAL

MALPRACTICE CHECKLIST

- Beware of the malpractice carrier's attorney who suggests going to arbitration because he does not want to meticulously prepare for a trial.
- Always attend a pretrial conference to emphasize to the judge how concerned you are about the lawsuit.
- Dress conservatively with little jewelry.
- Become as familiar as you can with the physical layout of the courtroom before the trial.
- Arrive at least 30 minutes before the court convenes.
- At selection of jurors, sit straight and look solemn and concerned.
- You should be consulted by your attorney during jury selection and can play a key role in who is seated.
- Do not show any sign that you recognize any potential juror.
- Your name does not begin with "Dr."
- It's essential that you look at the jury at all times— you are building rapport with eye contact.
- The jury's attention span is greatest during opening and closing statements— attorneys should open quickly.
- Face the jury squarely during closing arguments.
- Insisting on answering questions "off the cuff" instead of referring to medical records is a major error.

186

- Never volunteer information to the opposing attorney— answer only what is asked.
- Convey the impression that you are 100 percent convinced you followed the correct course of action.
- Be aware of your body language. Don't show signs of anxiety or uncertainty.
- When you leave the witness stand, do not convey what you are feeling. Don't grin or wave at friends or relatives.
- Your attorney must insist that the judge's instructions to the jury benefit you.

ANATOMY OF A TRIAL

When all the research for a deposition or trial is completed, when all the investigations are done, when all the experts are lined up in a row, the bottom line in the case is still the physician and how he will perform on the witness stand. The judge has set the case for trial, the case has been placed on the docket and a pretrial order has been issued. This pretrial order will require a listing of witnesses, the substance of the proposed testimony, a list of exhibits to be used, a statement of the case and the facts relevant to an affirmative defense. There will also be an order setting the date and the time at which jury selection will begin.

Set aside the preconceptions or misconceptions that the deposition or your reading of Franz Kafka have engendered about the trial. Away from their natural setting and unfamiliar with courtroom routine, many physicians find the prospect of testifying as a witness in their own case an intimidating experience. But like other aspects of the case, if you enter the courtroom as prepared for the trial as you were for the preliminary events, you will already feel tested for battle. The first part of that preparation is to become familiar with the ground rules. A jury trial is largely determined by state law and what your malpractice carrier's attorney elects. In some jurisdictions he can elect to go to binding arbitration or jury trial, and the physician may have little or no say about which course is followed. Although not always true, generally a physician stands a better chance with a jury trial. It is as if you are being tried by 6 or 12 of your patients.

Binding arbitration may leave you with a different and often unpredictable set of challenges. You could, for example, be faced with colleagues who "would never have done the procedure like that." They may be combined with a "blue ribbon" panel of attorneys who may resemble six vultures sitting on a fence. In many cases of binding arbitration the newest physician in town who uses the newest technologies has been sued for malpractice. An arbitration panel may be selected that includes physicians from the other two major surgical groups in town, who have a financial interest in seeing that the new physician is curbed because he has been attracting too many patients. The lawyers selected for the panel may be plaintiff's attorneys.

The malpractice carrier's attorney may suggest that you go to binding arbitration because he does not want to prepare for this case as meticulously and as painstakingly as he would if it were tried. As you have at previous stages along the way, consult with your personal malpractice defense attorney before it is determined whether you will have a jury trial or binding arbitration. If you are headed for trial, you need to be circumspect about a pretrial conference. Your carrier's attorney may suggest that it is not crucial for you to attend, that it is merely a "formality." A physician should always attend a pretrial conference to emphasize to the judge how concerned he is about the lawsuit. If he is not represented at this conference by a personal attorney, he should request copies of any pretrial orders or pretrial papers that are required to be filed.

How You Appear to Potential Jurors

It begins when you drive to the courthouse. If you have an older car, drive it. If you are married, bring your wife with you. Bear in mind that the people you see in the parking lot may be those who ultimately sit in judgment on the facts of your case. Dress conservatively with little jewelry— a wedding ring and a watch at most. Be well groomed and well dressed but not excessively. If you arrive with your wife in the family station wagon you will be perceived in a more favorable light than if you come barreling into the parking lot in your Ferrari.

Be Familiar with the Surroundings

Some attorneys recommend, and it may be a good idea, that physicians become as familiar as possible with the physical layout of the courtroom— who's who, who sits where or how you're supposed to move around. A few attorneys even go so far as to use photographs to help doctors feel at home in the courtroom. Photos taken from different angles in the courtroom can help a physician become oriented and acclimated to the jury box, the witness stand, the bench, the bailiff's seat and the counsels' tables where the litigants and the lawyers sit. If photographs are not available, your attorney may want to sketch a diagram that at least indicates where the physician will be sitting in relation to others in the courtroom.

Part of this general briefing should also include an explanation of court hours. This is crucial because nothing hurts a physician more— or any litigant, for that matter— in the eyes of a jury or judge than coming in late. Physicians should arrive at least 30 minutes before the court convenes. Generally there will be a 10-minute recess in the morning and afternoon sessions, enough time to visit the rest room or smoke a cigarette. But it is a poor idea to linger outside or in the hallways. If the court reconvenes at 11 a.m., the physician should be back at least several minutes before that time. Nothing is more embarrassing to an attorney than to have his client missing and the judge scolding him from the bench as the entire courtroom waits for the doctor to return, or for the attorney to find him.

Selection of Jurors

Up to 40 potential jurors could be sitting in the courtroom. The selection begins with the plaintiff. Sit straight in your chair and look interested, solemn and concerned. Do not slouch, lean back or appear casual because *you are on trial*: this is your chance to show the jury that you are another human who has dedicated his life's work to caring for those who suffer. It is not a time to display arrogance or convey the slightest suggestion of feeling superior. As a judicial assistant once said, "The higher a physician places himself, the farther a jury will cause him to fall."

Your attorney should consult with you during the jury selection because you may play an instrumental role in who is seated. For example, in some areas of the country, small towns where everyone knows one another, the physician may have treated the relatives or even the spouses of potential jurors. This does not necessarily mean that these people should be disqualified, but that the relationship that the physician had with them should be considered. Do not show any sign of recognition of any potential juror. If you have had a particularly unpleasant experience with any of them, however, point that out immediately to your attorney. For whatever reason, if there is something about a potential juror that you do not like or that makes you doubt his or her ability to be fair minded, consult with your attorney.

Types of Challenges to Jurors

All jurisdictions have two types of challenges. The first is for cause. This type of challenge would include persons who are related to the plaintiff or the defendant and who have already formed an opinion about the case and cannot be considered fair or impartial because of this relationship. Challenges for cause are found in two forms, statutory and discretionary. Those that are statutory are those in which the law enumerates certain factors that disqualify a potential juror. For those that are discretionary, the trial judge will ultimately decide whether a potential juror will be excused for cause.

The second challenge is preemptory. No reason need be given for this challenge. For whatever reason, you may feel a potential juror will be less than fair to you. It is the right and the duty of your attorney to excuse that person from sitting in judgment of your case. Since you are functioning as a member of the defense team, a good attorney will always consult you in these matters of selection. In terms of priorities, the pretrial deposition is the most critical factor in deciding the outcome of a malpractice case, but a close second is the jury that is selected. Jury selection is so crucial that the process has spawned a new breed of consultants who help attorneys make what they consider to be appropriate choices. Many attorneys debunk the work of jury consultants, arguing that there is no reliable way of predicting how to pick a jury that will be predisposed to one side or the other. But other attorneys are relying more heavily on these behavioral scientists, if not for input on whom to select then on how to tailor their courtroom presentation based on research that jury consultants conduct as the trial is being held. These jury consultants conduct what they call "focus group" sessions in which they ask groups of people within the community different questions so that they select the kinds of potential jurors who could be favorable to one side.

Jury consultants also help attorneys in phrasing questions put to potential jurors, the process called *voir dire* (to speak the truth). In some jurisdictions, attorneys can directly question prospective jurors, while in others they submit their questions to the judge who reads them. Invariably the judge will ask, "Is there anyone here who doesn't think he or she can render a fair and impartial verdict in this case?" Few people would answer yes to that question, so lawyers have to probe to uncover possible impartiality through the *voir dire* questioning. That's where jury consultants are carving out a niche for themselves. They sometimes help attorneys construct the questions. Consider these two ways of asking the same question: (1)"The plaintiff in this case is asking for $350,000. Do you believe anyone can be so injured that he should be awarded that amount of money?" It requires a yes or a no answer that may not reveal much about what a prospective juror is thinking. (2)"How do you feel about awarding a sum of $350,000 in a suit like this?" Thus rephrased, the question is certain to elicit more of a response.

During the *voir dire* questioning, the key response you are looking for may not even come from the potential juror who is being questioned. For example, you may notice that another potential juror is nodding or shaking his head in response to the question— a tipoff to his sentiments.

The Trial Begins

The sequence of the trial begins with opening statements by the plaintiff's attorney about what he expects to prove and by the defense counsel on what he expects to prove. The plaintiff calls the first witness because he has the burden of proof. He must prove by the greater weight of the evidence that he is correct. It is not uncommon for the defendant-physician to be called as an adverse witness. The posture you adopted during the deposition in which you showed no hostility toward the plaintiff or the plaintiff's attorney must be continued during the trial. But there are other aspects of your testimony that will also either score points with the jury or detract from your credibility. For example, your name does not begin with "Dr." You should reply to the opposing attorney's questions with a "Yes, sir" or a "No, sir." If you do not understand a question, you may turn to the court and say simply, "Your honor, I'm sorry, I just don't understand the question." By the time you take the stand, your attorneys should have you thoroughly briefed for every possible contingency that can arise— regardless of whether you are testifying for yourself or as an adverse witness. There is a striking difference between the two.

For example, as an adverse witness you may be called for only a limited purpose in building the plaintiff's case. The attorney may ask,"Doctor, you treated John Doe on March 20, 1985. On that date you did not know that the plaintiff was suffering from a ruptured appendicitis. Yes or No." Your answer should be direct and polite and you should look at the jury and answer with a crisp "Yes, sir" or "No, sir."

It is essential that you look at the jury at all times, because these are the men and women who will judge the facts of the case. If the jury views you as being honest, sincere and dedicated, you will have that much more credibility in their eyes. During these early stages of the trial, you are building rapport with the jury with eye contact. That eye contact will help you gauge whether they understand what you are saying and what impact it is having on them. Never talk down to them. Explain the medical facts of the case as you might describe them to a patient and in a way that they can understand. From time to time, you will perceive that they understand or do not understand what you are saying if they nod their heads or if they look confused.

The medical profession is filled, as are other professions, with jargon, technical terms, and profession-specific words. It is up to the physician and his attorney to communicate to the jury as clearly and precisely as they can. When possible, physicians should always use simple two or three syllable words instead of technical medical terms. It is useful to provide the attorney with a glossary of medical terms and their definitions specific to the particular court action. The attorney can then refer to this glossary when pleading the case.

It is also important to explain every medical term instead of taking for granted that the jury will know what even the simplest one means. For example, the term "normal sinus rhythm" has a specific medical connotation. Assuming the jury will know that the term refers to the heart and not the nasal passages is an error on the part of the physician and his attorney.

The physician's attorney should be an excellent barometer of what is difficult and beyond the common knowledge of most jurors. Again, the physician and his attorney should spend considerable time together planning and discussing the entire case presentation.

Throughout the trial you will not be allowed to talk to the jury except from the witness stand. Many juries are instructed not to have any contact with you or anyone involved in the case and if you do, it is a gross breach of ethics. However, if a juror looks at you and smiles, you may manage a weak smile back. Despite the lack of contact with the jurors, some attorneys try to crack the impervious shield that the court seeks to build around them. Jury consultants can and do play a role in advising attorneys based on their observations of jurors in groups. Certain jurors tend to dominate the others in the group and if they are observed before the court convenes— at lunch, outside the courthouse or wherever they gather— it can be determined which among them are the leaders or the persuaders. As a result, jury consultants may convey this information to an attorney, who then addresses his presentation to these "leaders" in the hope that they will convince the other jurors or at least influence their thinking.

Additional research has also shown that many jurors arrive at a decision early in the trial, then seek to support their conclusions. A jury's attention span, according to some medical-legal experts, tends to be greatest during the opening and closing statements. Mindful of this, attorneys open quickly, aware that a jury's attention is about at as high a level as it will be throughout the trial.

POLISHING YOUR PRESENTATION

Your choice of words, like your attorney's, is also crucial, and you may want to tailor your phraseology accordingly. For example, you may want to say "incident" instead of "accident." A witness testifying for you may want to refer to you as the physician rather than as the defendant. These are nuances that may not be apparent to you without some reflection on the impact of such words on the mind of a juror. As you have throughout the trial, it is also important for you to face the jury squarely during the closing arguments. Look directly at them, do not nod or shake your head when key points are being made, and maintain the same dignity and respect for the jury that you have had throughout the proceedings.

Demonstrative Evidence

Jurors, like everyone else in the video age, think more clearly when assisted by visual presentations, and demonstrative evidence can significantly help a physician. Your attorney may want to arrange to have a medical illustrator prepare overlays that can be used to demonstrate anatomical features to the jury. Nevertheless, physicians should be aware of how demonstrative evidence carries a degree of risk, especially when a mechanical apparatus or some other piece of equipment is used and its impact depends on its functioning properly in court. For example, one Florida attorney had what he considered a harrowing experience when his client placed a ring forceps on a 4 x 4 sponge and violently shook it to demonstrate that it would not slip off during a dilatation and curretage. He had, unknown to the attorney, brought two ring forceps in case he discovered that one was weak. It was powerful evidence and a convincing demonstration because it demonstrated precisely what the plaintiff's attorney had argued. The physician won the case, but the demonstration was so crucial that if it had failed, the doctor may have lost.

There is nothing quite as effective as bringing a skeleton, a graph or slides during a malpractice trial to help you illustrate certain aspects of testimony. Visual materials go a long way toward making medical terminology and procedures understandable, and therefore they enhance the chances that the doctor's choice of treatment or methods will be accepted by the jury. When a physician starts talking about an open reduction of a femur, for example, it is just so much medical jargon as far as the jury is concerned. But when that same physician brings out a couple of bones and pins and actually shows the jury what he did, then it makes his case much more understandable.

Also, the doctor should sit down before the trial with his attorney and give a "hands on" demonstration of what was done. This way, the latter will be better able to explain the procedure and technique to a jury. However, the physician should never use any visual material in court without first having cleared it with his attorney. Nothing startles an attorney more than having his client suddenly volunteer to draw a diagram to explain what was done. "No surprises" should be the rule of thumb to follow.

Finally, as part of the staging of the courtroom drama it is important for the physician to address the jury. Look at the jurors, focus on them one at a time, speak directly to them, make them understand what you, as the attending physician, did and why. One strategy, which often works to focus the attention of the physician on the jury, is for the defense attorney to position himself in a visual line with the jury box so that while the doctor is answering questions posed by his own attorney, he is also being forced to face and address the jury.

Don't Rely on Memory Alone

Despite the best preparation, physicians may be prone to a variety of mistakes that neither they nor their attorneys may have anticipated. Relying on memory alone is one of them. Insisting on answering questions "off the cuff" instead of referring to medical records is a major error that most physicians make during almost all stages of the malpractice suit. The physician should always insist that he has no independent memory of anything substantive regarding the patient and that to give an accurate and honest answer, he must refer to his medical records. Even though the physician may be well prepared, and familiar with both the case and his records, he should always refer to them and read from them directly.

Never Volunteer Information

This rule is as true at the trial stage as it is at deposition. Physicians need to bear in mind that they are not responsible for explaining everything in response to a single question. You will have a chance to explain points at other stages of the trial. By simply answering with a "yes" or "no" or an "I don't know," you are not evading the question.

A corollary to these guidelines is never answer a question from the other side with "yes, but..." What usually follows is a long, rambling qualification of the answer that opens up a new front for the plaintiff's lawyer to ask new questions. It's a geometric progression that can only harm you. Your attorney has the responsibility of bringing out all the information relevant to your defense. One simple answer will not determine the outcome of the case.

Do Not Waffle

At all times you must convey the impression that you are 100 percent convinced that the course of action you followed was the correct one. Even when the other side marshals expert witnesses who raise the possibility that there were other diagnostic or therapeutic choices available, the physician on trial must stick to his conviction that he took the best possible course under the unique and particular set of circumstances. To the question, "Doctor, is the other doctor— the expert— correct in what he says?" the doctor who is being sued must be able to answer, without hesitation, "No, the expert is not correct under the circumstances."

Be Aware of Your Body Language

Expelling breath.   People usually make a sound when expelling their breath which gives the impression of relief from a difficult and uncomfortable situation. The sound signifies that there was some tension in the situation and that the outcome was doubtful. This is not a positive sound for a physician to make when he is being questioned.

Clearing the throat.   This is a common sound and gesture in response to the mucus that forms in the throat during a period of stress or apprehension. However, the sound can be interpreted as a clear sign of excessive nervousness, or even as a nonverbal admonishment and criticism.

Rubbing.   Rubbing the arm of a chair, a shoe against the carpet, or even thumbs together is a clear signal of nervousness. The physician should be aware of the impression this creates with the jury and should avoid them.

The role that the physician himself plays as the central character of the malpractice drama should not be underestimated. All the resources and talent invested in the physician's defense can be negated by an impression that the physician is unable to cope maturely and professionally with the stress of the case or that he has a negative attitude. It can't be emphasized enough that the physician in a malpractice case is in a highly charged drama. Every gesture and every line count toward how the audience— the jury— views the production. A mistake, a flippant attitude, or a careless answer can not only cost the physician an enormous sum of money, but a hard-earned professional reputation as well.

You Must Account for A Bad Result

Physicians sometimes commit the error of failing to attribute a bad result to a particular cause. A jury may question his knowledge or assume that he is covering up something. Despite the fact that you cannot precisely explain what went wrong, you should offer an explanation that indicates you have analyzed what went wrong and are willing to suggest a reason for why it did. If you do not, the plaintiff can reap the benefit of the doubt.

Your Testimony Could Be Impeached

Often upon reviewing the deposition, your attorney may spot a potential minefield. This concerns statements that could leave you open to impeachment. This typically occurs when your testimony in court contradicts what you have said during the deposition.

The plaintiff's attorney will be quick to point out the contradiction and ask you whether you recalled saying something differently during the deposition. There is no way you can deny having done so because the attorney can prove that you did by using your prior deposition. Do not argue with the plaintiff's attorney about what you said in your deposition. All the attorney has to do is pick out that portion of your deposition and read it back. But that does not mean that you have just undermined your case. Let's assume that the plaintiff's attorney continues down the track with "How can you say this when six months ago you testified to the opposite?" One way to escape unscathed is to suggest that your answer today is different because it is based on current research not available when you gave your deposition. You may want to add that you were concerned about that previous response and returned to the testimony you gave during deposition, and reconsidered it. In the light of fresh data on the subject, you may want to say that your previous answer was based on your best judgment but that the revised testimony is the correct response.

How to Leave the Witness Stand

Some physicians have helped to snatch defeat from the jaws of victory by the way they leave the witness stand, destroying the image that they had carefully built through their testimony. When you leave the stand, do not convey what you are feeling. Thinking that you have won, it may be tempting to grin at spectators or wave to friends and relatives. If you anticipate victory, do not show it. Similarly, do not tag yourself as a loser by looking dejected or defeated. You are still being observed, so maintain the same composure that you have throughout other aspects of the trial.

JUDGES INSTRUCTIONS

The judge's instructions to the jury are also crucial to your case, and your personal attorney must be insistent that the instructions benefit you. During a charge conference, held prior to when the jury is charged, your attorney should renew the objections that he has raised during the trial so that you will be certain aspects of their deliberations do not pertain to you. For example, by requesting that certain instructions do not apply to you, your attorney will see to it that the jury will not consider certain aspects of the testimony as bearing on your negligence. It may be that they will consider testimony on the disconnection of anesthesia or certain aspects of hospital care that were not within your control. When the judge instructs the jury concerning these matters, it is crucial for him to convey the idea that these matters do not apply to your case and that the jury is not to consider them in determining whether you were negligent.

16

WHEN
TO SETTLE
A CASE

MALPRACTICE CHECKLIST

- The decision to settle a case is never one to be made alone or only based on the advice of an attorney.
- The barometer should be four colleagues, none of whom practice with you.
- View the plaintiff's case in the context of your duty, a breach of duty between you and the patient, the causal connection between the care and the injury and the extent of the injury.
- Are damages to the plaintiff severe enough to enable him to obtain a sympathetic jury?
- You can judge the potential size of the award by consulting a service that publishes jury verdict awards.
- Settle cases in which the potential for damages is great and your liability is either clear or marginal.
- Don't let the carrier's attorney manipulate you into an unwanted settlement.
- If you want to fight and the carrier is reluctant, put the carrier on notice that it has no authority to negotiate.
- There are no nuisance suits; none that should be considered frivolous.
- The most dangerous cases are those related to etiology— profound injuries in which you were only marginally involved.

- What is meritless in medicine may have nothing to do with what is meritless in law.
- Beware of cases that could swing toward the plaintiff based solely on a "sympathy factor."
- A case may lack merit in medicine or law but have "courtroom merit" because of sympathy for the plaintiff.
- Delay any decision to file a countersuit until your claim has been adjudicated.

Settling a malpractice claim may be harder for you than fighting the case in the courtroom. Few physicians are likely to settle a case without feeling uneasy. Your misgivings about settling may stem from the fact that for months you have geared for a fight, priming yourself for the day when you will take the witness stand. You may also have felt that your case had merit, and that you might have won, had you given it a chance to proceed to trial. What is perhaps most troublesome is this question: by settling, are you admitting to incompetence?

All of these feelings are entirely understandable during a time when you are most vulnerable to self-doubt and the emotional turmoil generated by a malpractice claim. For these reasons, the decision to settle a case is never one that you should make alone or only on the advice of your attorney, no matter how much you trust him and follow his advice. This is a time for you to rely on the counsel and candor of your colleagues, not those who practice with you, but others whose judgment and skill you also respect and whose opinions you can rely on.

FIRST STEP

Peer review is the first step you should take in evaluating the merits of settling a case. Let your medical colleagues review the facts of the case, even if they practice in other states. Simply tell them, "Look, I want your honest opinion. If you think I screwed up, tell me." The barometer should be four colleagues, none of whom practice with you, who can return to you and say, "We don't think you did anything wrong, and we will testify for you." With that kind of honesty and support, you know you are on solid ground.

On the other hand, their analysis can help you chart your way through ambiguities that might otherwise cloud your perception of the strength of your defense. For example, medical records may be ambiguous on critical points, or your defense may depend on the credibility of a witness, i.e., whether the patient disclosed certain information in his history. It may seem that you can bank on a clear and simple defense, such as a recognized complication after a major operation or a side effect of a commonly used drug. But other variables that you may not consider can chip away at the defense you thought was rock-ribbed. The location of a trial, the composition of the jury deciding the case, and the judge who presides are all elements that need to be assessed.

At the earliest possible time, you need to gauge the potential danger of not settling the case. Is it a case that will merely serve to educate the plaintiff and his attorney if it is dragged out, causing him to bring in other attorneys who may be looking for damages of $3 million to $4 million? The personality of the physician, the competence of opposing counsel and the injury to the patient are added ingredients that can stack the odds for or against you.

FOUR AREAS

In evaluating those odds, you need to view the plaintiff's case within the context of the four areas of negligence: (1) your duty to the patient; (2) a breach of the duty that exists between you and your patient; (3) the causal connection between your care and the injury to the patient; and (4) the extent of the injury or personal damages. In some cases, the duty is clear, the breach is clear, and the damages are bad. But the causal connection between the breach and the damages may be slim. Despite that tenuous connection, this case may be the kind in which your potential for getting hit far beyond your policy limits is real.

You need to examine the case and ask whether this is the type of plaintiff whom a jury will look at with tremendous sympathy because of the extent of the injury. This type of case, one in which the bridge between causal connection and damages is tenuous, but is enough to get to a sympathetic jury, should be settled early.

BUMBLING DILIGENCE

It is wise to conduct an independent evaluation at the outset, so that you don't get beyond the jury level and discover you have made a mistake. At that point, the defendant's attorney is deciding whether the plaintiff has a case. If he does, the physician had better settle before the plaintiff and his attorney understand their good fortune.

It is strongly recommended that you retain a personal attorney independent of the carrier's attorney. The reason you need your attorney is that many carrier attorneys are among the legions of malpractice defense "alchemists." They take a case that can be settled for $100,000 and, through their bumbling diligence and education of the plaintiff's attorney, turn it into a $1 million judgment.

NONMEDICAL FACTORS

The following nonmedical factors are to be considered before you make your decison as to whether to settle:

• You need to assess the severity of the damages to the plaintiff. Are they devastating enough, from a legal standpoint, so that the plaintiff can obtain a sympathetic jury?

• Is the judge pro-plaintiff?

• Is the jury sympathetic to you? Your attorney must be adept at discerning how the jury reacts and relates to plaintiff's counsel. Do they smile at him and scowl at you? It may seem superficial, but nonverbal body language is often a telltale sign of which way a jury is likely to decide. This sign should be an early warning to your attorney as to which way the wind is blowing.

• The magnitude of a potential verdict. Parameters exist, based on awards for similar injuries by different juries. There are numerous cases that describe what particular injuries are worth. A brain-damaged baby case, for example, may be worth $1.5 million in your locality. A missed fracture and gangrene infection may be worth $50,000.

Your attorney should be aware of services that publish jury verdict awards, from which you can judge the potential size of the award in your case. For example, if you know from your personal attorney's analysis that an award could be as high as $500,000, and your colleagues have told you that they consider your case indefensible or within a gray area, it is a good idea to begin negotiations for settlement. At that point, your personal attorney should contact your carrier's attorney and declare your position that the matter be settled for $25,000, or whatever sum you and your attorney agree is appropriate and within the limits of your policy. The negotiations with the plaintiff's attorney at this stage are delicate, and your attorney can ill afford to so enlighten your plaintiff and his attorney, through discovery, that the value of the case is increased. Mishandled, that $25,000 case can turn into a gold mine for the plaintiff.

TOUGH CALL

The tough call for many physicians is the case that can be settled for less than $10,000. It's often the kind of case in which the plaintiff has won a sizable award without having done much work. Lurking in the back of your mind is the fear that there may be a slim chance the plaintiff could parlay the facts in the case into a jumbo verdict. After all, every personal injury suggests the possibility that a plaintiff could win enough sympathy from the jury to be awarded much more than the amount he would have accepted as a pretrial settlement offer.

There is a school of thought among defense attorneys that says that, unless the physician is committed to digging in and fighting these cases, they should be settled because of the potential for risking a larger award and greater exposure. You are actually risking more if you *do* settle. Here's why. By settling, you are only encouraging other lawsuits, thus establishing a precedent that could leave the door open to more claims. For example, if you rendered a service to a patient and are owed $3000 for a cholecystectomy, you may want to sue the patient to collect that fee. However, after learning that you were previously sued by a patient who underwent this same operation, and that you settled the case for $3,000, this patient may suspect you are an easy mark and countersue for malpractice after your legal effort to collect the delinquent account. Settle those cases in which the potential for damage is great and your liability is either clear or marginal. If you have doubts about whether to settle these small cases, you may have forgotten that, in some jurisdictions, a pattern of settling, or even the tacit admission of guilt or negligence, could eventually result in the suspension of a medical license.

INSURANCE PREMIUMS

Contrary to what you might suspect, the decision to settle a case is not likely to significantly affect your insurance premium. Considering the rate at which premiums have been rising, other factors, such as your carrier's solvency and financial management, are probably more important. But if you are still worried about the effect of such a settlement on your premium, write the carrier and ask about that possibility, requesting a written response.

If more than one school of thought prevails in whether you should settle cases for $10,000 or less, the same is true for deciding the best time to settle any case. Some attorneys suggest that you should wait until during, or shortly after, the selection of a jury. The theory is that a plaintiff's settlement demand will drop considerably when a trial actually starts, because his attorney must confront the weaknesses in his case, the inadequacy of discovery, and his inability to produce the witnesses he had lined up at the outset. It may also be true in some jurisdictions that plaintiff's attorneys start negotiations by making inflated demands, which turn out fanciful when the moment of truth, the trial, approaches.

The best strategy to use, at least in the beginning, is to approach the opposing attorney and avoid indicating the potential for a large award. In a conciliatory manner and without drawing attention to the details of the case, but congenially noting that you "did your best and prefer not to go through a trial," your counsel can often keep a plaintiff's attorney from bringing in a big gun who may raise the stakes.

POKER-FACED

The last thing you want to do is educate the plaintiff's attorney if he appears relatively ignorant as to the potential hidden in the claim. This strategy doesn't always work, especially if you are up against a shrewd plaintiff's attorney who will recognize a gold mine when it is within his grasp. In these circumstances, your best strategy may be to apply the rules of poker: negotiate as if your hand is much stronger than it actually is. As in any bargaining process, settling a malpractice case to your advantage may hinge on your attorney's display of showmanship at the conference table as much as it does on your documentation of quality care. During these negotiations, you need to be adequately represented by personal counsel. Don't let your insurance carrier's attorney steal the show by manipulating you into a settlement you feel you don't want.

If you want to fight the case, and the carrier is reluctant, put the carrier on notice (with a certified letter) that it has no authority to negotiate. Your attorney should draft a letter to this effect:

```
This is to confirm my telephone conversation in which I
advised you that it is the position of my client that no
settlement or negotiations of any type be entered into
```

between your office and the plaintiff's attorney, and
that he has not breached any duty due and owing to his
patient.

Settling a case after you have followed the advice of a personal attorney
may not necessarily mean you have eliminated your misgivings about
doing so. You may always feel a twinge of doubt and guilt about settling,
and wonder what might have happened had the case been tried. But
whoever said that litigation, like some aspects of medicine, is predictable?

THE "NUISANCE" SUIT

Few claims arouse as much anger and frustration as the meritless case or
so-called "nuisance suit." There is no question about settling, because you
and your attorney are confident that you did nothing wrong. Medically and
legally you hold all the cards.

"This is a nuisance suit," he scoffs. "A fishing expedition. It's frivolous
and it will explode in the plaintiff's face as soon as the facts are put on the
table and the jury is set straight." But like the unsuspecting swimmer
oblivious of the Great White, you and your attorney may be misled by your
own complacency, victims of a deceptive and dangerous line of thinking
that assumes such a liability claim is a "nuisance suit." If the malpractice
crisis has taught us anything, it is that there are no nuisance suits, at least
none that can be considered frivolous. The supposedly meritless case may
indeed have merits beyond the realms of medicine and law. These claims
must be taken seriously because they may have merit in the courtroom,
gathering strength and building momentum from the chemistry between a
plaintiff who can arouse sympathy and the juries ready to reward them for
reasons you may not have initially considered.

There are other reasons for treating these cases seriously, however, and
among the most important is a growing trend: Depending on where you
practice, you could be investigated for a single act of malpractice. In some
states one malpractice suit could spark an investigation by licensing
authorities that raises implications not only for your licensure but for other
matters. For example, it could have implications for whether you will be
required to attend continuing medical education courses beyond what is already required. Hospital boards may also take notice of a single malpractice
suit, scrutinizing such cases and taking them into consideration when
weighing the granting of privileges.

A Step-wise Approach to Follow

Because of these implications, your posture toward a so-called "nuisance suit" should be no different than what it is toward other liability claims that you would tend to regard in a more serious light. The sequence of events for handling these suits should unfold as with all other liability claims (see Chapter 10).

All of these steps are as essential to fighting the so-called nuisance suit as they are to fighting those with merit, or those that eventually may be settled. It is easy to understand how the words "nuisance" and "frivolous" worked their way into the medical-legal lexicon. In the late 1970s, as the malpractice crisis mushroomed nationally, numerous suits were filed that were blatant attempts at a shakedown of some poor physician who had conformed to the standard of care but who was nevertheless willing to settle because he did not want to cope with the pressure of fighting a case or the public embarrassment of having his name exposed. But the situation has changed. First, the plaintiff's bar has become much more sophisticated, eschewing that kind of strategy because it is not likely to succeed in a climate where pretrial screening panels have helped to impose tougher standards on the adjudication of claims and where tort reform has contributed to an atmosphere in which such spurious claims are not given as much chance of getting to court. Secondly, physicians have developed more spunk. They are tired of serving as patsies.

Burden of Proof is on You

Instead of referring to these cases as "nuisance" or "frivolous" suits, a better term in today's climate is "meritless." Although the theory of law is that the plaintiff has the burden of proof, in a meritless suit the burden shifts and it is the physician who must prove his innocence. As an example, consider the case in which the attorneys are seeking to establish an etiology for an injury that resulted from the following circumstances: A patient crushed his ankle when he jumped over a hurdle. A plaster cast was applied and an open reduction and internal fixation were done. The patient started sloughing skin off the dorsum and it necrosed. The necrosis penetrated the muscles over the dorsum and the result was 70 percent permanently disabling. You may know that it was not caused by the tightness of the cast but by the six-hour delay when the patient was transferred from one hospital to another. The patient developed micro emboli and had peripheral vascular problems that caused it. The suit against you is meritless but the burden of proving your innocence is on you.

Meritless cases must be taken seriously but often are not. The danger is that complacency sets in and the knee-jerk response is to say to yourself, "Anybody should understand that there's no substance to this case." But physicians tend to lose sight of the fact that malpractice cases are not being tried by their peers but by 6 or 12 citizens. The underlying danger, and one that is often not immediately perceived, is that the plaintiff may transform something that appears meritless into a viable case. If the plaintiff produces something that is plausible and reasonable, especially in the etiology-related cases, you must prove that you were not negligent. For a defense attorney, it is sometimes more difficult to defend a physician from a meritless case because doctors are less apt to take these cases seriously.

Why Etiology Cases are Dangerous

The most dangerous of these cases are those related to etiology and in which there is the potential for severe damages. These are usually cases in which the plaintiff has suffered profound and irreversible injuries during the course of care, but in which you were only marginally involved. Another point that physicians lose sight of is that what is meritless in medicine may have nothing to do with what is meritless in law. The distinction turns on the fact that there may be no basis in medical evidence for a certain result being attributed or even partially attributed to you, but there are other plausible explanations in law for blaming you.

Consider, for example, the stabbed, indigent patient who arrives at a private hospital that refuses to treat him because of a lack of insurance. The physician on call instructs the ambulance personnel to transport him to the next hospital, a short distance away; but by the time he has arrived there, he has bled and is in shock. The physician did not assume a duty to act and did not establish a physician–patient relationship, yet the case may turn on a fine legal point: Did he delay the transfer so that he even marginally contributed to the bleeding problem?

As far as medical evidence is concerned, he may not be culpable. But the effect on the jury could be devastating when its members are confronted by the fact that the patient left a wife and four children, all of whom are sitting in the courtroom and looking pitiful. The jury's sympathy is likely to be aroused regardless of whether a case has merit in medicine. Beware of the potential for such cases to swing toward the plaintiff solely because of the "sympathy factor."

Don't Underestimate the Sympathy Factor

Perhaps the worst case to defend against is the one in which the physician is innocent, medically and legally, but the sympathy factor is so great, because of the damages to the patient, that there is bound to be a sizable award. The case may lack merit in medicine or law but it nevertheless must be taken seriously because it has "courtroom merit" and the potential for damages is massive. Perhaps 25 percent of cases are decided, at least partially, on the basis of sympathy.

Although the sympathy factor is important, there are additional elements to be aware of in planning your strategy when you are hit with these meritless cases. The "joint and several" rule, for example, can snare you even if you were marginally involved in a patient's care and could devastate you if other physicians also named in the suit are the ones who were negligent. This doctrine is neither new nor novel, but it is rapidly wreaking havoc. It specifies that if more than one defendant is negligent, all of those named in the suit are liable for the total damages. A jury may find you only 10 percent negligent in the care of a patient whose spleen ruptured after he was discharged, but the plaintiff conceivably could collect the entire judgment from you if the others are going "bare."

The joint and several rule is one factor that makes a physician think twice about discounting a suit as "frivolous." There is nothing frivolous about your possible exposure for a jumbo award even if you were only marginally involved in the care. And there is nothing frivolous about the possibility, in some states, that you could be investigated by licensing authorities for even a single act of malpractice. Such scrutiny by medical boards looms as a growing trend, especially in states where the climate for malpractice litigation is red hot. It seems that the real nuisance, indeed the danger, behind any malpractice suit, especially those that appear frivolous from a medical point of view, is the complacent attitude that keeps physicians from taking these claims seriously.

Countersuit: Knowing When to Hold Your Fire

The biggest tactical error in handling a meritless claim is filing a countersuit before a decision has been reached in the case. Not only does it antagonize the plaintiff, undermining your chances that he will drop the case, but it can backfire in court as it evokes more sympathy for the other side. By simultaneously filing a countersuit, accusing the plaintiff of abuse of process or malicious prosecution, you may convey the impression that the plaintiff is indeed being treated harshly by an indifferent physician. Delay any decision to file a countersuit until your claim has been adjudicated, and even then tread lightly because the likelihood of success is slim.

According to the medical-legal literature, the best cause of action is probably malicious prosecution, although some physicians have pursued a countersuit on other grounds as well. For example, some physicians have argued that besides malicious prosecution, the patient's attorneys were negligent in failing to investigate a claim and continuing to prosecute it even after they learned it was groundless.

In all cases, judges will seek to balance the interest of the patient to free and open access to the courts with the interest of the physician to be free from "frivolous" malpractice suits. Although the countersuit strategy has not met with great success, that has not deterred a growing number of physicians from trying. The important point to remember is not to file a countersuit in mid-stream while the meritless claim is still being adjudicated.

PHYSICIAN'S COUNTERSUITS:
ARE THEY WORTH IT?

So far, only three truly successful malicious prosecution cases, won by physicians, have been upheld on appeal. Those cases were filed in Kansas, Kentucky and Tennessee. However, these were egregious malpractice lawsuits. Overall, doctors' lawsuits for malicious prosecution have been highly unproductive. In all but these three states, the next malicious prosecution cases successfully brought by a physician will be the first. A few insignificant awards, certainly not worth the time and trouble, have also been won or settled.

DIFFICULT TO PROVE

A malicious prosecution case requires a doctor to prove not only that the malpractice action against him was brought with malice, but that the case was filed without probable cause. If sued, the lawyer's defense is likely to be the existence of probable cause. This is a question of law, *not fact*, which means that the case can be dismissed by the trial judge on a motion for summary judgment.

Even a directed verdict or dismissal for the original defendant physician does not establish lack of probable cause on the part of the plaintiff's lawyer. Furthermore, the physician must usually prove "special" damages, which do not include emotional injury and increased insurance costs. The physician must prove, an almost impossible task, that loss of patients and income occurred.

Other intentional torts alleged by doctors against litigious attorneys are abuse of process, invasion of privacy, intentional infliction of emotional distress, and libel and defamation. But the latter actions are usually premised on statements that occurred during the course of the litigation, which is normally privileged. These have been consistently rejected by the courts.

JUSTICE DELAYED

Another inequity for physicians is that they are normally precluded from bringing a counterclaim until the original lawsuit is decided, a rule that requires a defense for even the weakest suit before any claim for malicious prosecution can be made. Physicians are justified in their complaint that the judicial system is plaintiff-oriented, and that protections are inadequate against groundless litigation. Nonetheless, there is potential for reform, and some seems to be on the way. Some jurisdictions now require attorneys to conduct an investigation of the client's claim before filing suit. California, Florida, and Kentucky are examples. This requirement forces the attorney to think twice about filing if he knows that sanctions could be imposed for filing a suit without reasonable basis.

The Federal Rules of Civil Procedure are more supportive of these actions. Federal Rule 68 states that if the plaintiff receives a judgment after trial that is less than (or only equal to) the defendant's settlement offer before trial, the plaintiff must pay the doctor's attorneys' fees. However, Rule 68 is seldom used, and in 1981, the U.S. Supreme Court held that it does not apply when the plaintiff loses the case. Remember, judges, with or without Rule 68, still have the power to award attorneys' fees if provided for by contract or statute.

CAVEAT EMPTOR

Although it is likely that a countersuit can be successfully defended, most attorneys are still wary of them. The experience of being sued for malicious prosecution is emotionally disturbing and potentially expensive, and embroils the attorney in litigation where the usual objective is vengeance. For that reason, lawyers are now being advised to avoid "shotgun" pleading when prosecuting a malpractice action. (Shotgun pleading involves naming peripheral parties whose liability is questionable. Such parties are potential malicious prosecution or abuse of process plaintiffs.)

Another deserving cause for unhappy physician defendants is the seemingly irrational need for lawyers to plead every legal cause of action theoretically conceivable, although there may be no factual basis for doing so. For example, gratuitous allegations of fraud and deceit with claims for punitive damages often inspire malicious prosecution claims by doctors. Since courts have ruled that probable cause must exist for each cause of action alleged in the malpractice suit, it has also been suggested that plaintiff's lawyers have more pre-suit contact with their potential opponents to weed out meritless claims or build a record supporting probable cause.

Even though plaintiffs often expect a pot of gold at the end of their malpractice suits, facts show that is not the case; plaintiffs lose at least 85 percent of their cases. For that reason, plaintiffs may join their attorneys as defendants in a physician's countersuit. Then, should attorneys give their clients this information and obtain an "informed consent" before they bring suit? Absolutely! That knowledge could have a chilling, and restraining, effect on questionable lawsuits.

On the other hand, doctors must remember that being a plaintiff in a countersuit is no disgrace, but it may not be an honor, either. They too are going to have another agonizing, frustrating experience, not much different from the time they were defendants. Although you might receive financial assistance from a legal fund sponsored by your local medical society, more often the costs are yours. In any event, there is loss of time from practice and other activities, all with little likelihood of a successful outcome. In the final analysis, that first taste of victory, yourself as the victor in a malpractice action, should perhaps stand on its own.

PRETRIAL PANELS STILL UNRAVELING THEIR KINKS

Pretrial screening panels, one of the methods that tort reform advocates had hoped would help curb meritless claims, have run into administrative and judicial problems. The only areas where they have been effective are in those states that have mandated this screening system.

Pretrial panels were originally adopted in 30 states and have been upheld by 10 state supreme courts, struck down by four and repealed or permitted to expire by four state legislatures. Many states adopted a system that required review of all medical liability claims by a panel composed of physicians, lawyers and laypersons. After a panel's decision is given, either party can proceed to a jury trial. Usually, a panel's conclusions can be introduced as evidence at trial. It was hoped that if a panel indicated a claim was meritless, a plaintiff would have less incentive to pursue court action. Similarly, if a physician saw that a claim did indeed have merit, he would be more inclined to settle.

So far, pretrial screening panels have been the victim of a Catch-22. To be effective, say medical-legal experts, they should be mandatory. But in the states where they have been mandatory, they are apt to encounter tough challenges on their constitutionality. A recent AMA report on professional liability indicates that voluntary pretrial screening panels have usually passed constitutional muster. But in the states that have adopted them, pretrial screening panels are usually underutilized or inactive. With their dismal track record so far, pretrial screening panels have not had much of an effect on discouraging meritless claims, but tort reform advocates are still hopeful that variations in their structure and operation may yet make them effective. If you are fortunate enough to practice in a state that has a functioning and active pretrial screening panel system, the meritless claim against you may be defused before it does any damage. Consult with your attorney about whether a pretrial screen could offer you advantages.

17

POST-TRIAL

AFTER THE WAR
IS OVER

After the trial, your attorney may move for a directed verdict. At that stage, the court will weigh whether the evidence alone is sufficient for the matter to be decided by the jury. A denial of a motion for a directed verdict does not mean you will be found guilty by a jury. It simply means that in the Court's opinion, sufficient evidence has been produced to allow the case to be decided by the jury. Not all of the charges that have been made against you may be decided by the jury. For example, you may be sued on three counts with the judge directing the verdict on two of them. From a practical point of view, that weakens the plaintiff's case because of the psychological impact that his decision will have on the jury. There is no predicting how a jury will decide. The length of time it is out is never a yardstick for which way it is leaning.

After the verdict has been rendered, it is not uncommon for either side to move for a new trial. In some jurisdictions, you must move for a new trial immediately after the verdict has been rendered. In other states, however, the motion for a new trial can be filed for within specified time limits. Another motion commonly filed for is the entry of a judgment notwithstanding verdict, or as is known in law, Judgment N.O.V. This is a motion in which the plaintiff or defense contends that there is no basis on which the jury could have found "X" and therefore the court should enter a judgment notwithstanding the verdict. The converse may be true— that the verdict is inconsistent with the evidence. There may be other motions that can be filed. Your attorney may file one for remittur, which means a reduction for the amount awarded; while the plaintiff may file for additur, which means an increase in the amount awarded by the jury. Although there are a host of additional motions that may be filed post-trial, these are the major ones that you are most likely to encounter and with which you should be familiar.

If the case is to be appealed, your attorney will generally need to file within 30 days. The difference between an appeal and the trial is that the trial has tried the facts while an appeal tries the law that the court has applied to these facts. For example, did the judge exclude evidence favorable to you that should have been admitted? Did he fail to give the jury a critical and requested instruction? Because of questions such as these, it is essential that your trial attorney has properly preserved a record upon which an appeal can be made. In addition, an appeal will depend on other factors, too. Your attorney must have made timely objections during the trial, and offered testimony on the record yet out of the presence of the jury that the appellate court will need to review. At key points along the way, your attorney should have taken exception to certain rulings, which will also help form the basis of the appeal.

You could win at trial and see the case reversed on appeal, which means it has been remanded in favor of the plaintiff. Generally, any large malpractice award is appealed. The greater the amount of money involved, the longer is the trial and the greater the chance for error. As a result, the greater is the chance for reversing the results. Your personal attorney remains your best advisor if there is a possibility of an appeal, and you should rely on him instead of the carrier's attorney to preserve points that will serve as the basis for a new trial. It is unfortunate that when a court overturns a large award against a physician, the press generally will not report the results as vigorously as it did when the large award was announced. In any case, be prepared for a prolonged process if your attorney considers that it is worth appealing. The appellate process usually requires 6–18 months, and this period may vary depending on the court, its caseload and the complexity of the issues that are being considered.

Decisions to appeal should never be made hastily. If a verdict for $100,000 is returned and you may not have been guilty, the case should be appealed because the verdict may be overturned. The problem you may confront in such situations, however, is that your malpractice insurance carrier may not want to spend the additional money to see that the decision is reversed. Your insurance policy will usually not stipulate anything regarding an appeal. For these reasons, you need to be wary of the attorney who does not want to appeal a case when you lose.

It is, however, a new ball game if you reach the appellate stage. The appellate court may show less understanding and less interest in the medical factors and issues than the jury did. In most jurisdictions, appellate judges are political appointees. Regardless of the apprehension that you feel about the appeal, do not let the carrier dissuade you from following through if you and your personal attorney both believe that the verdict in your case could be reversed. If you want to appeal and your carrier refuses to consent, it may be a breach of their contract as stipulated in your policy with them. If that is the case, you could simultaneously appeal your case and sue them for breach of contract.

THE AFTERMATH

According to the AMA's American Medical Assurance Co., physicians win 80–90 percent of the malpractice suits that go to trial. But even if you are among the majority who win their cases, you may discover that the trial or at least certain things that were said about you during it will live on. Whether you turn into a Monday-morning quarterback will depend on how faithfully you followed your game plan and how well you maintained your cool in the courtroom. Even if you did keep your cool and everything went almost as planned, you are likely to replay in your mind what happened.

No matter how the case is resolved— by dismissal, settlement, or verdict— physicians generally feel greatly relieved to have it completed. There is a certain healing effect in the legal process. Regardless of any bitterness, physicians seldom want to countersue even though they may have harangued their attorneys for months about their being hell-bent on doing so as soon as the case is decided. As one attorney put it, "It's like going through a divorce. The day you move out, you're lucky that you don't shoot the person. But by the time you have finished dividing the property, you simply don't have much spunk left to fight." If you've won, you will probably feel a measure of vindication that will further deter you from the idea of countersuing unless the charges brought against you were blatantly malicious.

Despite the vindication and a sense that your besmirched reputation has attained a new luster, there will still be hard feelings. Residual anger is common and physicians use a variety of outlets to express it. For example, some physicians write about their experiences or offer to help local defense lawyers make it tougher for unscrupulous plaintiff's attorneys.

In her study, University of Illinois psychiatrist Sara C. Charles produced some interesting results when she surveyed 154 Cook County physicians who had been sued. She found that 96 percent of them reported some traumatic consequences of litigation. Yet only one-fifth said their practices had suffered. The effects of a suit had significant implications, however, for *how* they practiced. For example, 69 percent kept better records; 62 percent ordered more diagnostic tests; 42 percent stopped seeing certain patients; 28 percent quit doing some high risk procedures and sadly enough, more than one-third contemplated early retirement.

Another recent study conducted by the American College of Obstetricians and Gynecologists found a strikingly similar pattern as it gauged how OB/GYNs nationwide were reacting to the groundswell of claims that have hiked premiums as high as $80,000 for some members of this specialty. So many of them had eliminated obstetrics, according to this survey, that some areas of the country soon could be faced with a shortage of physicians in this specialty. Many physicians reveal similar transformations in their outlook. Up until they have been sued, their relationship with patients tends to be one of mutual trust. Then their attitude changes. They start treating the chart, perhaps wondering, "How will this look to a jury?" The chart becomes all-important, and some physicians become so obsessed with documentation that it detracts from the kind of attention that they might otherwise offer a patient. Still other physicians become too eager to refer a patient when a diagnosis or treatment begins to look complicated enough to them to trigger a lawsuit. They change their collection habits, reviewing their accounts receivable files more warily and do not pursue some bills that they should legitimately and aggressively pursue. In the extreme, some physicians dramatically alter their practice profiles, switching to low-risk specialties, becoming hospital administrators, teachers, researchers or insurance claim consultants.

These practice adjustments and career changes are part of the broad spectrum of reactions that may be triggered by the phenomenon of being sued. Despite the cook book-like guidelines that risk management specialists like to recommend for curbing the potential for liability in your practice, there are no handy prescriptions for learning to live and to continue to practice with the fact that you have been sued. The first time around is the most traumatic, and by now approximately one out of four physicians has been sued. That doesn't mean that the next time will be much easier, but it does suggest that you will know what to expect and will be much better prepared.

18
MALPRACTICE 2000
GET READY
TO BITE
THE BULLET

Predicting what your medical malpractice situation will look like by the turn of the century may seem similar to determining the diagnosis of a patient before learning his symptoms. Today's volatile medicolegal climate, increasing physician militancy and political activism appear to be raising the public's consciousness about premiums, awards and problems within the current insurance and tort systems. Sometimes these efforts will contribute to constructive change; inevitably others will backfire. As a result, it is sometimes difficult to foresee what will happen during the current legislative session, let alone to predict what the next 15 years will bring.

Given the vagaries in the medical legal system, speculation about what the malpractice beast will look like in 2000 is almost as much conjecture and fantasy as those that project visions of extraterrestrial life. Nevertheless, the job is made easier because many of the trends in malpractice and products liability can help suggest the shape of things to come. Also an understanding of the political process and the philosophical changes that are reflected in the courts as well as the legislatures sometimes aid in determining what will happen to otherwise unregulated trends.

While many people do not expect a dramatic change in the next few years and project a linear continuation of current trends, we disagree. Although the size and frequency of awards will continue to grow in general, they will level off in those states that have had the greatest amount of malpractice activity. The increase will occur in other jurisdictions where

216

cases are not now often brought. Litigation trends, like changes in the prices of real estate, are never uniform; wide regional differences rarely remain permanently fixed.

Unfortunately, the premiums for traditional professional liability insurance will continue to rise, with rates as well as claim experience becoming more uniform across the country. New products in that industry, however, will be made available at lower cost and with per unit pricing. Part-time practitioners, along with those just beginning and ending their careers, will enjoy special rate relief in many jurisdictions. In addition, carriers will offer policies that cover the physician on an "a la carte" basis. For example, under such a plan, a neurosurgeon will be able to separately insure each procedure performed on a "premium per event" or patient-by-patient basis. Thus, you will be able to secure added protection for high-risk patients, or choose less coverage in other cases. A specific premium will be attributable to the individual patient (and his bill). While prospective health insurance coverage will be the rule for those not enrolled in HMOs or other similar programs, time and visit allocations will be pared to the bone. All or a part of the "per procedure" or individual patient DRG malpractice premium will be passed directly on to the patient.

Doctors will also be able to purchase "a la carte" coverage at wholesale rates, paired with quantity discounts. Thus, at the beginning of the year you will be able to determine how many of a given procedure you wish to cover. Active members of a specialty will therefore be charged more than those with a lighter schedule. This type of insurance will be available either by itself or, more likely, as a supplement to a basic coverage package that would carry a lower rate. Speaking of primary insurance, the "occurrence coverage" that is currently on the decline in high activity states will give way to "claims made" policies in almost all jurisdictions.

FUNDAMENTAL CHANGES

At some point in the 1990s we will begin to see a major restructuring of the entire process of determining medical liability. There will be fundamental, maybe even sweeping, changes in how claims are resolved and a profound realignment of attitudes that affect physician–patient relationships. None of this will happen quickly, although some of it is beginning to occur already and may be evolving so gradually that we are unaware of it.

The good news for the year 2000 is that generally, most physicians will be in a better position than they are today in terms of malpractice exposure, claims resolution and insurance coverage. The not-so-good news is that this improvement in your situation will require noneconomic costs. There will be some trade-offs, some tough concessions that the medical community will have to make before major change is directed into our tort system. In that sense, physicians may have to accept government supervision and regulation far more intrusive than you might imagine, or a few years ago would have tolerated.

Physicians who are practicing good medicine will not be as affected as those whose patterns are slipshod. But everyone will come under closer scrutiny as government agencies tighten their policing of the profession and institute more quality of care evaluations, adopting some of the types of programs that we find today in acute care facilities. The cutting edge for governmental intervention will be at the licensing and reimbursement levels. It will take many forms, including mandated reporting of physician misconduct similar to the system that currently exists in New York. Before long, all states will adopt similar requirements.

In New York, physicians, nurses, dentists, pharmacists and hospital administrators are required by Section 230(11) of the Public Health Law to report to the state's Office of Professional Medical Conduct when they learn of physician misconduct. That process will be expanded. The state licensing agencies will become involved in more cases and at a much earlier stage, interfacing perhaps with the malpractice claim process. When a liability action is filed, state licensing boards may be put on notice so they can decide whether to launch their own investigations. By the year 2000, malpractice claims will no longer be solely a private encounter between patient and doctor. Even now that is no longer the case, as state and federal agencies build dynasties.

It's difficult to predict what forms punitive action may take. Plenty of options are open. For example, some states may develop programs similar to the point system that has been developed for penalizing errant automobile drivers. In New York, a physician's license may be jeopardized if he is found grossly negligent on one occasion or careless or negligent on more than one occasion (Education Law Section 6509). Within the next decade, more states will move aggressively in this area, adopting statutes for punitive action. If a malpractice case is brought alleging evidence of gross negligence, we may see a time when the state would be placed on notice and a determination made as to whether a summary action should be taken concerning a physician's license.

Restrictions on licensing may take other forms as well. Licensing boards may soon become agressive in requiring retraining, limiting the scope of a physician's practice or requiring that it be supervised by colleagues. The trends within the last few years have suggested that this is already in the works, and as the number of claims and the severity of awards continue to spiral, licensing boards will soon have a mandate in many states for the expansion of their powers. It is already apparent that more jurisdictions are taking a tougher stance on incompetence and the impaired physician. We will gradually see an expansion of these efforts to the point where hospitals in all states will be required to report to the regulatory authorities when they remove personnel from their staff because of incompetence or disability.

The old "conspiracy of silence" that long had sheltered incompetent physicians clearly has crumbled in recent years. The trend will be accelerated in the wake of new laws that have made it an offense if you fail to report cases of an impaired physician. It will grow stronger nationwide as drug and alcohol abuse among physicians become subject to closer scrutiny in all states.

TORT REFORM

Despite efforts in Congress to generate interest in a no-fault medical malpractice bill, this approach is grossly unaffordable; it will not be enacted in the next 15 years. National health insurance will, however, be a possible vehicle for implementing other changes.

Physicians can find encouraging signs in other areas of tort reform, however, notably in the arbitration process. Proponents of arbitration have been touting this approach for decades but it has never gathered the momentum that it deserves. That's going to change in the next 15 years. If we can arbitrate disputes involving thousands of people and hundreds of millions of dollars in labor disputes and in architectural and construction contracts, why can't we apply the same methods to medical malpractice? The answer is we can and should. Because it is fast, simple and can help limit the size of awards, the arbitration system will grow in popularity, aided by legislative initiatives. With arbitration, there will be less of a chance for a runaway verdict and the need for a verdict to be appealed. It may not dramatically affect the size of awards, but all parties will gravitate toward arbitration because of the speed and simplicity it can offer in resolving claims. A more knowledgeable public will demand this method of handling disputes.

Courts will take a sterner look at awards for pain and suffering. In so doing they will set standards that will have the effect of limiting such payments. Many states will also enact legislation placing a limit on pain and suffering awards in all tort actions, not just malpractice. While many of these efforts will not survive judicial scrutiny, others will receive approval and remain in effect.

Broad coalitions and new alliances formed between medicine, business and government are a driving force behind the tort reform movement and will be for years to come. A survey, for example, by *American Medical News* found that in the first few months of the 1986 legislative session, tort reform measures had passed in 12 states and are pending in 31 states and the District of Columbia. Legislation to cap damages was introduced in 31 states and Washington, D.C., in 1986. The fact that proposed laws that would modify joint and several liability were pending in 20 states is also encouraging. Joint and several liability enables plaintiff's attorneys to go after "deep pocket" defendants when other defendants— who may be more culpable— are not as well covered by malpractice insurance or have gone "bare."

CHANGES IN THE PRIVATE SECTOR

In the private sector, however, other developments could have a more profound impact than tort reform legislation. We may see private agreements between individuals and their health care providers affecting the rules of liability. The initial vehicle of change will be health maintenance organizations. As these and similar groups of physicians grow, forming associations organized for reimbursement purposes (IPAs, for example) there will be, as part of the patient contract, a degree of "private" tort reform. We will move even further away from the traditional delivery of health care, the old one-on-one basis with a single practitioner. It's happening to a large extent already, but this trend will accelerate as groups of employees and organizations of practitioners explore new arrangements in contracting for health services.

Subscriber contracts may also limit those occasions when a patient may recover against the health care provider. Under some agreements, the quality of care will be evaluated only as against that offered in similar organizations. With the aid of enabling legislation and financial consideration, injured patients may agree to sue only for gross negligence. Other contracts will place limits on the size and nature of awards. While these provisions will be challenged, full disclosure, the availability of competitive health plans and cost levels reflecting different malpractice options for the patient will support court decisions upholding the agreements.

This so-called "private" tort reform could take the form of shortening the statute of limitations or in imposing restrictions on damages. In other words, in exchange for concessions in certain health care costs, the groups of patients who contract with physicians and group plans may agree to limitations on filing malpractice claims. These changes will go considerably beyond what legislatures have been able to implement. Whereas the state's standard may be more liberal, these private agreements can be much more restrictive. For example, imagine the statute of limitations being cut to one year. Constitutional questions may still arise, but since the agreements are privately made, such challenges will have only limited success. We might see private agreements that provide for periodic payments instead of lump sums, therby allowing any verdict to be amortized. It's all part of a shakeup in the health care system that will continue in the 1990s.

FEWER FRIVOLOUS SUITS

In some jurisdictions, plaintiffs who bring irresponsible claims are required to pay attorneys' fees for the defendant. States will enact laws creating much stiffer penalties for frivolous suits. Unsuccessful plaintiffs will also have to pay court costs and maybe fines, too, as states aggressively move to curb nuisance suits and limit the overloading of trial courts. Currently there is little incentive for plaintiffs and defendants to reach a settlement at an early stage of litigation. This situation will change with earlier judicial intervention and special preference granted in the scheduling of malpractice trials. Some states will go much further, perhaps designating certain times during the course of litigation when the parties will pass a milestone, so to speak, and have an opportunity to resolve their differences. If one passes that point (at the termination of discovery, for example) without settling the case, penalties will be imposed on any party who unreasonably holds out. That side will be surcharged or required to pay their adversary's legal fees.

CHANGES IN INSURANCE COVERAGE

By the year 2000, the collateral source rule will be imposed nationwide. That will mean that plaintiffs will not be able to receive payments in a malpractice award for expenses already reimbursed from other sources such as health insurance. What's more, insurance carriers will all be authorized to surcharge physicians who are the targets of many compensable claims. In many states now, a physician who has never been sued pays the same premium as a physician who has been sued successfully on many occasions.

Look for a shakeout in the number of companies who are insuring physicians. This is so volatile an area now that it's difficult to even speculate on what it might be like at the turn of the century. But it seems that the medical society captive insurance companies are now at the height of their popularity. They currently insure about half of the physicians nationwide. But a new wave of claims and large payouts are testing the mettle of these doctor-owned carriers in much the same way that commercial carriers were tested in 1975. It remains to be seen whether some of them will survive this crunch. Regardless of whether they do, they will be met with competition from private sources, some physician-based. The ground rules of underwriting will also undergo some substantial changes. Among new conditions for insurance will be madatory continuing education, ongoing chart reviews, and agreements on limitations of practice. The carrier will engage in tighter scrutiny of its insured, moving in to limit the scope of practices when a physician has not performed well in certain areas.

High technology will play a larger role in the peer review process and in the monitoring of physicians by carriers and state agencies. It's all part of the trade-off alluded to earlier, as doctors will need to accept more scrutiny in exchange for an easing of the crisis. High-tech evaluation tools will become a part of the screening process, as hospitals develop liability profiles on computer to grant or deny physicians privileges. Underwriting decisions will be made the same way, drawing on practice data as well as information from the hospitals and third-party payors. Just as computers are currently tracking length of stay and other pertinent information for DRGs, the computer will also be applied to patterns that suggest a heightened risk for physician liability. We already have the concept of "generic" screening of events in the hospital. These are incidents that trigger a review. Insurance companies and physicians will utilize similar techniques to monitor their own practices, adjust premiums and determine who is to be eligible for coverage, as well as premium cost. With increased competition due to the growth in the physician supply, hospitals will get even tougher on privileges. The state and the insurance industry will pool their information with one another, as their computers exchange data on professional activities of physicians. These profiles will include untoward events, infection rates, lengths of stay and patient complaints.

SETTING A PRICE ON INJURY

The wide variation in awards for the same injury will disappear as we are given specific dollar amounts for certain injuries. This is what happened with worker's compensation. Under current law, if you lose the use of an organ or limb, you receive a specified number of weeks pay as your award. The same standardization of payments will be extended to malpractice verdicts. If someone loses a leg due to a therapeutic misadventure, that leg will be deemed worth much the same to everybody, unless you're a runner or a professional athlete. These awards will have to be adjusted for a cost-of-living index. In addition, the gap between what you receive for an injury in an auto accident versus what you receive for the same injury in a malpractice action will disappear. We are headed for a categorizaton of all compensable events in which the amounts will be set by the standards in non-malpractice actions.

While such standardization may sound good to physicians, the other changes that are suggested here—increased surveillance and tougher policies on licensing—may be hard to live with. But then, what is the alternative— an extension of the malpractice crisis that has already cast a pall over medicine for more than 10 years? To be sure, for the physician who practices slipshod medicine, these changes *will* be hard to live with, but for the vast majority of physicians who practice good medicine it will be worth biting the bullet. By the year 2000, the malpractice monkey may not be off your back, but it will feel much lighter.

INDEX